THE INSPIRING STORY
OF ZION ORPHANAGE
AND ITS FOUNDER,
RABBI AVRAHAM
YOCHANAN BLUMENTHAL

Home of Miracles

MOSAICA PRESS

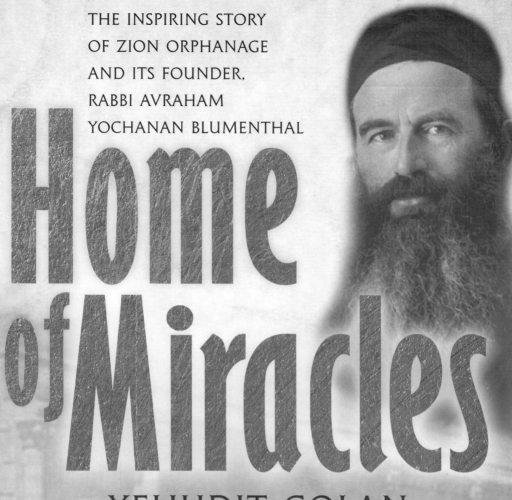

THE INSPIRING STORY
OF ZION ORPHANAGE
AND ITS FOUNDER,
RABBI AVRAHAM
YOCHANAN BLUMENTHAL

Home of Miracles

YEHUDIT GOLAN

Mosaica Press, Inc.
© 2017 by Mosaica Press
Designed by Daniella Kirsch
Typeset by Brocha Mirel Strizower

Published and distributed by:
Mosaica Press, Inc.
www.mosaicapress.com
info@mosaicapress.com

Adapted from the Hebrew *Elef Olamot* by Yehudit Golan
Based on the testimony of Rabbi Blumenthal's daughter, Yocheved Solomon
Translated by Esther Friedman
Edited by C.B. Lieber

Table of Contents

Foreword

A LIVING LEGACY

When my grandfather, Rabbi Avraham Yochanan Blumenthal, of blessed memory, established his orphanage close to 120 years ago together with my grandmother, Chana Shaina, they had one single goal: to give every homeless orphan who needed it love and warmth, a home and a family.

When I was a young girl, I knew that Grandfather was not only mine but also the grandfather of many hundreds of other children. It was so natural that my grandparents called Moshe Sitton, one of the orphans in the orphanage, their own "Moishy." That's how they were, completely devoted to the children.

Their incredible devotion has continued down the chain of generations in this great and hallowed home, the Zion Blumenthal Orphanage.

7

The love and care have continued until today, with the same atmosphere and goals. Grandfather wouldn't have had it any other way.

My husband, Rabbi Eliezer Rakovsky, of blessed memory, assumed the job of running the orphanage at Grandfather's request. After his passing, my son, Rabbi Baruch Rakovsky, took up the reins, continuing the family tradition while at the same time ensuring that the orphanage keeps up with the times.

The voices of the children playing in the courtyard and the happiness radiating from their faces is the best testimony that Grandfather's vision remains alive and well!

Writing with deep emotion,

Rivka Rakovsky
Jerusalem, January 2017

Preface to the Hebrew Edition

A FATHER TO THOUSANDS

This book is the story of my father, Rabbi Avraham Yochanan Blumenthal, who served as a father to thousands of children. As founder and head of Zion Orphanage (also known as the Zion Blumenthal Orphanage, in his memory), my father created a unique institution where children found a home after being orphaned of one or both parents, left alone in the world with no one to care for them. Father loved them and cared for them as his own, raising them to adulthood as only a parent could.

Father received this calling from his spiritual guide, Rabbi Yehoshua Leib Diskin (1818–1898), a leader of the religious community of Jerusalem in the nineteenth century. At a time when Jerusalem was being ravaged by disease, war, starvation, and rampant poverty, Father embraced this role and dedicated himself to the children, heart and soul.

A born-and-bred Jerusalemite, Father began educating youngsters in 1899 with the establishment of the Educational Home for Boys (in Hebrew, Beit Chinuch Ne'arim), a program that prevented many boys from falling into a wayward lifestyle. During World War I, he accepted the charge of building the orphanage, one of the first homes of its kind in Jerusalem and the only one still in existence today, saving many children from certain death by disease and starvation. His educational career continued throughout the British Mandate of Palestine, when his influence began to spread through the city. With the establishment of the State of Israel, Zion Orphanage created an open-door policy for children of various backgrounds who immigrated to Israel, providing them with a home when their parents could not.

For close to seventy years, Father viewed it as his obligation and privilege to raise "his" children and lead them on the proper path. Under the most trying conditions, he enabled these orphaned youngsters to grow to adulthood in an environment of warmth and care. Like a captain tirelessly leading his ship through stormy waters, he navigated difficult times with calmness and fortitude.

As a social activist as well, he never stopped working on behalf of his community, the Old Yishuv of Jerusalem, always ready to assist private individuals and the public alike. With every new endeavor, his lips murmured a prayer, "Please, God, enable us to succeed!"

His life's work has not been quickly forgotten, and it is for that reason that I encouraged writer Yehudit Golan to take pen to paper to illuminate the life and times of my father, Rabbi Avraham Yochanan Blumenthal, of blessed memory.

Yocheved Solomon
Jerusalem, 2003

Preface

Eliyahu was seven years old when he came to live at Zion Orphanage. Victim of a dysfunctional and unstable home, Eliyahu had watched as his mother lost her mind and was institutionalized. His father, unable to cope, chose the destructive path of drugs, which soon became an addiction. Their child was bereft of normal parental care — no one to hug him, attend to a scraped knee, or sing him to sleep. Struggling to survive was the only world Eliyahu knew.

When Israel's Ministry of Social Welfare brought Eliyahu to Zion Orphanage, he was extremely withdrawn and distrustful. He was barely speaking, shut off from the world around him.

Our first step was to place Eliyahu in a Family Unit on our Jerusalem campus. There he joined a young, energetic couple who lived in an apartment with their own young children as well as a group of twelve Zion Orphanage boys aged seven to fourteen. It was here that Eliyahu first encountered caring, responsible adults worthy of trust. In his desperate need for a secure and loving home, this was Eliyahu's new beginning.

Our next step was to help Eliyahu emerge from his shell and begin communicating. We tried various activities and therapies to build his confidence: arts and crafts, martial arts, musical instruments, computer proficiency, and gymnastics, as well as speech and play therapies.

Beyond meeting every basic physical need, we focused on Eliyahu's deep psychological need for a unique sense of importance. Already eighty years ago, Rabbi A.Y. Blumenthal taught public speaking to Zion Orphanage boys as a way to instill self-confidence. His goal was to get the boys to articulate: Who am I? What do I stand for? What is my message to the world?

For Eliyahu, the answer was music. Over the next nine years, Eliyahu's latent talent emerged full force. He began composing music and became the lead singer in our Zion Choir. Today, Eliyahu displays such sensitivity, confidence, and joy that you would never imagine the dark, cold, and unpredictable world in which he spent his first tender years of life.

At Zion Orphanage, our definition of success is when a boy gains fresh perspective: that the world is beautiful, filled with good and caring people. A world where he understands he has something valuable to offer.

Today, Eliyahu is headed for a career in music.

EVER SINCE RABBI Avraham Yochanan Blumenthal began caring for the orphaned, homeless, and underprivileged children of Israel in 1899, Zion Orphanage has stood for turning challenges into opportunities. Each boy — despite a rough start in life — is given a second chance to reach his potential and achieve greatness. We facilitate this by emphasizing the standards of a stable, healthy home: clean and dignified premises, caring, nurturing warmth and joy — all driven by a belief in the greatness of every human being.

Avraham Ravitz, born in Tel Aviv in 1934, lived in Zion Orphanage together with his brother. Rising above a challenging beginning, he became a popular member of the Israeli Knesset, where he served faithfully for twenty years. Similarly, David Azoulay, born in Morocco in 1954, spent his formative years at Zion Orphanage and has served as a member of Knesset since 1996.

The list goes on: Moshe Abutbul was born in Beersheba and came to Zion Orphanage at age ten. He is now the mayor of Beit Shemesh, one of Israel's largest cities. With the tender guidance of Zion Orphanage, the boys' deeply ingrained fighting spirit remained as they matured and reentered the world, this time from a position of strength. There are thousands of such Zion Orphanage success stories.

The Talmud teaches: "Whoever saves a life [is considered] as if he has saved an entire world" (*Sanhedrin* 37a). Every day at Zion Orphanage, we see this adage literally playing out in front of our eyes.

TWELVE YEARS AGO, I was privileged to join Zion Orphanage as its director. I became drawn to this mission by observing the secret of how Zion Orphanage has continued to thrive and expand for well over a century: It runs with genuine honesty, integrity, and standards of excellence. Perhaps most significantly, everyone at Zion Orphanage has the same goal and priority: to care for these children and provide the best environment for them to grow and thrive.

This family tradition continues generation after generation, and today Zion Orphanage is run by Rabbi Blumenthal's great-grandson, Rabbi Baruch Rakovsky.

This continuity is providential. In 1965, Rabbi Blumenthal was walking with his grandson-in-law, Rabbi Eliezer Rakovsky, who asked for a blessing for a son following four daughters. With loving warmth, Rabbi Blumenthal said, "Next year you will have a son, and I want you to honor me with serving as his *sandak*." And so it was — one year later to the day, little Baruch Rakovsky was born, and Rabbi Blumenthal served as the *sandak* at his great-grandson's circumcision. A few months later, Rabbi Blumenthal passed away — leaving the key to continuity in place.

We find this continuity in our financial supporters as well, some of whom have donated to the orphanage for multiple generations. They, like the staff at Zion Orphanage, are driven by a passionate belief that we can inspire these boys and transform their lives.

The book in your hands tells the story of the world's longest-running Jewish orphanage. Yet, much more, it tells of one man's passion for caring, hope, and love, and how that ignited a tradition that grows ever brighter — day by day, child after child. We hope this legacy will inspire you, as it inspires all of us.

Gershon Unger
Jerusalem, January 2017

Rabbi
Avraham Yochanan
Blumenthal

Founder and director of the Zion Orphanage,
born in Jerusalem June 18, 1877,
died November 30, 1966

Prologue

Jerusalem, February 1917

The moonlight streamed in through the window, casting a weak glow on the iron beds where two thin, ragged boys lay marveling at the change in their fortunes that had unfolded over the last twenty-four hours.

A tall figure soundlessly approached the room, then stood still, concealed by the shadows.

"Psst, Uri," whispered the boy in the bed nearest the door.

"What?" A dark head raised itself from the next bed.

"Remember where we were at this time last night?"

"We were sitting near the vegetable crates in the open-air market, trying to fall asleep, Shimon. It was so cold, and we were so hungry…"

"And now we're here." Shimon took up the tale. "They gave us a bath and clean clothing, and now we're in real beds instead of outside with the rats."

The two boys lay silently, too overwhelmed to speak. Finally, Shimon spoke again. "It's like a miracle…"

The tall figure detached itself from the shadows and entered the room. Shimon gulped. "Rabbi Blumenthal?"

The director smiled into his thick beard. He stroked Uri's head, adjusted Shimon's blanket, and asked, "Tell me, children, what did you do to merit this miracle? Do you know?"

"Yes," said Shimon, without a moment's hesitation. "When we were lying in the marketplace, a man passed by. We recognized him as a missionary. He saw us begging for a slice of bread, and he said, 'Do you want to come with me, children? Do you want to come to my nice house?'

"We looked at one another. Uri was ready to go, but I stopped him. The man continued, 'You won't go hungry in my house. Leave the Jews behind. Leave poverty and hunger… Convert to my faith and you'll only stand to gain.'

"'No way!' I shouted. 'We prefer to die of hunger than to go with you.'

"After he left, Uri asked me if we would really die of hunger. I told him that I didn't know, but perhaps God would make a miracle for us… And the very next day, someone came and brought us here."

Only the moon bore witness to the tears that shone in the director's eyes. *The Father of orphans has performed miracles for all the children in this building,* he thought as he tiptoed out of the room.

CHAPTER 1

Jerusalem of Old

The Jewish community of Jerusalem in the mid-nineteenth century was largely religious, a mix of Ashkenazic and Sephardic Jews who had returned to their homeland after centuries in exile. With the rise of Zionism and the resulting wave of immigration from Europe, referred to as the First Aliyah, in the late 1800s, this community became known as the "Old Yishuv." Jews of the Old Yishuv lived for the most part in dire poverty, suffering from the overcrowded, primitive housing in the Old City and oppressive Ottoman rule.

The majority of these Jews dedicated their time to Torah study, subsisting largely on the donations sent by their brethren in the Diaspora. Many pious individuals made aliyah during this period, with the intent of living out their remaining years in the Holy Land. Younger families came in an effort to protect their children from dangerous forces sweeping through Europe, believing that in Jerusalem their children could be raised in a safe Jewish environment.

Into this latter category fell Yaakov and Leah Blumenthal, who in 1876 arrived in what was then known as Palestine with their three young sons, Simcha, Meir, and Hershel, leaving behind their native Hungary and its relative comforts in search of a brighter future.

Yaakov was a community activist and Torah scholar. He and Leah were married in 1868. Fear of physical and spiritual dangers led them to the Holy Land, where they rented a tiny apartment that was a far cry from their former comfortable home. Although physical amenities were lacking, the family did not struggle for survival like many of its neighbors; in addition to a sizable inheritance from Yaakov's parents, they supported themselves by selling textiles that Leah's mother, Feigele Wosner, shipped from Hungary.

Avraham Yochanan, born on June 18, 1877 (7 Tammuz 5637), was the couple's fourth son and their first child born in Jerusalem. He was later followed by a daughter, Hindel.

OUTSIDE THE WALLS

Ever the communal activist, Yaakov Blumenthal established a free-loan society and served as sexton (*gabbai*) of Yeshivat Torat Chaim in the Old City of Jerusalem. He forged close ties with many of Jerusalem's leaders, including Rabbi Yehoshua Leib Diskin, a leading figure of the Old Yishuv, and Rabbi Shmuel Salant, Ashkenazic Chief Rabbi of Jerusalem from 1840 to 1909. He was a close confidant of Rabbi Yosef Chaim Sonnenfeld, renowned leader of the Ashkenazic community during that period, accompanying him on visits to foreign dignitaries and consulates.

Rabbi Yosef Chaim Sonnenfeld, leader of the Ashkenazic Jews of the Old Yishuv

The overcrowding of the Old City of Jerusalem during the

mid-to-late nineteenth century necessitated the Blumenthals' move outside of the city's walls — an undertaking fraught with danger, as marauders and wild animals roamed the countryside. Yet a few brave pioneering spirits persisted, and over several decades, new neighborhoods were successfully established outside the walls. Yaakov Blumenthal played a key role in the development of one of these new neighborhoods, named "Beit Yaakov" in recognition of his efforts. (The neighborhood eventually merged with several others and became known as Machane Yehuda, home of the famous Jerusalem *shuk*.)

Yaakov's next project was the creation of the Jewish settlement of Petach Tikva in central Israel, about six miles east of Tel Aviv, purchasing a fifth of the land set aside for the town. The Blumenthals originally intended to settle in Petach Tikva themselves, but when many of the settlers were stricken with malaria, they reluctantly reconsidered their plans. Yaakov sold his land to the hardy pioneers who remained.

Turning his sights back to Jerusalem, Yaakov joined Rabbi Yosef Chaim Sonnenfeld in petitioning a wealthy philanthropist for help in building another neighborhood outside of the Old City. With the sizable sum of money they received, they purchased a large plot adjacent to the newly built Meah Shearim. The homes in the new neighborhood, named Batei Ungarin ("Hungarian Houses"), were large, comfortable, and surrounded by spacious courtyards.

The Blumenthal family moved into Batei Ungarin in the early 1890s, as soon as it was habitable. By this time, the older children had married, and Avraham Yochanan had blossomed from a sweet young boy into a fine Torah scholar. He spent many hours poring over the Talmud, studying long into the night. As he reached adulthood, it became clear that his passion in life was not only to learn but also to teach.

BATTLEGROUND FOR SOULS

In addition to physical growth, the Jewish community of Jerusalem was experiencing growing pains of another sort. The First Aliyah, which brought approximately thirty thousand Jews to Palestine, was the first wave of mass immigration from Europe. Unlike the Jews of the Old Yishuv, the immigrants of the First Aliyah came for ideological reasons, feeling it was time for the Jewish people to have a homeland once again. While some of these immigrants were religious, the vast majority were not.

The pioneers of the First Aliyah had an impassioned vision for the future, leading to the establishment of Tel Aviv, then called *Achuzat Bayit* ("Homestead"), and many other towns and cities. Swept away by the idealism of these newcomers, as well as the wave of modernity that had reached the Holy Land in the latter half of the nineteenth century, many young Jews abandoned their heritage and joined the pioneering efforts. Others, however, remained strong, upholding their traditions.

One of these staunchly observant young men was Avraham Yochanan Blumenthal. Even as a youngster, he had stood out among his peers for his love of Torah study. Having been raised in a home that valued and supported community activism, he didn't hesitate to reach out to others, encouraging them to follow his example.

Slowly but surely, he drew others close to the Judaism he knew and loved, to the holy books he knew so well, setting the stage for a lifetime career in education.

CHAPTER 2

Early Years

I n 1896, at the age of eighteen, Avraham Yochanan celebrated his engagement to Chana Shaina Rosenberg, who had been born in Lomza, Poland, and had immigrated to Jerusalem as a child. The couple's wedding took place several months later and was officiated by Rabbi Yehoshua Leib Diskin, Avraham Yochanan's teacher and spiritual guide. Rabbi Diskin gifted the couple with a silver goblet, which remained a treasured possession of the young couple for years to come.

Rabbi Yehoshua Leib Diskin, Avraham Yochanan's mentor

By the time he married, Avraham Yochanan was already conducting regular study sessions with young boys. After several years, these sessions formalized into the Educational Home for Boys, founded in 1899

with the express goal of creating a warm educational environment for young boys. The fledgling institution had a small dormitory and attracted students from all over the country, from as far away as Tiberias and Safed.

While the initial group was small, the bonds Avraham Yochanan formed with these boys remained strong for years to come. Some of them later assisted him in transforming the educational home into a full-fledged orphanage, serving as dorm counselors and helping with fundraising.

Avraham Yochanan as a young man

DESTINATION: VIENNA

On the home front, Avraham Yochanan and Chana Shaina were blessed with four children in quick succession, two daughters and two sons. The happy sounds of young children filled their home for several years, until tragedy struck. In those years of primitive medical care and high infant mortality rates, first a son, then a daughter, succumbed to illness, leaving the bereaved parents stunned at the suddenness of their loss.

When Yisrael Chaim, the youngest, began burning with fever as well, Chana Shaina panicked. "Master of the Universe," she wept, "You took two children from me, and now the third is ill. Please, have pity on me!"

Miraculously, little Yisrael recovered, but the young family's cup of sorrows had not yet been filled, as Chana Shaina suddenly lost her hearing.

The Blumenthals consulted several doctors, but no one could explain her deafness nor offer a viable means of treatment. Avraham Yochanan then fell ill too, the strain of his strenuous schedule along with his family's suffering proving too much for his system.

In the midst of this challenging time, the family was blessed with a small measure of consolation as they celebrated the birth of a baby girl whom they named Nechama, meaning "comfort."

"Travel to Vienna, home of the largest medical center in Europe," the doctors advised the couple. "Perhaps you will both be cured of your illnesses."

Weary yet hopeful, Avraham Yochanan and his wife left the Holy Land and traveled to Vienna with their two younger children, Yisrael and Nechama, leaving their nine-year-old eldest, Chaya Sima, with her grandparents in Jerusalem. After an extended stay at the world-renowned medical center, Avraham Yochanan recuperated, but Chana Shaina's hearing, unfortunately, remained impaired until the end of her life.

LEARNING, TEACHING, AND TRAVELING

In addition to his convalescence, Avraham Yochanan utilized his time in Europe to study in Satmar (Satu Mare), Transylvania, and to become acquainted with his extended family in Hungary and his wife's family in Poland. When his wife and children returned to Jerusalem, Avraham Yochanan remained behind for several months to raise funds for his educational home and to meet with several Torah scholars in Europe, including Rabbi Chaim Soloveitchik, father of the renowned Brisker Rav, Rabbi Yitzhak Zev (Velvel) Soloveitchik.

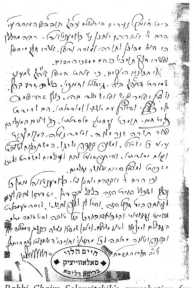

Rabbi Chaim Soloveitchik's approbation for the Educational Home

But the time had come to return home to his waiting family and to his young students who needed his steady hand and guidance. With his return to Palestine, Avraham Yochanan resumed his Torah studies with renowned scholars in the Holy Land, turning his attention to the study of Talmud and Kabbalah. Yet the Educational Home received the lion's share of his attention, and the institution grew steadily, acquiring a building on Yoel Street in today's Geulah neighborhood.

Blessed with a keen pedagogical sense, Avraham Yochanan could always discern when his students needed to air out. He would take them by donkey — the main method of transport at the time — for a change of scenery. One memorable trip was to the Cave of the Patriarchs in Hebron.

Teacher and students stood on the steps outside the building, as close as Jewish worshippers were allowed to approach. There they recited Psalms, while the Arab guard yelled at frequent intervals, "*Yahla imshu* (leave already)!"

Once they had left, Chaim Spitzer, who served as the school's dorm counselor, asked Avraham Yochanan what he had prayed for.

"I asked that I succeed in educating the boys to study Torah and always live as proud Jews," responded the ever-devoted teacher.

A postcard from 1915, complete with stamps from the Turkish postal system, addressed to the Educational Home

Embarrassed, Chaim admitted that he had prayed solely for an improvement in the home's financial situation so that it could survive.

Despite financial woes and heavy debt, the Educational Home for Boys remained active as the years passed. Her handicap notwithstanding, Chana Shaina stood at her husband's side and assisted him in the institution's upkeep. Meanwhile, the Blumenthal family grew; two more daughters, Naomi and Yocheved, and a son, Shmuel, were born in the succeeding years.

MALARIA

Life in the Holy Land at the time was precarious even in the good times. One morning, the teenage Chaya Sima awoke with a strange heaviness in her limbs, along with fever, dizziness, and shivers. The doctor was duly summoned. He examined Chaya Sima and then issued a verdict: malaria. He instructed Chana Shaina to give the girl quinine, the only known cure for the dreaded disease.

For three turbulent days, Chaya Sima burned with fever, alternating between shivers and sweat. Finally, her fever began to subside, to the family's great relief.

But after two days of recovery, her fever returned. Again the doctor was summoned; again he prescribed quinine. Chaya Sima began to recover, but three days later, relapsed once again. The doctor prescribed yet more quinine.

With each successive attack, Chaya Sima's body grew weaker. The family feared for her health, yet the doctor had nothing else to suggest.

Relief came at last from a most unexpected source.

Every evening, after many hours at pasture, an old Arab shepherd named Abu Eref would lead his flock toward Batei Ungarin, where women would emerge from their homes, metal pots in hand, to purchase fresh milk. It was usually the teenage Chaya Sima's job to wait in line, toss the coins into Abu Eref's tin can, and watch him milk one of the sheep. She would carefully carry the frothing milk home, to be placed over the coals and pasteurized.

Now, however, Chana Shaina had to do the task herself. "Where is the girl who used to come?" Abu Eref asked one day.

"She is ill," her mother responded.

"Still?" the Arab asked. "What ails her?"

"Malaria," Chana Shaina admitted. "Her fever comes and goes every few days."

Abu Eref's eyes narrowed. "I have a cure for her," he said. "In our village, the cure for this form of malaria is a snake. It's not poisonous, and if one wraps it around one's neck, the illness disappears, never to return."

"I'll ask the girl if she wants to try it," Chana Shaina said politely, without much faith in the Arab's words. Upon her return home, she related Abu Eref's strange proposal to the family only as a point of curiosity.

Chaya Sima, however, whose face was yellow from the massive doses of quinine, announced that she was prepared to give it a try. "I'm sick of this disease! I have no energy left, and the quinine hasn't helped! Let's try Abu Eref's snake. I just want to get better already!"

With much reservation, Avraham Yochanan reluctantly agreed to allow her to try it. "Perhaps G-d's salvation will come through this strange treatment," he reasoned.

Abu Eref was duly summoned. When he arrived at the Blumenthal home, he wrapped the snake around his own neck to prove it was harmless. Then, he gently placed it around Chaya Sima's neck. The cool sensation of the scaly serpent nearly caused her to faint, but her mother held her upright.

Several minutes later, the nightmare was over. The Arab was offered some food. Before he left, he announced, "In several days the girl will be completely well."

A day passed, then two. The feverish symptoms subsided. The Blumenthals waited with bated breath for the next attack, but it never came. Slowly the color returned to Chaya Sima's cheeks. Only the memory of the snake wrapped around her neck remained to haunt her.

CHAPTER 3

War Breaks Out

The Blumenthal family, along with the rest of Jerusalem's citizens, was about to face its next major trauma: World War I, a period of four terrible years that devastated Europe and parts of Asia, including the Middle East. Four major empires crumbled in the wake of the war — the German, Russian, Austro-Hungarian, and Ottoman Empires, the last of which had ruled Palestine for the past four centuries.

War broke out in the summer of 1914 following the assassination of Archduke Franz Ferdinand, heir to the Austro-Hungarian throne. The Ottoman Empire, eager to regain some of the territory it had lost in the Russo-Turkish War, joined the war that November on the side of Germany and Austria, the Central Powers. Yet even before the war spread to the Middle East, the Jews of Palestine were hurting: With the outbreak of war, the routes through which the Jewish community received essential aid from Europe were blocked, prices on regular staples rose drastically, and basic food products became scarce. Poverty and illness raged throughout the struggling settlements.

In addition, the Ottoman Empire declared that every Jewish inhabitant of Palestine had two choices: accept Ottoman citizenship or be expelled from the country. For the Jewish inhabitants, who often retained citizenship of their countries of origin, both alternatives posed grave dangers. While expulsion was a bitter and potentially perilous option, accepting Ottoman citizenship meant being subject to the draft and forced to go to war.

Turkish general Djemal Pasha

Toward the end of 1914, soldiers began to arrest all Jewish males in Jaffa and Tel Aviv who weren't Turkish citizens. In a chaotic and heartrending scene, these unfortunate men were loaded onto a boat and exiled to Egypt. While Avraham Yochanan held only Czechoslovakian citizenship, the edict of expulsion had not yet reached Jerusalem, and he preferred not to become an Ottoman citizen.

In the following weeks, the Turks began drafting hundreds of young Jews who were Ottoman citizens. Many were killed in battles they had no interest in fighting. Others simply vanished, their fates unknown. Still others were badly wounded in battle and returned home, weak and broken, months or years later.

Turkish soldiers eating a meal together

Desperate to avoid the battlefield, some men managed to escape the draft through bribery. Others, who couldn't afford this option, went into hiding, living in mortal fear of the punishment for draft evasion: death by hanging at Jaffa Gate.

FOOD AND MONEY SHORTAGES

As the war progressed, the value of the Turkish lira decreased daily, and the prices of basic food supplies rose alarmingly. Staples imported from other areas were sold on the black market for huge sums. Organizations were established to provide aid and distribute bread and other staples to people who had none.

Soon, the middle class and even the wealthy were affected by food shortages and hunger. Throughout the country, people bartered household items like linen and clothing in exchange for bread to feed their families.

Avraham Yochanan later described these degrading markets:

> People sold whatever possessions they had, even the clothes on their backs, for a slice of bread to give their children. Anyone who never witnessed the frenzied marketplace, the tumultuous fairs that took place outside the city, and the "wool marketplace" in the city, where refined Jewish girls stood in line with articles of clothing for sale over their arms, with young Arab urchins surrounding them, mocking them in an appalling and shameful way — a person who never saw all this never saw sadness in his life...

Distinguished Jewish men were now forced to frequent Arab villages, a sack of possessions on their shoulders, wearily announcing their wares. Avraham Yochanan wrote:

> We would often walk through the marketplace and see Arab women wrapped in fringed tallitot (prayer shawls), which they had purchased or stolen from Jews. Toward the war's end, these women refused clothing and accepted only gold, silver, and copper, which they purchased for half, a third, or a quarter of the market price.
>
> Sometimes, people had to empty the feathers from their blankets and pillows. The feathers no longer had value, but the blanket and pillow covers could be sold for a few coins. The feathers would fly up in the air and shower down upon the earth like a flurry of white rain.

The hunger, dirt, and shortage of water led inevitably to disease. Jerusalemites of that era drew water from rainwater wells that stood in their courtyards and stored it in large clay containers, which were scrubbed once a week to remove the dirt that had accumulated inside. When these wells dried up, the Arabs would bring water from distant springs and sell it for a hefty price. Neither method was especially hygienic, and disease spread quickly. Typhoid, typhus, malaria, and cholera raged mercilessly in the tiny homes.

When an infectious disease broke out, the affected house and its adjacent courtyard were boarded up immediately to prevent the disease from spreading. Soon afterwards, Turkish legionnaires would appear and lead the ill to the hospital, where they were often placed in quarantine.

The bodies of those who succumbed to illness were coated in plaster to avoid contagion. At funerals, people would steer clear of the coffin. Only those wearing protective gear would participate in the actual burial.

In Batei Ungarin, as in the surrounding neighborhoods, the mortality rate was alarmingly high. According to the Sephardic Chevrah Kaddisha (burial society), the death rate for children in Jerusalem during the war went from six to eight children per month to upwards of one hundred and twenty children per month!

TRAGEDY STRIKES AGAIN

In the Blumenthal home, eleven-year-old Nechama and seven-year-old Naomi fell ill. The patients lay silently, their bodies burning with fever. Chana Shaina moved from one bed to the next, wetting parched lips and rearranging their blankets. But while Nechama gradually began to recover, Naomi did not.

One dark night, the Angel of Death visited the Blumenthal home once again, and little Naomi breathed her last.

The mourning that settled upon the Blumenthal home went largely unnoticed in the streets of the city, where death continued its assault.

Barely a month later, Chaya Sima noticed that the baby, Shmulik, was burning with fever. With no medication available, the doctor could only suggest one thing: "Pray!"

Chaya Sima, Yisrael Chaim, Nechama, and even little Yocheved recited Psalms diligently, but the baby faded away before their very eyes. By morning, he was no longer with them.

He was the fourth Blumenthal child laid to rest in the local cemetery. Even as Chana Shaina lifted her tearful eyes to the heavens to accept the terrible decree, she begged, "Master of the Universe, You took half of my children. Please don't take the other half, too."

Returning home to Batei Ungarin was difficult. The rooms where Chana Shaina had watched four of her children breathe their last were a constant reminder of her great pain. The Blumenthals therefore decided to rent an apartment in a new neighborhood, Achva (to the north of today's Zichron Moshe neighborhood), established several years earlier.

MORE LOSS

For Avraham Yochanan's father, Yaakov Blumenthal, the war years took their toll as well. The poor and hungry knew that he would never turn anyone away, and they frequently came knocking at his door. Even as his wealth diminished, he put others' needs ahead of his own and distributed most of his earthly belongings, all the while lending a listening ear and a good word to those who sought help.

In the summer of 1915, Yaakov developed an intestinal illness due to the lack of proper nutrition. He was unable to digest the coarse flour that was available during the war, and he could no longer afford to pay the exorbitant price of wheat. After Sukkot of that year, his strength waned, and on October 20, 1916 (12 Cheshvan 5676), at the age of seventy, his holy soul ascended to the heavens. Rabbi Yosef Chaim Sonnenfeld was among those who eulogized him at the funeral.

The Blumenthals were not alone in their suffering. At the outbreak of war, approximately fifty thousand Jews lived in Jerusalem. By the end of the war, the population had diminished by fifty percent, with malnourishment and disease claiming twenty-five thousand lives.

EYE AFFLICTIONS

Many Jerusalem citizens in those years were afflicted with eye problems. Prior to the war, the one recognized eye doctor in Jerusalem was an unsympathetic German gentile whose waiting room was consistently overflowing with patients hoping to find a solution for their painful eyes.

One morning, Chaya Sima awoke with a terrible pain in her eyes, which refused to open. The family sought out the non-Jewish doctor, who treated her harshly. Later, it became evident that the so-called treatment had damaged Chaya Sima's eye irreparably.

It wasn't long before people put two and two together and realized that the anti-Semitic doctor was deliberately inflicting harm on his patients. A complaint was filed with the Turkish police, who arrested the doctor and deported him from the country.

COMMUNAL MISFORTUNE

New troubles befell Jewish settlements in the Holy Land with the arrival of a plague of locusts in March 1916. The locusts speedily devoured leaves, peeled away at tree bark, and demolished the grass. There was little relief when they left, as the locusts had laid eggs in every crack and crevice. Once the eggs hatched, a new generation devoured everything the original locusts had left behind.

The Turkish police announced that every adult was required to collect and destroy five kilograms of locust eggs. Some quick thinkers turned the new law into a profitable business. They collected huge amounts of locust eggs and sold five kilograms for half a Turkish lira to anyone who did not want to personally go out to the fields to collect eggs. After purchasing five kilograms from these "merchants," people presented them to the police and received a pass.

At times, the police drafted all male adults for an entire day of gathering and destroying eggs. Despite these efforts, not all the eggs were collected, and after a short while new locusts began to emerge. Once again, the citizens were called upon to destroy the insects as the Turkish police stood over them.

As it was wartime and the country was cut off from the world, there was no way to import food staples from overseas, and the locust plague meant that food was even scarcer than before. Children stood at the sides of the road, their hands outstretched, crying out in Arabic, "*Jawan, jawan* (hungry, hungry)..."

CHAPTER 4

The Zion War Orphanage Is Born

With the end of war nowhere in sight, hunger racked the city. In school, young children lay inert on wooden benches as they studied, lacking the energy to sit up. People resorted to eating orange peels when the oranges themselves were long gone.

American aid stepped in, allotting a daily ration of one hundred eighty grams of bread (about a quarter-loaf) to each child in the city who was registered in school. Rather than eating the bread at school, however, many children saved their rations and brought them home at the day's end, where it was divided among their starving siblings.

Each Friday afternoon, teenage boys would go from house to house in the Jewish neighborhoods, making sure that each family had at least one loaf of bread to honor the Shabbat. The loaves were donated by kind people who responded to appeals in synagogues around the city. The bread was gathered into large sacks, which the youngsters slung over their backs as they went from door to door, repeating their refrain, "Either give [a loaf] or take!"

A general committee to aid the poor lent money to poverty-stricken families and wrote letters of appeal to Jews in other countries. Through the generosity of Nathan Strauss, a wealthy American Jewish philanthropist, centers were established to distribute bread and tea to the needy, and to arrange for shiploads of basic staples to be sent from America. Community activists used every connection at their disposal to acquire food for the hungry masses.

Children with eyes glazed over from hunger roamed the streets of Jerusalem. Hunger chased them outdoors, where they hoped to find a scrap of food to quiet the starvation that gnawed at their innards. Crumpling into street corners, they stretched out limp hands to passersby, begging for something, anything, to eat.

A PRECIOUS "FIND"

The Blumenthal family fared no better. One morning, Chaya Sima went out to buy flour. When she asked the grocer permission to buy the flour on credit, he said, "Tell your mother to pay up the huge debt she has already, and then I will sell her flour." Chaya Sima left the store in shame, empty-handed.

She dragged herself home, eyes downcast. Suddenly she saw a row of black olives in the street. Excitedly, she thought, *I'll bring them home and we'll have something to eat!* She began gathering the olives into the folds of her long skirt.

Arriving home, Chaya Sima rolled her treasure onto the table. "The grocer refused to give us flour on credit," she said. "But look, I found olives."

Chana Shaina turned to study her daughter's find by the weak light of the kerosene lamp. Quickly, she discerned the truth. The "olives" her daughter had gathered were none other than goat manure!

SAVING THE CHILDREN

The Turkish mayor of Jerusalem, Hussein Bey al-Husayni, could no longer ignore the suffering of the Jewish children. In the autocratic manner of the day, he penned a letter to the Sephardic chief rabbi, Chacham

Nissim Danon, ordering him to arrange suitable housing for the orphaned children filling the streets. Along with a veiled threat of consequences if the matter was not attended to, he added that he had asked the Jewish Syndicate to allot each child half a kilogram of wheat per day.[1]

An anxious Chacham Danon turned to several institutions in the hope they would accept responsibility for these suffering children, but each responded that it was full to capacity and hard-pressed to feed even the children already in its care. Desperate, Danon appealed to Avraham Yochanan Blumenthal, director of the Educational Home for Boys, which until that time was known as a refuge for disadvantaged boys. If Rabbi Blumenthal did not accept the task, he feared the children would be turned over to various non-Jewish institutions in the city.

The request proved to be one that changed history. Chacham Danon's written supplication, sent by messenger to the Blumenthal home, pierced Avraham Yochanan's soft heart. Despite the wretchedness around him and the hunger in his own home, Avraham Yochanan envisioned the starving children standing in the streets, palms outstretched, desperate eyes pleading for help.

Can I really handle the extra burden of caring for dozens, if not hundreds, of homeless children? he wondered. On the other hand, at this difficult time, with no one else willing or able to act, perhaps he was required to accept the task.

Rabbi Blumenthal weighed out the issue:

> *We are children of Abraham who taught humanity that "even greater than speaking with God is to emulate Him, and do whatever possible to help others." This is why I accepted the recommendation of Rabbi Diskin to open the Educational Institute in the first place. I have embraced the task, despite the overwhelming challenges.*
>
> *The need to expand the operation is clearly needed, to provide for children from dysfunctional homes who would otherwise be lost to their people. And the Torah enjoins us to care especially for orphans. But how can I possibly handle such responsibility?*

---

1   The Jewish Syndicate was an organization created by the Turkish government to provide its citizens with bread during the war. Originally three-and-a-half kilograms were allotted per week, but the amount gradually decreased over the course of the war until it ceased entirely.

*The current burden is already so great! Then again, our Sages
teach that in a situation where no one is taking responsibility,
we must make the effort to be that person.*

With these conflicting thoughts in mind, Avraham Yochanan presented the dilemma to his mentor, Rabbi Yosef Chaim Sonnenfeld. The
response was unequivocal: "You must open the doors of the Educational
Institute and take in these children. It is a challenging task, but the
Almighty will stand by your side!"

With his wife's support, Avraham Yochanan sat down to pen his
response to Chacham Danon with a sure and steady hand. He would
devote himself entirely to these children; he would open his home and
heart to them, no matter what it entailed.

"My heart bleeds," he wrote to Chacham Danon, "when I walk the streets
of Jerusalem, and the precious children of Zion are rolling like dung in the
fields...I am prepared to devote my energies to the aid of my young brethren...

"[You are] surely aware that the care and education of these children,
especially children as neglected as these, requires tremendous exertion
and effort, which I will devote willingly to rescue hundreds of children
from the fangs of destruction, and [to save] Jerusalem from her shame,
and the glory of our nation from disgrace..."

Avraham Yochanan then requested that Chacham Danon aid him
in establishing a financial base to provide for the children, asking that
several committees in existence at the time — the American Committee,
the Committee to Aid German Jews, the Committee to Aid Jews from
Amsterdam, and the Nathan Strauss Committee — each set aside a weekly sum to enable opening the doors of his institute to these children.

Chacham Danon and Avraham Yochanan met several days later, on
February 20, 1917, in the headquarters of the American Committee,
together with several other community activists. Chacham Danon
promised to establish a committee that would provide a financial base
for the children and asked Avraham Yochanan to start by accepting
fifteen orphaned children into his school by the next morning.

Avraham Yochanan agreed, and Chacham Danon wrote out a check
covering the children's provisions. The orphanage was now a reality.

CHAPTER 5

Off the Streets at Last

After the meeting, events moved quickly. Chacham Danon penned his response to Mayor al-Husayni. The next morning, a message was conveyed to the police commissioner, who ordered two police officers to gather fifteen Jewish boys from the marketplace and bring them to the Educational Institute, on the corner of Yoel and Avinoam Yellin Streets (part of today's Geulah neighborhood).

Fifteen boys — most of them orphans, clad in rags or even blankets, and on the verge of collapse from starvation — were duly chosen from the masses and marched through the streets by the two Turkish officers. The pitiful parade of terrified children soon arrived at the gate of the institute, where Avraham Yochanan anticipated their arrival.

"Come, children," he invited them inside. The frightened boys hesitantly followed him into the building, where a long table had been set with sliced bread and cups of hot tea — a veritable feast for their hungry eyes.

40

Avraham Yochanan could not take his eyes off them. The children's bare feet were swollen from cold, their hair was tangled and lice infested, and their clothing was mostly rags.

"My dear children," Avraham Yochanan declared emotionally once they had eaten, "from this day forward, you will no longer roam the streets. This house will be your home. Here we will provide all your needs — food, clothing, and schooling so that you will grow up happy and successful. If you follow the rules and listen to your counselors, you will blossom."

He said nothing about the layers of dirt covering the neglected children, his loving gaze seeing beyond the filth and despair. He saw straight to their souls, as pure as diamonds, and prayed for the ability to clean those diamonds of the muck that covered them.

BATH AND BEDTIME

The entire Blumenthal family quickly rallied to the cause. Chana Shaina and Chaya Sima made the beds and organized the kitchen and laundry for the new arrivals. Yisrael Chaim, who had recently turned bar mitzvah, lent a hand as well. Avraham Yochanan had hired several counselors to attend to the youngsters' needs, most of them alumni of the Educational Institute, including Binyamin Hausman, Pinchas Segal, and Zeidel Hollander.

After lunch, the counselors directed the children to bathe in the tubs of heated water that had been prepared for them. This was an enormous task, as many of the children had not seen soap and water for days or even weeks. Working with ceaseless devotion, the counselors scrubbed them clean, examining every scratch and bandaging every wound.

The children returned to the dining room hours later, looking significantly more civilized than the group that had arrived earlier in the afternoon.

After supper, each child was assigned a bed with fresh linen. The food, baths, beds, and most of all the knowledge that someone cared about them and their needs comforted the boys. One by one, they drifted off to a peaceful slumber for the first time in many months.

SWEET DREAMS

Later that evening, Avraham Yochanan tiptoed into the room to look at the exhausted faces. In their sleep, the children's worries and pain momentarily eased. Just yesterday, they had slept out in the streets, with nary a wall or window to shield them from the cold winds. Now, they belonged to him. They had no parents to care for them, and it was his task to be their father.

He tried to remember their names: Shalom Suisa, Eliyahu Manola, Mordechai Ben Chanuka, Nissim Ben Aga, Yosef and Moshe Braha, Shmuel Abu, David Ben Menashe, Avraham and Yaakov Hasson, little Yosef Ben Refael, Eliyahu and Baruch Mizrahi, Shalom Chavshush, and Chaim Sved…

He had four children at home, and now another fifteen had been delivered to him in one day. How many more would join their ranks?

Avraham Yochanan left the room quietly. In addition to the joy he felt at the heartwarming sight, the full burden of responsibility now weighed on his shoulders. Not only would he have to provide the children's physical needs — food, clothing, proper housing, and clean beds — but he also had to establish a new type of educational framework and guide them to becoming functional adults.

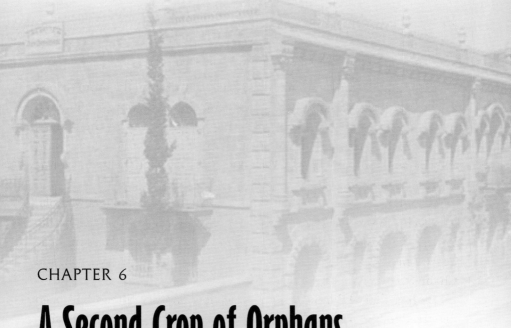

CHAPTER 6

A Second Crop of Orphans

That same evening, Chacham Danon called a meeting to establish a firm financial base for the brand-new orphanage. Each of the four committees invited to the meeting pledged a monthly sum to support the orphans, and it was decided that another fifteen orphans could be absorbed into the fledgling institution.

In order to avoid involving the Turkish authorities, three men were appointed to send Jewish representatives to the marketplace the next morning and gather up fifteen new children.

NEW ARRIVALS

In the orphanage, a new day dawned, and the children were awakened by their counselors, directed to wash up, and given breakfast. Their weary bodies refreshed, they were ready to start a new day. Outside, however, there were still dozens of youngsters, bereft of parents and home, waiting for someone to take notice of them.

One by one, new children began arriving at the orphanage building, accompanied by a messenger who handed Avraham Yochanan a short note with the child's name. The notes read as follows:

> As per the request of the chief rabbi [Chacham Danon], I request that his honor take in the orphan Avraham Ponis. His parents have died, and he is out in the streets. Kindly accept him (as per our arrangements).
>
> Respectfully yours,
> Yosef Elyashir, President of the Sephardic community

> To the honorable citizen, Avraham Yochanan Blumenthal:
> As room has been set aside in your institute for children roaming the streets, I am requesting that you take in Avraham Lari, son of Binyamin, whose father died in the army and whose mother is blind. He is thus left to fend for himself.
>
> Respectfully yours,
> Halil Bey, Police Commissioner

KADDISH

One boy did not walk into the orphanage but was carried in, burning with fever, by a messenger sent by Rabbi David Agababa, principal of the Sephardic school Tifereth Jerusalem. The child, Yom Tov Crispin, had been orphaned of his mother three months earlier. His father had been drafted into the army at the start of the war and knew nothing of the fate of his family.

Realizing that the boy was very ill, Avraham Yochanan immediately made arrangements to have him transferred to the hospital to avoid infecting the other children. Two of the orphanage's employees began to lift the feverish boy onto a stretcher.

When Yom Tov grasped what was happening, his flushed face paled. "No!" he protested weakly. "No, not the hospital! I need to say Kaddish!"

The employees hesitated. Avraham Yochanan leaned over and asked gently, "What's that, my child?"

"Father is in the army," Yom Tov mumbled, his words barely audible. "Mother is dead, and I must say Kaddish for her! There is no one else... Soon it will be time for afternoon prayers. I want to say Kaddish, and afterward you can take me to the hospital..."

No one could refuse such a heartrending request. The boy was carried to the orphanage prayer room where — with superhuman strength — he uttered the words of Kaddish, "*Yitgadal veyitkadash Shmei Rabba.*"

Afterward, he was carried to the hospital, where he remained for several weeks. Fully recovered, he returned to the orphanage, which became his new home.

"MOTHER, YOU'RE HUNGRY"

Like their contemporaries the previous day, the new group of children hungrily inhaled the black bread that was served in the dining room. A hum of conversation filled the room as the "old-timers" related their experiences to the new arrivals.

Later that evening, as the children prepared for bed, Avraham Yochanan heard the sound of quiet sobbing. In the corner of one of the dormitory rooms, a thin form sat huddled. It was Avraham Lari, the boy who had been brought to the orphanage on the police commissioner's command.

Placing a hand on the boy's shoulder, Avraham Yochanan asked softly, "Why are you crying, my son?"

Slowly, the child lifted his tear-stained face and related, "My mother is blind and has nothing to eat. Until now, we survived by begging for coins from passersby, but now I am here and she is home alone..."

He showed Avraham Yochanan a crumbled piece of black bread. "I saved this for my mother. Can you bring it to her so she won't starve?"

The tears rose to Avraham Yochanan's eyes. He stroked the child's cheek and assured him that he would help his mother in whatever way he could.

Later that night, as he made his rounds through the rooms again, he stopped near little Avraham's bed. Even in his sleep, the child was moaning. "Mother, you're hungry..."

CHAPTER 7

Funding Needed

B y the end of their first week in the orphanage, the thirty children had become a lively group, with little trace of the weak apparitions who had been begging for bread just days earlier. Responding to the devoted care of Mrs. Blumenthal and her staff, the comforting rhythm of a daily routine, and Avraham Yochanan's loving guidance, the children blossomed.

Outside the orphanage, however, dozens of neglected children still scrounged the garbage bins in the vain hope of finding a scrap of food. Eyewitnesses of the time recall these desperate children collecting orange peels and thorny sabra fruit, looking for any possible source of nourishment. People wandered the streets with bodies swollen from hunger, and entire homes were emptied of inhabitants. If both parents were gone, the children had almost no hope of survival; extended families had vanished to the vicissitudes of war.

MORE CHILDREN, MORE EFFORTS

On February 27, 1917, only a week after its initial meeting, the committee established to aid the orphans gathered again and decided unanimously that it could not rest on its laurels. The committee members would spare no effort to ensure that other children roaming the streets would be placed in Rabbi Blumenthal's care as well. (As the Educational Institute only took in boys, girls were sent to Rabbi David Weingarten's orphanage for girls, the GIOH, established in 1902.)

A six-year-old child in the orphanage

Avraham Yochanan agreed to accept more children, though his building was already filled to capacity. "If we take in more children, we will need a larger building," he informed the committee members. "I need your assistance in financing these efforts."

The committee members concluded that Rabbi Blumenthal should rent a larger building, with half of the rent increase covered by the committee and the other half to be covered personally by Chacham Danon.

The meeting was adjourned, with the members feeling well on their way to expanding the Educational Institute. Their joy, however, was premature.

FINANCIAL WOES

Two months earlier, the Turkish police had conducted a thorough search of the offices of the American Committee and discovered a cache of gold coins. It was illegal to possess gold at that time, and the Turks confiscated everything. Now, mere days after the committee had promised to assist in covering the orphanage's costs, an order arrived from

Istanbul for the American Committee to be disbanded immediately. The committee's records were confiscated and its resources transferred to the American Consulate, which would henceforth preside over the distribution of charity arriving from the United States.

Meanwhile, the Committee to Aid German Jews, which had originally pledged twenty-five Turkish liras per month in support of the orphans, was forced to close as well, and in time, the Committee to Aid Jews from Amsterdam also dissolved. Only the Nathan Strauss Committee was still able to stand by its commitments.

Though the Nathan Strauss Committee continued to cover the cost of bread for the orphans, Avraham Yochanan suddenly found himself with no other steady source of income. Meanwhile, the children kept coming.

RECORDKEEPING

As the children poured in, Avraham Yochanan carefully recorded each child's personal information in a special notebook. Each entry included, in Avraham Yochanan's clear script, the boy's name, his parents' names, his origins, and any other known details:

> *Name: Shalom Samivasya*
> *Age: 14*
> *Parents: Orphaned of father (Massoud) and mother (Sara)*
> *Origins: Yemenite*
> *Citizenship: Turkish*
> *Place of Birth: Jerusalem*
> *Place of Residence: Beit Yisrael neighborhood*
> *Relatives in Israel: None*
> *Doctor's examination: Dr. Yarmons*
> *Date of admission: Wednesday, March 23, 1917 (29 Adar 5677)*
> *Means of admission: By order of the government, Police Officer*
> *#112 (Halil Efendi)*

On the adjacent page Avraham Yochanan left space for notes on the boy's studies, the date of his bar mitzvah, and other information to be added later. The notebook filled rapidly, its pages including many question marks where records were unavailable.

"WELCOME HOME"

By the end of its first month, the number of children in the Blumenthals' care had climbed to a staggering 128. The children quickly filled every inch of space of the larger building that Avraham Yochanan had rented in the Achva neighborhood. Even so, orphans continued to arrive. Despite the desperate financial situation and crowded conditions, Avraham Yochanan did not have the heart to send any child away.

With limited outside funding to rely upon, Avraham Yochanan began to use his personal resources for the orphanage's upkeep. When

A letter from the Turkish commissar, requesting that a child be accepted into the orphanage

that too was consumed, he borrowed money, giving his personal items of value as collateral — even pawning the heirloom silver candlesticks his wife had inherited from her grandmother. Anything to nourish the orphans in his care.

A new routine developed: Upon arrival at the orphanage, children would be seated in a heated room and wrapped in a blanket, waiting for their ragged clothes to be laundered. The clothing was immersed in boiling water to remove the lice, vigorously scrubbed free of dust and stains, and finally dried before being returned. New clothing was not yet part of the orphanage budget.

Some children arrived with open wounds buzzing with flies. Others were feverish and ill. When there was reason to suspect that a child was contagious, he was placed in quarantine so as not to endanger the others. After receiving proper medical attention, he would be allowed to join his peers.

While most of the new arrivals ranged in age from six to fourteen, a few older teens joined the group as well. Two teenage brothers, a silent plea in their eyes, knocked on the door one morning in March, handing Rabbi Blumenthal a letter they had written, along with a note from Chacham Danon.

> To the honorable Rabbi Nissim Danon:
>
> We left our father's house many months ago, filled with dreams and faith. Our ambition was to bring life to the youth of our hometown by providing them with a Jewish education. We traveled to the Land of Israel, and our father supplied us with all we required, both physically and spiritually.
>
> In Jerusalem, we began to study [Torah]. At first we lacked nothing, but with the arrival of war, our situation rapidly deteriorated. Our father tried to provide for us, but the aid he sent was a drop in the ocean due to the staggering expense of food. As the war progressed, his aid ceased to arrive altogether, and we began to feel the pangs of hunger. We are alone and bereft, with no acquaintances or relatives in the country.
>
> Our hunger increases daily, and there are times when we do not eat for a full day. Our classmates have pity on us and occasionally bring us a slice of bread...
>
> We beg of you to come to our aid, for we no longer have the strength to continue.
>
> > Yosef and Shimon Pesach,
> > sons of Rabbi Moshe Pesach of Greece

Chacham Danon's request was attached to this letter, "Please accept these unfortunate young men. It is evident from their letter that they are sons of noble people and they arrived in Jerusalem for a lofty purpose."

Avraham Yochanan's gaze took in the two youths, who appeared to be about sixteen and seventeen years old. "Welcome home," he said.

FUNDS FOR THE HOLIDAY

Spring approached, heralding the Passover holiday. As housewives beat straw mattresses on their tiny balconies, scoured their pots, and repainted their walls in anticipation of the holiday, new children continued to arrive at the orphanage doors.

Although he knew the facilities were too small to hold them all, and there were scant resources for their upkeep, the situation was so dire that Chacham Danon continued to send children — accompanied by a note that read, "Please accept this child until we have another solution," or "Please make this one exception." The many exceptions became the new rule.

Avraham Yochanan could no longer ignore the glaring lack of funds for his newly founded orphanage. He penned a desperate letter to Chacham Danon: "Passover is approaching, and I have no way of obtaining everything needed for the holiday…"

In response, Chacham Danon urged Avraham Yochanan to "be patient" in light of the difficult circumstances. "There are still children who are worse off than those in the orphanage," he wrote, "and we must attempt to find a solution for all of them…"

Avraham Yochanan then requested that the orphanage committee ask the American Consulate for funding for the orphanage upkeep. The committee, despairing of the situation, decided to disband. Avraham Yochanan had to meet with the American consul himself.

On April 2, just four days before Passover, Avraham Yochanan met with the American consul, Dr. Otis Glazebrook, who promised that each orphan would receive a stipend of forty *grush* (one-hundredth of the Turkish lira) for food and a kilogram and a half of matzah for the holiday, when they could not eat bread. After the holiday, he would establish a committee to care for the orphans' needs.

With great effort, Avraham Yochanan succeeded in attaining another seventy-five kilograms of matzah, courtesy of another charity organization in the city, and procured wine for the Seder from the Carmel Winery, which donated one thousand liters of wine to the city's poor each year. The orphans would have food for the holiday.

CHAPTER 8

Preparing for Passover

A week before Passover, a boy named Yaakov Cohen was carried into the orphanage, bearing a note from Rabbi Agababa, principal of Tifereth Jerusalem: "Kindly accept this boy, Yaakov, son of Shlomo and Rivka Cohen. His mother is dead and his father is in the army."

Avraham Yochanan placed a hand on the boy's forehead and discovered that he was burning with fever. He quickly directed two of his assistants to take the boy to the hospital. The next day, he went to see how the child was faring.

"He has typhus," the hospital staff informed him. "We're doing the best we can."

The hospital's "best" was, unfortunately, not much. With most of the hospitals in the city shut down by the Turks and the remaining ones combating various contagious diseases — without electricity, indoor plumbing, central heating, gas cooking stoves, or sufficient staff — little could be done to help the ill. Young Yaakov grew weaker and weaker, passing away just before the onset of the holiday.

Upon hearing the bitter news, Avraham Yochanan realized that he could no longer send the children in his charge to the hospital. With no parents to sit by their sides and ensure that they received proper care, orphaned children had almost no hope of survival in the understaffed public hospitals. The orphanage would need an infirmary of its own.

Avraham Yochanan hired a doctor and a pharmacist to make daily rounds in the orphanage, and the very next day — the day before the holiday — the infirmary became a reality. The next child who arrived at the orphanage with signs of typhus, Avraham Rekanati, was cared for in the infirmary where he fortunately recovered.

A COLLATERAL FOR MATZAH

At last, the holiday arrived. One hundred children recited evening prayers and entered the dining room dressed in freshly laundered clothing, their excitement over the holiday tempered by longing and sorrow as they recalled past Seder nights spent with their parents. But as Avraham Yochanan led the Seder, songs of hope and praise echoed through the room. The matzah, wine, and feeling of togetherness enveloped the children with joy.

Yet during the intermediate days of the holiday, Avraham Yochanan realized that the orphanage's supply of matzah was dwindling quickly. Another two days of the holiday remained, and they had almost nothing left.

He approached Shmuel Moshayoff, who worked for the American Consulate, and asked if the consulate could cover the cost of more matzah. Moshayoff regretfully explained that he had nothing left to give. "All the monetary aid allotted by the consulate for the holiday has long been distributed."

Not feeding the children for the next three days wasn't a possibility. Suddenly, a solution occurred to the distressed director. A temporary solution at best, but it was all he had.

In addition to undertaking responsibility for the orphanage, the Blumenthals had celebrated a joyous occasion that winter: Chaya Sima had become engaged to a young man named Fischel Zaks. As the family had scrubbed the orphanage in anticipation of the holiday, a messenger arrived with a beautiful gold necklace, a gift for Chaya Sima from her future husband.

Returning home, Avraham Yochanan turned to his daughter. "Chaya Sima, we have no matzahs for the remainder of the holiday, and our money has been exhausted. Can we pawn your necklace to buy matzahs?"

The girl's hands flew to her neck. With barely a moment's hesitation, she removed the necklace and handed it to her father.

"The kind deed you have done is the greatest jewel of all," Avraham Yochanan assured her, "and it will stand you in good stead as you build your own home. I pray that we will be able to reclaim it quickly."

Necklace in hand, Avraham Yochanan returned to Mr. Moshayoff. "This is my daughter's," he explained. "I brought it as a collateral, in exchange for your note instructing the matzah bakery to provide the orphanage with matzahs for the rest of the holiday."

Mr. Moshayoff immediately wrote the note, telling Avraham Yochanan, "After the holiday, when I have funds available, I'll pay for these additional matzahs and return the necklace."

Avraham Yochanan redeemed the necklace at the first opportunity. Chaya Sima, however, insisted on giving it as a collateral when the orphanage's coffers emptied yet again. She would borrow it back whenever her fiancé visited. Only after the war was over did she reclaim it permanently.

BREAD AT LAST

On Sunday morning, the day after the holiday, the counselors announced to the children, "Today you'll be getting bread!" After a week of matzah, bread was a special treat.

Two boys were sent to Shlomo Roth, director of the Nathan Strauss Committee, which had committed to providing bread for the orphans. But they returned to the orphanage empty-handed. The committee had exhausted its funds, and Rabbi Roth could no longer provide the orphanage with its needs.

With one hundred children waiting for bread, Avraham Yochanan quickly called upon Mr. Moshayoff and Dr. Helena Kagan, a pediatrician and community activist affiliated with the consulate. The three met with Rabbi Roth, who apologetically explained, "I promised to provide bread for the children only until a proper committee was established to care for them. Now that the consulate is organizing such a committee, my aid is no longer necessary."

He agreed, however, to temporarily continue providing bread until the new committee was operational. Meanwhile, Dr. Kagan asked Avraham Yochanan to draw up a list of all the orphans in the city and present it to the consulate, to assist in establishing a committee.

When the bread finally arrived at the orphanage that day, the children greeted it with whoops of joy, oblivious to the battle their director had fought to obtain it.

CHAPTER 9

Typhus

A s the scent of spring filled the air, Avraham Yochanan was preoccupied with the myriad responsibilities on his head. Then, just two days after Passover, he awoke weak and feverish. The doctor who came to examine the children checked Avraham Yochanan and issued a somber verdict: typhus. Avraham Yochanan had become infected by the highly contagious virus while caring for young Avraham Rekanati, who had arrived at the orphanage only a short while earlier.

Within days, his daughter Chaya Sima and a teacher tending to young Avraham both fell ill as well. Chana Shaina was left to care for the three patients, in addition to managing the orphanage in her husband's place. Young Yisrael Chaim stepped in to help out, lending a hand to his mother and to Binyamin Hausman, the head counselor, who worked tirelessly to keep the institution running.

At first, the orphans were skeptical of the new "director." Eventually, however, they formed a close connection with Yisrael Chaim, who served as a loving older brother to many of them. Under his supervision and that of the devoted counselors, the daily routine in the orphanage continued with prayers, meals, and studies.

"GO HOME"

When news of Avraham Yochanan's illness reached Dr. Moshe Wallach, founder and director of Shaare Zedek Hospital, he immediately dispatched a private nurse to help care for the patients. Yet in those pre-antibiotics days, there was little they could do.

Avraham Yochanan's fever raged for over two weeks. His wife followed his progress apprehensively, her lips murmuring prayers. Less than a year after the loss of two of her children, would the Angel of Death once more approach the stricken household and steal away more precious souls?

The orphans too tearfully recited Psalms for their director's speedy recovery. "Our father is sick," they cried, sensing instinctively that Avraham Yochanan's illness placed their lives in danger as well.

Dr. Moshe Wallach, founder of Shaare Zedek Hospital

As the disease took its toll, Avraham Yochanan lost consciousness. After three days, rumor spread that he had died. Neighbors began gathering outside the building, whispering words of eulogy about the beloved man and casting pitying glances at the children.

The nurse, however, held onto the hope that her patient would recover. Taking matters into her own hands, she rolled up a wet towel and began to strike her patient in an effort to revive him. Incredibly, Avraham Yochanan's eyes opened. In a weak voice, he said, "No hitting!"

"He's alive," the cry burst out of the nurse's mouth. The news spread like wildfire down the hallway, to the children, the counselors, and the neighbors who had solemnly crowded outside. It was a miracle!

As soon as the nurse ascertained that Avraham Yochanan was truly awake, she hurried to Chaya Sima, in the process of recovery herself.

The nurse prepared a cup of black coffee and instructed the girl to spoon-feed it to her father to help him regain strength.

Later, Avraham Yochanan related an out-of-body experience that occurred as he lay unconscious and delirious. His father, Yaakov, had appeared and began leading him toward a series of magnificent galleries. As he attempted to enter one of them, Yaakov said, "It's not for you now. Go home."

At that point, he felt the nurse's blows and regained consciousness. There was still work to be done on earth.

BACK TO WORK

The process of recovery was slow but steady. Although Chaya Sima remained in bed, Avraham Yochanan felt he could not allow himself the luxury of resting. His responsibilities beckoned.

Still weak, he began to review the list of orphans he had begun to compile the day before the typhus struck, which his assistants had completed as he lay ill.

The tally revealed a shocking three thousand seven hundred Jewish orphans in Jerusalem. These unfortunate souls were divided into five categories: children orphaned of both parents; children orphaned of their father; children orphaned of their mother; children orphaned of their mother and abandoned by a father who had been drafted or forced to travel abroad; and children abandoned by both parents, either because they had traveled abroad or because they had lost contact in the havoc of war.

Avraham Yochanan submitted the list to Dr. Kagan and turned to the challenge of feeding and clothing over one hundred children on almost no budget. Every new child accepted to the orphanage came with the inevitable dilemma of how to provide a bed, a blanket, and a set of clothing. Every meal on the orphanage table was the result of endless strategizing.

HOT SOUP AND TEXTBOOKS

Rabbi Roth, who managed many of the city's charity funds, continued to provide daily rations of bread, which the children ate three times a day. Hot soup for the afternoon meal came from the Strauss Soup Kitchen. A few children were appointed to carry oversized metal containers to the soup kitchen, where they were filled with either hot vegetable soup or beans, and then carefully carried back to the orphanage.

When the other children saw the food coming, they sang out in Arabic, "*Adza shurba! Adza shurba!* (Hot soup! Hot soup!)"

The only other "luxury" the children enjoyed was tea, the Middle Eastern drink of choice. Due to the lack of sugar, the hot beverage was served with a fig, which the children sucked between sips in order to sweeten the bitter drink.

No less important than food to Avraham Yochanan was the children's spiritual welfare. He hired teachers and sought out prayer books, Bibles, and other Jewish texts. Since the city's printing presses had been shut down due to the war and bookstores were nonexistent, he had to collect used books, not an easy feat in an impoverished city, where few families owned more than they needed. Often, several children used one book together.

CHAPTER 10

The First Summer

Another incident that stands out in the Blumenthal family chronicles was the shocking disappearance of three-year-old Yocheved one morning. The little girl had been playing with a friend, Chayala Heller, and the two of them could not be found in either home or in the communal courtyard.

A search began, with cries of "Chayala! Yocheved!" ringing through the yard. But to no avail. The two little girls had vanished.

When the entire house had been searched from top to bottom, the search spread outdoors. "I saw them over there in the morning," one of the children suddenly recalled, pointing toward the street. No one else had seen them since. The two girls had last been seen strolling hand in hand away from home.

The search parties turned westward, toward the barren fields at the edge of the neighborhood, calling the girls' names with increasing urgency. Had they been kidnapped? No one dared to voice the frightening thought, but as the hours passed, the possibility became ever more plausible.

Suddenly, the search party discerned a suspicious figure near a mound of sand in the distance. The group quickly advanced, catching by surprise the Arab who was spreading sand over the earth. They heard a whimper and a muffled cough. "They're here!"

The little girls were almost completely buried in sand and had nearly lost consciousness. They were quickly lifted out and carried home, to the relief of their horrified parents. The Arab, meanwhile, took advantage of the momentary confusion to escape.

THE DOCTORS' COMMITTEE

Realizing he had been spared from yet another potential tragedy, Avraham Yochanan renewed his efforts to help the orphans, feeling the hand of God protecting him and his family.

Although Turkish law forbade the formation of new committees during wartime, medical committees were the one exception. Doctors were allowed to form committees in order to consult and implement new ways of ensuring the health and safety of the city's citizens.

Using the law to its advantage, the American Consulate established a committee of local Jewish doctors charged with finding a solution to the thousands of Jewish orphans — among them Dr. Moshe Wallach, director of Shaare Zedek Hospital; Dr. Abraham Ticho, a well-known ophthalmologist; Dr. Arieh Behem, a founder of the Hebrew-Speaking Physicians' Society; and Dr. Helena Kagan.

At first, Dr. Ticho suggested placing many more orphans in Avraham Yochanan's care. This would require renting a suitably larger facility and providing a monthly stipend for each child. But it soon became clear that this was impossible, as there were too many people dependent on the monies distributed by the committee and not enough money to go around.

With fierce fighting between the British and Ottoman forces in southern Palestine during March and April of 1917, followed by a six-month stalemate as the two armies reinforced their military positions, there was little relief for the beleaguered and war-weary residents of Jerusalem. If anything, the situation only worsened.

DESPERATE TIMES

Boys filled every corner of the Educational Institute, which had long since outgrown its new building. The children slept in shifts, with four children sharing each bed and each of them sleeping for a quarter of the night. No child had more than one set of clothing. When their clothes needed washing, they would sit huddled in blankets until the freshly laundered garments were returned.

In bed at night

Despite the orphanage's grave financial situation, new children kept arriving. Meanwhile, the ration of bread provided by the Doctors' Committee kept decreasing. Each child now received only three-quarters of an *oka* (a Turkish measurement, the equivalent of 240 grams) of bread each day.

One morning in July, two brothers, Alter and Moshe Cohen, arrived at the orphanage bearing a note from Dr. Kagan stating she was shocked to learn the boys were subsisting on an *oka* and a half of bread per day. She requested that the children be immediately accepted into the orphanage, where she assumed they'd receive better nourishment.

Reading the letter, Avraham Yochanan spread his arms in despair. "I have nothing to give them!" The children of the orphanage themselves only received the ration of bread provided by the Doctors' Committee. What would these brothers gain by joining the others?

In desperation, Avraham Yochanan wrote to the committee again, which finally decided to increase the bread ration for each child for four weeks, "since we have no information regarding future funds arriving from America."

NEW CLOTHES

Having secured the promise of a reasonable supply of bread for the coming weeks, Avraham Yochanan decided to devote a sum of money

donated by Dr. Ticho to properly dressing the children and buying
them shoes.

He informed Rabbi Elyashir, head of the Sephardic community, and
the heads of the Jewish Syndicate of his plans. Both were touched by
his concern for the boys and immediately donated an additional sum of
their own for this need.

Fabric was purchased, despite the wartime conditions, and seamstresses were hired. The Blumenthal girls excitedly joined in the efforts
of sewing underwear, pants, shirts, and *kippot* for the boys. The local
shoemakers measured the children's feet and outfitted each one with a
proper pair of shoes.

The pile of finished clothing grew and grew. Although it was the beginning of the Hebrew month of Av, when new clothes are traditionally
not bought or sewn, the rabbis ruled that in light of circumstances the
seamstresses could continue their work.

CELEBRATION

On the morning of the fifteenth day of Av, a semi-holiday known as
Tu B'Av, there was much activity in the orphanage. The children bathed
and dressed in their new clothing. Then they trooped into the dining
room, where important guests awaited, including members of the
Doctors' Committee and many others who had been involved in helping
to provide their needs.

Together, the children recited the *Shehecheyanu* blessing on donning
a new garment, as many of the guests wiped away tears. Rabbi Ben Zion
Uziel, the chief rabbi of Jaffa (later to become the Sephardic chief rabbi
of Israel), a close friend of Avraham Yochanan's, arrived especially for
the occasion. He lovingly blessed the children to grow up to be good, upright Jews. A modest celebratory meal followed, gladdening the hearts
of all those present.

Cut Off from the Consulate

Despite the children's joy over their new clothing, the orphanage's precarious financial situation remained unresolved. The United States had joined the war on the side of the Allied Forces and against the Ottoman-Turks, forcing the American consul, Dr. Glazebrook, to leave the city. In mid-July, Avraham Yochanan discovered that all the American aid sent to Jerusalem would now be managed by the Spanish consul, Antonio de la Cierva Lewita Ballobar. Avraham Yochanan would have to begin anew his quest for funding, providing the consul with records of the orphanage's activities and explaining its urgent need for food and supplies.

Prior to his hasty departure from the Middle East, the American consul promised that as soon as he arrived in Switzerland, he would contact the US government and ask it to find new ways to send the badly needed funds to Jerusalem. Weeks passed, however, with no sign of the promised aid.

A month after the grand clothing inauguration, Avraham Yochanan sent an urgent appeal to Mr. Moshayoff, while Chacham Danon appealed to the Doctors' Committee. As a result, Avraham Yochanan was summoned to the Doctors' Committee and given a small sum of money to tide the orphanage over for another short period.

A NEW YEAR

The fall breeze replaced the dry heat of summer as the Jewish New Year approached. The children awoke each morning at dawn to recite the special pre-holiday prayers. Throughout Jerusalem, residents hoped and prayed for a new year of blessing and joy.

Meanwhile, the small sum of money Avraham Yochanan received had long vanished, and there was no communication from Jewish activists in the United States, who feared that letters to Jerusalem might result in charges of espionage.

To avoid Turkish censoring of his mail, the Spanish consul Ballobar valiantly traveled to Istanbul to personally relay the difficult situation of Jerusalem's citizens. Ballobar met with the Spanish consul in Istanbul, who had

One of the first children to arrive at the orphanage, barefoot and in rags

greater diplomatic immunity than Ballobar and whose letters were less likely to be intercepted. It was hoped that he could write to the Spanish consul in Switzerland, who would pass on the appeal to Dr. Glazebrook.

In the meantime, the Doctors' Committee persuaded Eliezer Hoffein, a Dutch Jew who managed the Anglo-Palestine Company (precursor to today's Bank Leumi) and an important political figure of the era, to lend a large sum of money to enable continued distribution of daily bread to the city's poor.

Mr. Hoffein distributed sums of money sent from abroad to various institutions around Jerusalem. The week before Rosh Hashanah, his generosity allowed the Doctors' Committee to send the orphanage an unexpectedly large sum, and Avraham Yochanan was able to provide the children with proper holiday meals.

APPEALING TO THE SWEDISH CONSUL

Sukkot passed, along with the last vestiges of summer. The scorching Jerusalem heat made way for cooler mornings and white clouds of the coming winter. But the generous loan Eliezer Hoffein had given the committee was exhausted, and there was no further communication from the United States.

A meal in the dining room

In despair, Avraham Yochanan decided to appeal to the Spanish vice consul, who was responsible for the city's poor in Ballobar's absence.

The vice consul welcomed Avraham Yochanan pleasantly but had little to offer. He showed Avraham Yochanan a letter sent by Ballobar, who wrote that he planned to return to Jerusalem shortly, but he mentioned nothing about money.

"The only thing I can do," the vice consul said, "is write a letter to the

Doctors' Committee appealing to them to find some source of money for you."

Armed with this letter, Avraham Yochanan hurried toward Dr. Wallach's home. Upon reading the letter, Dr. Wallach decided, "We'll take another loan from Hoffein." In response to the unspoken questions that filled the room, he added, "God will help."

RENEWED SOURCES OF AID

When Ballobar returned to Jerusalem several days later, he brought a pleasant surprise: the promised money from Dr. Glazebrook. He had not mentioned it in his letter to his vice consul for fear of it being intercepted and read by Turkish authorities.

Ballobar appointed Mr. Hoffein to manage the distribution of the funds, providing him with an office in the Spanish consulate building. A modest plaque was hung outside the door: *Spanish Consulate, Department of Aid*. Mr. Hoffein now became the address for all of the orphanage's monetary needs.

CHAPTER 12

War Encroaches

With the orphanage's financial situation finally somewhat stabilized, it was time to think about moving to a bigger building. By now, there were close to one hundred fifty orphans in Avraham Yochanan's care, and the current facilities were wholly inadequate. Soon, winter would be upon them, and the children would have to spend more time indoors. They needed more space.

Avraham Yochanan appealed to Mr. Hoffein, who agreed to allocate a modest sum toward renting a larger building. A grateful Avraham Yochanan signed a contract on a two-floor building on Eshtori HaParchi Street, also in the Achva neighborhood (today part of Geulah, off Malchei Yisrael Street). The cost of rent was one hundred sixty Turkish liras for the year.

While Mr. Hoffein made good on his promise to supply rent money, he also began sending new children to join the orphanage. In a note accompanying a group of boys on October 22, he wrote:

> Dear Blumenthal Orphanage,
> I am sending you the following five children: two Kaldiron

brothers, two Braha brothers, and one child named Manovela.
They were found this evening in the streets. Please accept them
into the orphanage for tonight and provide them with food.
This is not a commitment on your part for the future. See me
tomorrow at the consulate to discuss this issue.

Respectfully,
Eliezer Z. Hoffein

Needless to say, "tonight" turned into several weeks, then months, then years.

While Mr. Hoffein had promised to establish a committee to care for all the orphanage's needs, it seemed that Heaven had decreed that these plans be delayed yet again.

THE TIDE TURNS FOR THE BRITISH

With the end of October, the battles in southern Palestine renewed, as the British conquered Beersheba from the Ottoman-Turks and moved on to Gaza. The residents of Jerusalem watched from afar, praying for release from their cruel Turkish rulers. The Turks, however, were determined to push back the British advance.

Meal distribution in the Turkish army. Note the ragtag uniforms

The Balfour Declaration, stating that the British government would look favorably upon "the establishment in Palestine of a National Home for the Jewish people," was

Turkish infantry

publicized in England on November 9, 1917. Upon hearing this news, euphoria reigned in the hearts of the Jewish inhabitants, as many hoped the British arrival would herald the formation of an independent Jewish state.

On November 12, the news arrived in Jerusalem: "The British have broken through the Turkish front in Gaza. They are advancing northward. They will soon be here!"

A sense of anticipation filled the air. Within days, the British captured Ramla, in the center of the country. They were now at Sha'ar HaGai, just outside of Jerusalem, and surrounding the Judean Mountains.

PREPARATIONS FOR WAR

With each passing day, the chaos in Jerusalem increased. Members of the Turkish government began clearing out their offices. The orphanage children sat outside for hours, watching the parade of camels leaving the city.

A Turkish field hospital

Turkish soldiers in the trenches

The Turkish soldiers sang as they marched, "*Bal-adi bal-adi valla bidi ashuf bal-adi bal-adi* (My homeland, my homeland, my soul longs to see you, my homeland)." The monotonous tune accompanied the clouds of dust that billowed up into the air.

From time to time, the children joined in the singing, bringing a smile to the faces of passersby.

But the smiles were fleeting. For the people of Jerusalem, the difficulties grew by the day. Since the German bank holding the orphanage funds had closed down, there was no way to release the badly needed funds. In all the confusion, no one had the time or wherewithal to establish a committee to back the orphanage. With no idea how long the war would last, people tried to hoard whatever provisions they could for the coming days.

Mr. Hoffein provided funds to cover the orphanage's needs for the next three months. With this money, Avraham Yochanan attempted to prepare for his charges' immediate future.

"The Turks are planning to destroy all the flour in the city," the rumors spread one day. "They're going to take all the wheat from the mills so it doesn't fall into British hands."

Fear of this catastrophe buoyed the local committees to quickly distribute all available flour to needy institutions, including the Blumenthal Orphanage.

Strange indeed was the sight of Turkish soldiers, who had not received their own rations, going from door to door begging for bread. Again and again, they repeated the pitiful request: "*Ekmek, ekmek* (bread, bread)."

The smell of smoke hung in the air, along with a tangible air of fear and tension. As British troops gathered in the hills surrounding Jerusalem, the Turks fortified themselves in an attempt to halt the British advance and maintain their tenuous hold on the city. Their stronghold was in the Rama, a mountainous area to the north of Jerusalem, with the Arab village Nabi Samwil (so named for its proximity to the burial place of Samuel the Prophet) at its peak. The city's future would be determined by the impending battle.

CHAPTER 13

The City Surrenders

Although its chances of winning the battle of Jerusalem were slight, the Ottoman Empire continued to cast terror over its hapless citizens. Rumors filled the city that all the Jews would be expelled from Jerusalem. To a nation whose history was replete with homelessness and exile, this fear was very real.

As the British and Turkish troops prepared for battle outside the city, Jewish religious leaders, communal activists, and those holding American citizenship began receiving Turkish edicts of expulsion from Jerusalem. The first to be expelled were Chacham Nissim Danon and Rabbi Ben Zion Uziel, who were escorted to Damascus by Turkish guard as battle broke out in Nabi Samwil.

A British army platoon in Palestine

On November 22, 1917, the British captured the strategic Rama mountaintop from the Turks. Now controlling the road to Jerusalem, they were poised to gain control of the city.

MORE EXPULSIONS

Rabbis Danon and Uziel were permitted to return to Jerusalem after two weeks, but new edicts of expulsion continued to arrive. In addition, mortar shells began to rain down on the city, adding to the dread and fear.

On December 5, Eliezer Hoffein, head of the Yishuv's aid committee, received his order of expulsion. In the days before his scheduled departure, he devoted himself to the needs of the public. The night before he left, he sent a number of sacks of flour to the orphanage to feed the children.

That same night, many Jerusalem citizens were exiled to Damascus, some forcibly pulled out of their beds, never to return. The Austrian consul, in an attempt to "save" all Austro-Hungarian citizens — Avraham Yochanan among them — planned to transport them to Damascus the next day, Sunday, before the city fell into British hands.

Fortunately, the plan failed. The Jewish citizens, many of whom were already dressed in travel clothes and resigned themselves to their fate, were stunned when the British troops took over Jerusalem the following morning, much earlier than anticipated.

The Turkish troops made a hasty escape, and Hussein Bey al-Husayni, mayor of Jerusalem, attempted to surrender to the British. Accompanied by a group of Turkish officers, the mayor walked toward the city's outskirts to greet its British conquerors, a large white flag of surrender raised in his hands.

In a historic moment, the Turkish officials attempted to deliver the governor's letter of surrender to two young British officers, Sergeants James Sedgewick and Frederick Hurcomb. The officers refused to take the letter, which was eventually accepted by Brigadier General C. F. Watson, commander of the 180th Brigade.

A HANUKKAH MIRACLE

With General Watson at their head, the British soldiers marched into the city. Their first stop was Shaare Zedek Hospital, then situated at the entrance to the city on Jaffa Road. There, the mayor signed an official agreement handing over Jerusalem to British military control, thus putting an end to the Ottoman reign of four centuries. A new chapter had begun for the holy city.

The British reached Jaffa Gate in the early afternoon. Despite the bitter cold, people rushed out to the streets to see the soldiers in their bright uniforms. In just a few hours, the first lights of Hanukkah would be kindled. As evening fell on December 9, 1917, the Jews of Israel celebrated the convergence of miracles, past and present.

CHAPTER 14

From Joy to Near Tragedy

As the city celebrated its freedom from Ottoman rule, Avraham Yochanan gathered the orphanage children to pray and recite Psalms, pleading with the Almighty that the new reign over their city prove beneficial for its Jewish citizens. His family — Chana Shaina and the four children — stood outside watching the mighty British army march into Jerusalem. Wearing neat uniforms and friendly smiles, the young soldiers sang with patriotic fervor as they streamed into the city to the tune of steady drumbeats.

Standing with his mother and sisters, the teenage Yisrael Chaim Blumenthal could sense the relief and wonder in the air, as if the community was collectively taking its first deep breath after years of near-suffocation.

The small, battle-worn city at that time was a patchwork of neighborhoods and communities, huddled together for protection. The future neighborhoods of Sanhedria, Ramat Eshkol, Ramot, and others were still barren fields filled with weeds and thorns, with nary a hint to the multitude of buildings that would eventually fill the area.

Yisrael Chaim's attention was suddenly drawn to a flash of copper that glistened under a small bush. Bending down, he discovered a partially hidden metal sphere, large and cool to the touch. He innocently lifted the strange object, wondering what it was.

The procession of British soldiers had receded into the distance. The street was emptying. He hurried to follow his mother and sisters homeward, his newfound treasure in hand.

"The gate is locked!" Nechama, who had arrived at the house first, called out. "Someone locked it from the inside!"

The girls began banging on the door, their knocks growing increasingly louder as the moments ticked by.

"No one can hear you inside," Yisrael Chaim said. He looked at the copper sphere in his hands. The perfect find! If he knocked it against the metal gate, the harsh clang of metal on metal would summon someone from within.

He lifted his copper sphere and banged it roundly on the gate. Suddenly, he felt a sensation of heat on his face. The metal ball was emitting a dense cloud of smoke! Instinctively, he hurled it as far away as he could. A deafening explosion rent the air. The copper sphere — a hand grenade — shattered into a thousand shards.

Mrs. Blumenthal and all four children were wounded in the blast.

RECOVERY

Mrs. Blumenthal, whose condition was the most critical, was rushed to Shaare Zedek Hospital, where she was treated by Dr. Wallach. Meanwhile, at home, the others suffered from fear, pain, and agonizing treatments.

Yocheved, a young child, had been wounded only very lightly in her legs. Yisrael Chaim had been struck in the face, and the doctor worried that his vision had been affected. After a few days, however, it became clear that his eyesight had miraculously been spared, and his wounds began to heal.

A shard had entered Nechama's foot and come out the other side, while metal fragments were embedded in her hands, where they remained for the rest of her life.

Chaya Sima, meanwhile, lay bedridden with a metal shard embedded in her leg. With surgery impossible due to the primitive medical conditions, her fever rose and the leg swelled to monstrous proportions, turning blue and discolored. The medic attending her, Mr. Brochstein, tried everything he could think of, but there were no signs of improvement.

Realizing that the girl's life was in danger, Mr. Brochstein hurried out of the house to seek the advice of a more experienced medical personnel. Chaya Sima was left alone, groaning in pain and burning with fever. Gradually her pains were overpowered by a tremendous thirst. She looked around for assistance, but there was no one in sight.

The thirst cut her throat like a knife and emerged as a desperate plea. "Water!"

When only silence greeted her cry, Chaya Sima realized there was no choice but to get up herself. With superhuman exertion, she lifted her aching body from the bed. Clutching the wall for support, she hobbled toward the water basin in the courtyard, biting her lips to stifle the cries of pain.

After reaching the basin and drinking her fill, she made her way back to the house, her injured leg shooting waves of pain into her trembling body. With her final bit of strength, Chaya Sima reached out to pull herself onto the bed. Her swollen leg folded beneath her, and suddenly, the wound burst.

Along with the stream of puss and blood, the metal shard was released as well. Immediately, the pain subsided, and her fever began to drop.

When the medic returned, he immediately noted the change in his patient. New life glistened in her eyes, which had been dulled by pain and fever.

"What happened?" he asked in amazement.

Chaya Sima pointed to the shard on the floor and explained.

Years later, when Chaya Sima would recall her miraculous recovery, she would comment, "God works in marvelous ways. My healing came about precisely because there was no one around to tend to me and bring the drink I needed!"

ALLENBY ENTERS THE CITY

While the Blumenthals were preoccupied with recuperating from the explosion, the British army established itself in the city. On December 11, British Field Marshal Edmund Allenby entered Jerusalem with much pomp and ceremony. To demonstrate his respect for the holy city, Allenby dismounted before entering on foot through Jaffa Gate, accompanied by French and Italian high commanders.

Allenby was greeted with joy and respect by Jewish, Arab, and Christian representatives of Jerusalem. Rabbi Yosef Chaim Sonnenfeld and Chacham Nissim Danon, the Ashkenazic and Sephardic chief rabbis, stood at attention alongside Allenby and his commanders during the welcoming ceremony.

On an elevated platform outside the Tower of David, just inside Jaffa Gate, Allenby proclaimed the capture of Jerusalem by the British army and requested that its citizens help to preserve its historic and holy sites. The proclamation was repeated in several languages.

LIFE GOES ON

With the confusion of wartime finally receding, the Jews of Jerusalem were left to contend with the devastating aftermath of the war years. Loved ones had been exiled, drafted, or lost. Hundreds of widows and orphans remained alone. Rows and rows of fresh headstones filled the Mount of Olives cemetery.

A mother bringing her two children to the orphanage

As the people attempted to piece their shattered lives back together, organizations were established to aid the impoverished. The nascent Zionist Organization — today known as the World Zionist Organization — gained power during this time, taking control of key positions of authority in the city.

New children arrived at the orphanage on an almost daily basis. Despite

Avraham Yochanan's many responsibilities, however, he didn't neglect his own children, monitoring their progress with warmth and love, telling them stories of Jewish leaders of old, asking riddles about the weekly Torah portion at the Shabbat table, and showering them with attention.

CHAPTER 15

The War Is Over

The cherubic little boy who entered Avraham Yochanan's office looked like he belonged in a preschool rather than an institution for young boys. He had been sent by Mr. Moshayoff, along with a note that read:

January 24, 1918
Kindly accept the orphan Tzion into your institute. We will provide him with the daily ration for bread that we provide for all the boys in the orphanage.

Who were his parents? Where was he from? Little Tzion could not answer any of these questions. The only thing he knew was his first name.

When Avraham Yochanan next met with Mr. Moshayoff, he asked for more information about the new orphan.

"We know very little about him," Mr. Moshayoff admitted. "A year ago he was found outside the American Committee headquarters, his

80

A page from the orphanage records

stomach bloated from hunger and his body shriveled and emaciated. He appeared to be under three years old. Because he was circumcised, we knew he was Jewish. We named him Tzion because his pitiful state re-minded us of Rabbi Judah Halevi's famous poem, *'Tzion, halo tishali lishlom asirayich* — Zion, will you not ask about the welfare of your captives?'

"We hired a woman to care for him in her home," continued Mr. Moshayoff. "Now that he's grown a bit, we've decided it would be best to place him in the orphanage."

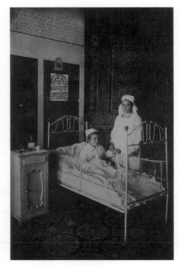

The orphanage infirmary

Returning to the orphanage, Avraham Yochanan learned that little Tzioni, as he was affectionately known, had been examined by the orphanage doctor and found to be weak and sickly, most likely the result of his early years of deprivation. The doctor prescribed several medications and a special diet to help him gain strength.

Tzioni was placed in the infirmary, with a nurse to attend to him. As the months passed, he grew stronger and healthier, testimony to the love and attention he received.

Little Tzion, bearing a sign with his name

Meanwhile, Avraham Yochanan began to search for information about the boy's background. Eventually, he discovered that the boy had been born in Kurdistan to a couple named Moshe and Rachel Mizrahi. Moshe had traveled with his young son to Jerusalem and settled in the Beit Yisrael neighborhood, with Rachel slated to join them a short while later. Tragically, she collapsed and died on the way, never reaching the Holy Land.

Meanwhile, Moshe succumbed to typhus, leaving the young boy completely alone in the world. Tzion eventually wandered out of his home in search of food and was brought by strangers to the American Committee headquarters.

This child with no home, no parents, and no siblings became part and parcel of the orphanage, attending school with others his age. In fourth grade, when he outgrew the orphanage school, he was enrolled in the Bnei Zion school in Jerusalem's Bukharian Quarter.

A CLOUD OF MOURNING

Yet young Tzion's suffering was not over. At age eleven, the kidney disease from which he had suffered as a small child returned. He was taken to the orphanage infirmary, and from there to the pediatrics department of Bikur Cholim Hospital, where doctors began to battle for his life. They tried their utmost to save him, to no avail. On March 30, 1925, Tzion Mizrahi left this world.

The following letter, written by researcher Pinchas Griyevski, was discovered in the orphanage archives:

> *A cloud of mourning settled upon the pediatrics department of Bikur Cholim Hospital today. At bed number thirteen, the faithful nurse Leah Cohen sat alongside Dr. Tziporah Slutzkin. Their eyes shed silent tears over the pitiful child Tzion, whose days on this earth were coming to an end. The father who had cared for him mercifully for the past seven years, Avraham Yochanan Blumenthal, stood sorrowfully nearby...*
>
> *At the funeral, Aryeh Geiger, one of the older boys in the orphanage, delivered a short yet heartbreaking eulogy. He enjoined all to cry out for the young sapling uprooted in the midst of its blossoming years. In a choked voice, he turned to the bier and cried, "Tzioni! Look at these poles! They are too long for you! They don't fit you at all!"*
>
> *The wails of the children and of all those present grew stronger when [Rabbi Blumenthal], who had stood silent and withdrawn until then, approached the coffin and began to speak... His voice trembled, but his words rent the air with their strength. The children looked on in grief, their choked sobs filling the air.*

A brokenhearted procession accompanied Tzioni to his final resting place on the Mount of Olives.

The Educational Institution for Boys had been renamed the Zion Orphanage during the war years. The name now seemed most fitting, as it perpetuated the memory of this pure young child.

PEACE AT LAST

Although the war continued to rage in Europe, in Jerusalem at last there was peace. Avraham Yochanan therefore tried again to tap into additional resources to help provide for the children. After much effort, he obtained a few meters of material to have underwear sewn for the boys. In addition, clothing for the needy began to arrive from the

United States, and a significant portion of these packages were set aside for the orphanage.

With the war behind them, another happy event was celebrated in the orphanage. Chaya Sima and Fischel Zaks's wedding ceremony could finally be held. Many guests arrived for the meal, which took place in the orphanage dining room. The orphans all participated in the festivities, with the air of brothers of the bride. Chaya Sima was, after all, a beloved older sister who had cared for all their needs.

After her marriage, Chaya Sima relinquished her responsibilities in the orphanage to her younger sisters, Nechama and Yocheved. She opened a small hotel, which she managed with aplomb. Her husband, meanwhile, assisted his father-in-law in the orphanage's administration for several years. When he moved on, he calculated the sum he had received over the years as salary and returned the entire amount to his father-in-law. "I do not want to benefit from charity funds," he explained.[2]

---

2   Fischel Zaks later established a free-loan society known as "Idud" (encouragement). He spent his days helping others and was known as an upright, God-fearing individual. Their son, Dr. Moshe Zaks, is renowned for his important contributions to the Israeli Agricultural Research Organization (ARO) and as the past director of the Institute for Agricultural Research According to Torah.

CHAPTER 16

The Palace

O nce again, the orphanage had outgrown its quarters. With the building's rental contract almost up, Avraham Yochanan realized it was time to relocate. After some searching, he discovered a magnificent structure in the Bukharian Quarter that was available for rent.

The Quarter had been built some twenty years earlier, at the end of the nineteenth century, by wealthy Jews from Bukhara, who wanted to create a Jerusalem neighborhood styled after Europe's major cities. It boasted large houses surrounded by spacious lots and streets three times wider than the average Jerusalem road of the time.

Yehudayoff Hefetz House, nicknamed "the Palace" for its majestic appearance, towered above the neighborhood on 19 Ezra Street. At one hundred eighty feet long, it was the most magnificent building in the neighborhood and had been built by Elisha Yehudayoff and his son-in-law Yisrael Hefetz. The building, which had served as headquarters of the Turkish army during the war, was rented to the orphanage for the grand sum of one hundred twenty liras a year.

The orphanage moved into the building in October 1918. Although it stood abandoned and empty, it still boasted some of its former glory in the form of arched ceilings, marble pillars, and curving staircases, as

Yehudayoff Hefetz House ("the Palace"), on Ezra Street

well as the iron Magen Davids that crowned the spikes on its gates. The children ran up and down the hallways excitedly, exclaiming in glee over each magical discovery.

"Come up to the roof! Look how much space there is to play!" called one young boy.

"Here's where we can build a sukkah!" cried another. "There's a removable glass roof over metal tracks near the courtyard!"

But to the children's dismay, one thing was missing: "The rooms have no doors!"

Inside Yehudayoff House; note the artistic renderings on the walls. On the left are Chaya Sima, Binyamin Hausman, and Alter Levsky. On the right is Yocheved; Nechama is at the end of the hall.

Apparently, the Turkish soldiers had removed the magnificent doors from their hinges and used them for firewood during the cold winter. The doors were replaced and the Palace became habitable.

A FOX IN THE COURTYARD

At last, there was ample space for one hundred fifty children, with a spacious courtyard, a large room to serve as a synagogue, bedrooms, study halls, a laundry room, a storage area, and a large dining room.

The Palace, however, was at the edge of Jerusalem, facing the vast expanse of barren fields filled with thistles and rocks. Wild animals roamed the countryside, and on the first few nights in their new abode, the children could not sleep from fear. They shivered at howls that sounded dangerously close to their windows, and the younger children cried.

The counselors hastened to explain that these were only foxes and jackals that roamed the nearby fields. "Don't worry," they reassured the children. "They can't get in."

A few days passed. The children grew accustomed to the pitch blackness of night, and even to the occasional howls from the fields beyond. Then, one night, one of the older boys ran in from the courtyard, panting. "I just saw an animal in the back courtyard," he said breathlessly. "Close all the doors so it doesn't get in!"

Yisrael Chaim bravely stepped outside, armed with a box of matches. Quickly, he identified the wild fox dashing around the courtyard. After he flung the lit matches in its direction, the fox hastily retreated.

"We have to hire a watchman," Avraham Yochanan said when he heard the story. A few days later, an Arab named Ali was hired as the orphanage's guard, maintenance man, and janitor.

WATER FROM THE WELLS

Another luxury in the Palace was its water system. Water was drawn from two large wells in the courtyard by turning a large wheel that sent the water up to cisterns on the roof. From the cisterns, it flowed through modernized pipes to the faucets in the kitchen and bathtubs on the building's two floors. The wide bathtubs were an attraction in themselves, the likes of which the children had never seen in their lives. Ali, the Arab worker, took sole responsibility for drawing the water, a process that required great exertion and physical strength.

Ali served the orphanage faithfully for the next year and a half, keeping it safe from wild animals and attending to repairs and maintenance. His service came to an end in April 1920, when, as a result of Arab riots, the Histadrut — a newly founded organization of Jewish trade unions — demanded that he be fired.

Left with no choice, Avraham Yochanan expressed his deep appre-ciation to the devoted worker and even accompanied him on his way to ensure that no harm would befall him. He provided Ali with food for his journey and a sum of money to tide him over, and stood watching until he disappeared over the hills toward the land that would later become Jordan.

Twenty-five years later, in 1945, Ali suddenly appeared at the or-phanage for a visit. He had come to express his thanks for those bygone days, when Rabbi Blumenthal had stood by in his difficult hour.

WINTER IN THE PALACE

With the arrival of winter, it was clear that the huge wood-burning stoves used by the Turkish soldiers would not be of any use to the or-phanage. It seemed that once the Turkish soldiers had burned all the doors, they had used the stoves to store ammunition, and Avraham Yochanan did not want to endanger the children by attempting to light stoves that most likely contained leftover bits of gunpowder. Instead, the premises were heated with coal-burning stoves. The lively orange fire danced within, providing warmth to those gathered around it.

In the corner of the Palace courtyard stood a chicken shed. During the day, the chickens traipsed around the yard, pecking at bowls of wa-ter and seeds. In the evening, they were herded back to the shed, where they snuggled down and slept until dawn. The hens laid an abundance of eggs, which were delivered to the orphanage kitchen to enrich the children's diets.

MORE NEW CHILDREN

With the move to the Palace, many new children continued to arrive, both war refugees and other orphaned or abandoned children.

Little Netanel was one of these new children. A shy and delicate child, he barely participated in the others' rambunctious games. When Avraham Yochanan passed the crowd of lively children in the evening, he immediately noticed little Netanel's detachment.

He approached the boy and placed a hand on his shoulder. "Netanel, why aren't you playing with the other children?"

"I...I can't see so well at night," the child stammered in an embarrassed whisper.

Suddenly, Avraham Yochanan remembered how Netanel barely looked into his prayer book in the orphanage synagogue. He immediately sent him to be examined by an eye doctor.

"His vision is weak due to nutritional deficiency," the doctor pronounced. "He must be fed a nutrient-rich diet, including a daily portion of beef liver. Before he eats the liver, it should be passed in front of his face so the hot vapor enters his eyes."

Beef liver? In Jerusalem? Every day? Avraham Yochanan wondered how he would get hold of the exorbitantly expensive item. But even as he uttered the words, he knew he would expend the effort — and the money — to help the child get well.

In the pre-refrigerator era, fresh liver had to be purchased every day. Each morning, Avraham Yochanan sent a special messenger to the butcher to purchase liver for little Netanel, whose vision slowly cleared. In due time, he became part of the group, frolicking and playing with all the rest.

CHAPTER 17

Two Years of Calm

With peace returning to the city, Avraham Yochanan stood at the window and gazed out at the large empty field behind the Palace. Only the sounds of the wind blowing over the wildflowers and the chirping birds disturbed the vast silence.

Suddenly, a thought occurred to him: The ownerless plot of land could be used for planting wheat for matzah to be used the following Passover!

Excitedly, he shared his plans with the children, who caught his enthusiasm. The very next day, an Arab with a herd of oxen arrived to plow the land. The fresh smell of newly plowed earth filled the air, and the once-barren field began to show signs of life.

Winter arrived, along with cloudy skies, rolling thunder, and blessed rain. The dry, cracked earth soaked in the droplets. One unforgettable morning, the children peered out at their field and saw a carpet of green shoots covering the brown earth.

The orphaned children diligently watched over the tiny buds as they blossomed from week to week. They built a scarecrow to guard their fledgling grain from pecking birds, checked that the earth was sufficiently loose, and exclaimed over the wheat's progress.

By the start of summer 1919, the rows of golden wheat were a sight to behold. The grain was harvested and gathered with joy and care. It was, after all, wheat that had been set aside for Passover matzah!

After the threshing, Arab women arrived with heavy stones that were used to grind the kernels into flour. The grinding stones were washed and dried for a full day, to ensure that not a drop of moisture remained, which would render the flour *chametz*, forbidden on Passover. Then the flour was carefully packed to ensure that no moisture seeped in.

The day before Passover, Avraham Yochanan left the orphanage early in the morning, accompanied by a select group of young men, heading for the Shimanovitz matzah bakery. The finished matzahs were placed in a spotless white sheet, prepared by Mrs. Blumenthal, and brought home in a wagon.

Back in the orphanage, Avraham Yochanan carefully examined each individual matzah. He removed those that did not pass his scrupulous inspection and placed the others in a separate sheet.

"Father needs nothing for himself," Mrs. Blumenthal once told her children, laughing, "other than two clean handkerchiefs — one for his matzahs, and the other for his *lulav!*"

On Seder night, Avraham Yochanan sat at the head of the table, his face glowing. His joy at eating the matzahs, which he had supervised through each stage of the process, was intense. As the children bit into the crispy crackers, the sweet taste of accomplishment filled their mouths. These were *their* matzahs, made from the wheat that had grown right outside their windows. Pride and joy permeated the air.

LIFE IN THE ORPHANAGE

Mrs. Blumenthal stood faithfully at her husband's side in raising their huge "family." She supervised the kitchen, helping the cook prepare nutritious and tasty dishes. She was the one who noticed every child's torn or dirty clothing, every broken chair, and every small altercation between the boys. Each one would receive her immediate and loving attention.

The Blumenthal children were integral partners in running the orphanage as well, helping out wherever necessary. The family lived in a small apartment inside the Palace, part and parcel of life in the home.

Lunch in Yehudayoff House

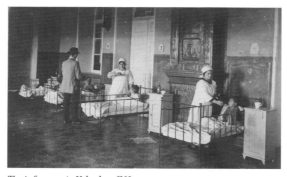

The infirmary in Yehudayoff House

The orphanage had an unwavering daily routine. The children awoke each morning to find clean clothes laid out near their beds. In those pre–washing machine days, with running water a scarcity, this was no small feat. The washerwomen occasionally had to work through the night so the clothing would dry by morning and ready to be worn again.

Soon, the pleasant sounds of the children raising their voices in prayer could be heard from the synagogue. After morning prayers, the children would enter the dining room for their breakfast of fresh bread, milk, and, during the summer, fresh vegetables. Meals, though simple, were delicious and prepared with scrupulous hygienic standards.

Some of the children attended the orphanage's school, while others were sent to other schools that Avraham Yochanan deemed more suitable for them. He invested much thought and consideration before placing each child in school. Where would the child's father have wanted him to study? Which institution would be best for him? Where would he advance in his studies and continue the legacy of his forefathers?

Avraham Yochanan made the following comment in the orphanage records regarding eight-year-old Yaakov Berkowitz, who had been orphaned of his Ashkenazic father and Sephardic mother:

Yaakov has been educated to this day in Sephardic institutions. His method of Torah study, his prayer, and his pronunciation is according to Sephardic tradition. We have therefore placed him in a Sephardic school, so as not to create unnecessary confusion for this tender youngster.

Yosef Gafni, who spent six years in the orphanage, testifies:

The children in the orphanage in my time were of varied origins, Sephardic, Persian, Bukharian, Yemenite, and Ashkenazic. It was customary to send each child to the school most suitable to him, his language, and his culture. In addition, there was no attempt made to assimilate the Sephardim [into Ashkenazic culture]. I see this as [indicative of] the rabbi's liberality. His approach differed entirely from that of both the secular and religious sectors in the '50s.

The children would all eat lunch together in the dining room, where the counselors supervised them carefully and told them riveting stories. In the evening, they would chat in bed until lights-out, when only a few kerosene lamps were left burning in the hallways. Avraham Yochanan would often walk through the corridors during this

Children studying in the orphanage school

time, listening to their thoughts and experiences and connecting to their hearts.

LIKE A REAL FATHER

The children often jokingly remarked that the director hid in their closets and listened in on their conversations. They were so used to his fatherly presence that they felt he was with them even when he wasn't, as though he could read their thoughts and understand their feelings from afar.

Avraham Yochanan was a beloved authority figure. The children would come to him whenever there was an unresolved dispute, trusting him to bring the truth to light and resolve all issues.

Avraham Yochanan Blumenthal

"Go call Yosef," the director would instruct after hearing out young Chaim's accusation. The summoned child would appear, and Avraham Yochanan would hear him out as well. He would treat the children's petty squabbles with utmost seriousness, as if he were resolving a complicated case between two litigants.

"Yosef?" the director would turn to the accused after a thorough investigation had revealed him guilty as charged. "Did you really do something like that? Is it possible? I find it hard to believe!"

Yosef would nod silently, holding back tears. How had he disappointed the director so?

The two sides would leave the room appeased, but not before Avraham Yochanan had hidden a small treat in each child's pocket.

Avraham Yochanan's measured actions were a model for the children. They witnessed his self-control time after time and they internalized his example.

Sometimes, a child was told to repeat a statement from Ethics of the Fathers, usually one having to do with the nature of his misdeed. Then he would be tested on it by the director. The children often recalled the teaching for years to come, and the warmth with which the "punishment" was meted out left an indelible impression in their hearts.

Avraham Yochanan also complimented the children often. Some even merited loving nicknames. Yosef Meyuchas, for example, was nicknamed "Bubbale" (sweetheart, in Yiddish), for his gentle and pleasant demeanor.

SPECIAL TIMES, SPECIAL MEMORIES

The neighbors in the houses around the orphanage regularly heard the children singing together.

"Our house was directly across the street from the orphanage," recalls Cheftziba Levinsky. "Every morning and evening, especially on Shabbat and holidays, the children's prayers would echo through the streets. I loved listening to the pleasant tunes, especially the Shabbat melody 'Kah Ribon Olam.' The tune was accompanied by intense sweetness and longing."

Saturday night in the orphanage was a special time. After evening prayers and Havdallah, Avraham Yochanan would sit at the table and pour out his soul in song. The children joined in, their pure young voices blending with his deep baritone. As the rows of children swayed back and forth, it seemed as if the very heavens were opening. Avraham Yochanan's voice grew stronger as he sang the words of the Saturday night melody, "Lead me to Zion, my holy portion/O God, hear my voice..."

The Blumenthal family and the orphanage employees stood and watched. Often, passersby were lured into the building by the magnetism of the singing. They would stand transfixed by the harmonious blend of voices, the love and holiness that permeated the room.

After the Saturday night meal, which often consisted of cake sent by Binyamin Hausman, the head counselor, who ran a family-owned bakery, Avraham Yochanan would take out the items forbidden to be handled on Shabbat (muktzeh), which the children carefully labeled and deposited with him to safeguard. Each child in turn was given his items, along with a heartfelt wish for a good week. In this way, Avraham Yochanan ensured they would have the greatest respect and honor for Shabbat.

MESSIAH'S HOUSE

Temira Volkni, a close friend of Yocheved Blumenthal, penned her memories as a little girl growing up in the shadow of the orphanage:

> We lived in a corner house in the Bukharian Quarter. Across from our home stood a large majestic building made of pink stone, with two floors, a flat roof, and a courtyard surrounded by a tall fence with a wide iron gate. This was the Zion Orphanage. The children of the orphanage — Shammai, David, Tzion — played marbles with my brothers right outside our window. My friends and I would play inside on the curving staircase that led up to the second floor, bouncing our balls from one step to the next.
>
> Every Shabbat eve, the awesome sound of prayer would burst forth from the orphanage, like a choir: "Lecha Dodi..." On Saturday night, we heard, "[Speedily may he come,] Elijah the Prophet...with Messiah, son of David." It never surprised me that the building was called the "House of Messiah."

SCORPION STING!

One day, two of the orphanage employees sat at a small table near the kitchen, chatting over lunch. One was the Yemenite cook who created tasty meals for the children each day, the other a cleaning woman.

Suddenly, the second woman leaped to her feet, screaming, "Help! My foot — a scorpion!"

The cook jumped up in alarm and immediately beheld the toxic yellow scorpion on the floor near her friend's foot. Acting swiftly, she ran to the kitchen and grabbed a pair of tongs. Lifting the deadly creature with the tongs, the cook hurriedly filled a small pot with olive oil and placed it on the stovetop. When the oil began to bubble, she dropped the scorpion into the pot and waited.

Meanwhile, the other woman's leg had turned red and begun to swell from the scorpion sting. The crowd that had gathered called instructions, "Call a doctor! She could die from the venom!"

The cook took no heed of their concerns. "In my village in Yemen, there were many scorpions, and we were stung often. I know what needs to be done. The best antidote is this oil."

When the scorpion had boiled long enough, she put the pot into a large container of cold water to cool, then soaked a large cloth in the oil. She then wrapped the woman's leg in the cloth and applied pressure to the wound.

Immediately, the other woman's groans subsided. Once the first cloth had worked its magic, the cook switched to a second, oil-soaked cloth. After several hours of this treatment, the leg had returned to its original size and the woman's pain was gone.

The oil, with the boiled scorpion inside, was transferred to a glass container and stored on a shelf in the corner of the orphanage kitchen for many years, a reminder of the Yemenite cook's wondrous cure.

CHAPTER 18

Adventures in the Orphanage

Winter 1919. A heavy snowstorm descended upon Jerusalem — which sees snow only rarely — and paralyzed the city. The snow began on a Monday and fell for three days. A blanket of whiteness covered the city, turning the streets into a frozen wilderness.

The children peered out at the storm from their windows, amazed at the sight of the snow reaching almost to the top of the fence surrounding their courtyard. It was impossible to distinguish the yard from the street. On the second floor, the sukkah's removable roof had been open; now the snow had piled onto the metal tracks and frozen over, preventing the roof from being closed. The porch was covered in over three feet of snow.

Bread was delivered to the orphanage via a wagon harnessed to a shivering horse that plodded through the snow with great difficulty. The children occupied themselves by roasting chestnuts, the pleasant smell filling the rooms.

"Let's build a snowman," said the lively Shmuel Winkler to his friends. The boys got to work enthusiastically, and in no time a tall snowman stood in the yard, with two black coals for eyes.

Days passed before the snow melted, but the bitter cold remained. The children bundled up in every possible garment, but the cold pierced through their clothes, cut their breath short, and made their hands dry and chapped. It was a winter that went down in the annals of the orphanage.

TZVI IS GONE!

"Tzvi has disappeared!" the counselor blurted out as he burst into Avraham Yochanan's office one spring afternoon in 1920.

"Have you searched the building?" the director asked.

"Yes," the counselor said. "We checked the yard, the chicken coop, the roof, even the storage rooms."

Tzvi Dinenberg, a tall and stocky twelve-year-old, had come to the orphanage from Jaffa after the passing of his mother, his penniless father unable to care for him. Outwardly, the boy appeared strong and confident, but he sorely missed his father and privately shed many tears. Several times he had begged Avraham Yochanan to send him home.

Avraham Yochanan immediately questioned Tzvi's close friends. "Did Tzvi fight with someone? Did someone insult him?" he probed gently.

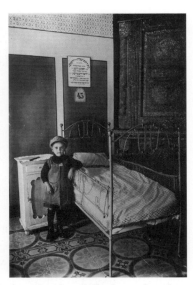

An orphan from Jaffa who was brought to the orphanage from a Christian mission

While the children initially shrugged their shoulders, a closer investigation revealed that Tzvi had fought with several of the boys that afternoon, coming to blows. One of the children recalled that Tzvi had angrily announced that he was going home. No one had paid him any particular attention, since boys who had homes to go to occasionally made threats of this sort.

Could Tzvi have actually left the orphanage? Avraham Yochanan decided to notify the police and initiate a city-wide search, since it seemed unlikely that a twelve-year-old could travel alone to another city without money or provisions.

Night fell, with no sign of Tzvi. A feeling of uneasiness spread through the orphanage. The children whispered among themselves, while the counselors searched the building again in the vain hope that he was hiding somewhere on the premises.

Unable to sleep, Avraham Yochanan wondered if the boy could have attempted the near-impossible. But in those pre-telephone days, there was no way to investigate until morning.

Early the next morning, Avraham Yochanan hurried to the post office and sent a telegram to Tzvi's father. Knowing the man's dire financial situation, he included money for a return telegram, which arrived several hours later.

"Tzvi is home."

The three short words dispelled the cloud of worry that had settled over the orphanage. Tzvi was home!

It soon transpired that after the fight, Tzvi had left the orphanage without informing anyone. With no money for transportation, he had walked through the night, in pitch darkness, for forty miles — reaching his home in Jaffa tired and hungry early the next morning.

Should the boy be returned to the orphanage? Avraham Yochanan realized that it was mission impossible. "I cannot take responsibility for him," he said. "He is too homesick and unable to be apart from his father."

Fortunately, some relatives overseas began sending Mr. Dinenberg money, enabling him to provide for his son.[3]

HUNCHBACK

Chaim Shvili, a Georgian-born boy, presented Avraham Yochanan with a concern of a different nature. He arrived at the orphanage with

---

3   During the Arab uprisings of 1936, Tzvi was working in Hadera as a bus driver when a group of Arab ruffians descended on his bus, murdering him along with his passengers. May God avenge his blood.

another boy by the same last name, Ephraim Shvili, but aside from their family names, they were complete opposites. While Ephraim was tall and sturdy, Chaim was thin and delicate.

Chaim Shvili as a youth

Avraham Yochanan followed Chaim's development with some concern. He was pleased to see a certain liveliness in his face, but concerned about his pale features and overall weakness.

One day, Avraham Yochanan noticed that Chaim was developing an acute hunchback. When questioned, Chaim related that while still in Georgia, he had fallen off a horse and hurt his back. The hunchback was the probable result of the fall.

Avraham Yochanan quickly arranged for the boy to see a doctor. After a thorough exam, the doctor decided to fit Chaim with a special body cast to be worn through the night for a full year, along with a supportive brace to be worn during the day.

Despite this regimen, Chaim's hunchback only worsened. Yet the boy's spirit did not waver. His personality and character became ever more refined, and his skills in Torah study were apparent as well. An excellent public speaker, he delivered eloquent speeches to his peers in the orphanage.[4]

SNAKE!

The uproar in the yard was different from the chatter and noise that ordinarily filled the orphanage. Avraham Yochanan hurried out to see what had happened.

---

4   Chaim Shvili eventually became a gifted Torah scholar, in addition to marrying and raising a beautiful family. He went on to write several Torah works, including *Chazon Chaim*, a commentary on the book of Daniel, and *Cheshbonot HaGeula*, about the future redemption. He also taught for several years in the orphanage school and remained connected to Avraham Yochanan, to whom he related as a father, all his life.

Outside, a circle of frightened children had gathered around a long, black snake that lay coiled on the ground, flicking its thin tongue at them.

Ali, the Arab worker, had discovered the snake inside the chicken coop, and in the confusion left the coop's door wide open. The chickens had dispersed throughout the yard, with the snake close behind.

"Where is it?" Moshe Tourgeman yelled as he burst through the circle of boys, followed by his brothers, Avraham and Montefiore. (The boy's unusual name had been given to him in memory of Moses Montefiore.) The three, who hailed from Argentina, were orphaned of both parents and had recently been placed in the orphanage by the Argentinean consul.

Moshe unhesitatingly grasped the snake by the neck in a tight vise, thus preventing it from turning its head to bite him. He then hurried up to the roof of the building, a jostling crowd of excited boys behind him. Standing like a commander leading his troops to battle, he began waving the snake back and forth in the air. Then, with a swift and powerful motion, he hurled it over the fence.

At that moment, Avraham Yochanan arrived at the scene, just in time to see the reptile flying through the air toward the open field beyond the orphanage.

"Moshe," he exclaimed in shock, "what are you doing?"

"We have many snakes in Argentina," Moshe replied calmly. "We're used to them. Whenever we find a snake, we throw it as far away as we can and it never returns. That snake wasn't even poisonous."

"Nonetheless," said Avraham Yochanan, "I prefer that you don't touch snakes again. Only an expert can tell if they're venomous, and even a bite from a harmless snake is no joke."

Sometime after this incident, another snake seemed to appear in the yard. Thankfully, it turned out to be nothing more than a snakeskin, shed by the reptile once in several years. The boys gleefully carried it inside and preserved it in a container with alcohol. They placed it on the shelf in the orphanage kitchen, alongside the roasted scorpion.

ACCIDENT IN THE YARD

In another frightening incident, Egyptian-born Aaron Avusdan, a rambunctious youngster who was orphaned of his father, decided to climb up one of the marble pillars in the orphanage courtyard while the boys were flying kites one Friday. He scaled the pillar easily and let his string up, excited at the new heights the kite could reach. Suddenly, he lost his balance and careened to the ground, landing painfully on the stone floor below.

His friends' initial shock quickly became genuine fear as they crowded around Aaron, attempting to gauge how badly he was injured. To their dismay, the boy was unconscious, blood dribbling from his mouth. The counselors attempted to revive him by wetting his face and calling his name, but he remained unresponsive.

Avraham Yochanan quickly summoned an ambulance horse and buggy and accompanied the injured child to the nearby Hadassah clinic. There he was examined by Dr. Nachum Kook, a religious doctor who was a nephew of the famed Rabbi Avraham Yitzhak HaKohein Kook. The doctor determined that the boy had suffered severe brain trauma and instructed that he be hospitalized immediately.

"I suspect that we need to operate on the child," the doctor told Avraham Yochanan.

Avraham Yochanan was hesitant. He had always resisted extreme medical intervention, and surgery on an unconscious child seemed risky. After much deliberation and consultation, he told the doctor, "Please push off surgery until after Shabbat."

Dr. Kook consented. Meanwhile, Aaron's mother was summoned, and she sat by his bedside the entire Shabbat, alternately praying and weeping.

Back at the orphanage, Avraham Yochanan instructed the children to pray for their friend. That night and the next morning, he walked to the clinic to see if there was any noticeable improvement.

"Well?" the doctor pressed Avraham Yochanan on one of his visits to the hospital. "Don't you think we should operate already?"

"No, not yet," Avraham Yochanan said, attempting to buy the boy some more time.

After several days, the prayers on Aaron's behalf were answered, and unbelievably, he opened his eyes. "He's coming to," his mother cried.

The doctors hurried over, checked his pulse and blood pressure, and tested his reflexes. Soon, it became apparent that while Aaron had regained consciousness, he was completely deaf. Yet the decision was reached not to operate on the boy, but rather to allow him to recuperate in the hospital for several more days. He was released, sound of mind and body, aside from his hearing loss, with instructions to rest.

Instead of returning the boy to the orphanage, Avraham Yochanan "hired" the boy's mother, who had been working as a cleaning lady, and paid her a salary to stay at home and care for her son.

Weeks turned into months, then years. Amazingly, Aaron's hearing improved until he was able to hear normally.

"Had we operated, it is doubtful he would have survived," Dr. Kook told Avraham Yochanan sometime later. "And even if he'd survived, I doubt he'd have recovered his hearing."

CHAPTER 19

Travel to the United States

oncurrent with the orphanage's growing pains, political events continued to unfold in Jerusalem. For two years after the Ottoman defeat, Palestine was governed by British military rule. A civilian government was finally established in July 1920, with Lord Herbert Samuel, a traditional Jew from England, appointed high commissioner, to the Jewish community's delight.

The fall holiday of Sukkot arrived in Jerusalem. Little wooden huts dotted the city. Joining in the holiday celebrations, Lord Samuel left his home on Mount Scopus for the prayer services in

A welcoming ceremony for British high commissioner Lord Herbert Samuel

the Hurva synagogue in the Old City. From there, he continued to the Bukharian Quarter, where a reception had been prepared in his honor in the spacious sukkah of the Blumenthal Orphanage, whose engraved marble pillars and artistic décor contributed to the sukkah's grandeur.

Excited masses assembled to greet the high commissioner as he ascended the stone steps of the orphanage. Seated at the head of the table, he commented on the sukkah's beauty. The many local rabbis and public officials in attendance stood up one at a time to bless the new leader and wish him success.

The Balfour Declaration — signed in November 1917 — and the appointment of a Jewish high commissioner initially filled the hearts of the citizens of Jerusalem with hope. Over the course of the thirty years of British Mandate, however, this initial euphoria died away, as politics led British sympathies to often lie with the Arabs rather than the Jews.

LOOKING HEAVENWARD

All was not well in the orphanage.

"The cook says there's not enough food for Shabbat," devoted head counselor Binyamin Hausman reported to Avraham Yochanan one Thursday afternoon.

The financial situation of the orphanage, shaky at best, had become dire. Sustaining over a hundred children was no simple matter, and the orphanage had sunk into debt.

"Perhaps you should approach So-and-So?" Avraham Yochanan suggested. "Ask him for a loan."

Binyamin hurried to the man's home, only to be told he had no spare funds available. He returned to the orphanage, where Avraham Yochanan instructed him to approach another kind donor.

Once again, the answer was negative. "He says we still owe him money from previous loans," Binyamin reported.

Avraham Yochanan suggested a third name, but again Binyamin returned empty-handed.

What to do? thought Avraham Yochanan desperately. They had exhausted all resources. He looked out the window and turned his eyes heavenward. "Master of the Universe," he said out loud, "the children are asking the cook for food, the cook is asking the counselor to help, the counselor is turning to me, and I have nothing to give him. Please, God, everything is Yours. These children are Yours as well. How am I to feed them?"

Several minutes passed before Avraham Yochanan thought of another avenue, a well-to-do individual who had lent the orphanage money in the past. He dispatched Binyamin for the fourth time that morning. To the counselor's utter surprise, the man swiftly placed a sizable sum in his hand.

"God has answered our prayers!" Avraham Yochanan uttered in amazement upon Binyamin's triumphant return.

FASTING FOR SALVATION

Avraham Yochanan had taken an enormous responsibility upon himself, which he often bore completely alone. Only the knowledge that the Father of all orphans was at his side, providing for the children, gave him the strength to continue. When the orphanage was in need of a specific salvation, he would occasionally fast for three days in a row, morning to evening, beseeching the Almighty for help.

On the third day of one of these fasts, he once passed a kiosk and requested a cup of seltzer, completely forgetting that he was fasting.

The kiosk owner pressed the siphon and a stream of soda water filled the cup. Suddenly recalling his fast, Avraham Yochanan paid for the drink and left the kiosk without it.

"Excuse me, sir, you forgot your drink!" the man called after him.

"It's okay," Avraham Yochanan responded. He walked away, leaving the kiosk owner shaking his head in confusion.

NEW VENTURES

With the orphanage's debts rising to astronomical proportions, Avraham Yochanan realized he had no choice but to travel overseas to create a solid financial base for his institution. As 1920 drew to a close, he set out for the United States together with his son Yisrael Chaim, leaving his son-in-law, Fischel Zaks, as the orphanage's acting director.

The children at the entrance to Yehudayoff House, with Fischel Zaks on the left

Avraham Yochanan and Yisrael took a train to Egypt, where they transferred to a second train that would bring them to Alexandria. In Alexandria, they boarded a ship bound for Marseilles, France.

"Send us in peace, and bring us back in peace..." Avraham Yochanan

Rabbi Zeidel Hollander

prayed as the ship departed, little dreaming that three and a half long years would pass before he would again set eyes on the Holy Land.

Avraham Yochanan and Yisrael spent a number of days in France, where Avraham Yochanan forged a close bond with Mr. Meyer, a leader of the Paris Jewish community who had visited the orphanage many years later. Then, father and son boarded another ship, this one bound for the United States.

The journey lasted four weeks. When the Blumenthals finally arrived in America, they were thrilled to see a familiar face among the crowd gathered at the dock. Zeidel Hollander, who had served as a counselor in the early days of the orphanage, was there to greet them.

Although Rabbi Hollander ran an orphanage in Rochester, New York, he devoted himself to Avraham Yochanan and his fundraising efforts. Before long, Avraham Yochanan had opened an office in New York and appointed his brother Simcha to manage it. An additional office was established in Chicago and managed by his brother-in-law, Dr. Avraham Levsky.

Avraham Yochanan traveled from city to city, making appeals and forging connections with various rabbis and lay leaders, many of whom became supportive friends of the orphanage. Yisrael Chaim, meanwhile, was enrolled in Yeshivat Rabbeinu Yitzhak Elchanan (today Yeshiva University).

SATISFYING THE POOR

Passionate about his cause, Avraham Yochanan spoke boldly and firmly, bringing to light the plight of the orphans in his care. He would size up each audience and deliver a tailor-made address, careful to temper his words with his trademark warmth.

On one occasion, he was invited to speak at a wealthy synagogue built with much opulence. He was greeted with respect and affection, as the synagogue members were eager to connect to the Holy Land. Avraham Yochanan opened a book of Psalms and read aloud chapter 132, which speaks of the Holy Temple.

"King David promised that he would not enter his own tent nor rest his weary eyes nor sleep in his own bed until he found a place for the Divine Presence to rest," he related. "God told him: 'Before the priests can serve in the Temple, you must first worry for the poor,' as the verse says, 'Her poor I will satisfy with bread,' and only afterwards, 'and her priests I will clothe.'

"Before building a beautiful House of God, we must first provide for the poor and the hungry, the widows and orphans," he continued.

"You must first address the needs of the orphans who are awaiting your help, in need of bread, clothing, and shelter. If you assist your brethren in this way, God will enable you to continue glorifying your synagogue."

His words penetrated, and the donations poured in.

Several times, he quoted the words of Rabbi Judah Halevi, "How can I take pleasure in eating and drinking when I witness the dogs dragging your young sons?" Avraham Yochanan would plead, "My dear brothers! How can you eat and drink when the city of God and her sons are hungry, sick, and in pain? Come and see with your own eyes the poverty and pain that reigns in Jerusalem. The city is filled with widows and orphans, poverty-stricken families who struggle to bring home bread for their children!"

Avraham Yochanan's travels were exhausting. Each overture was accompanied by heartfelt prayers that God lead him on the right path and put the right words in his mouth.

On one occasion, the president of a certain synagogue refused to allow Avraham Yochanan to speak to his congregants, claiming that they had to fend for orphans in their own community. Avraham Yochanan found himself in an uncomfortable position, yet he felt he could not leave the community without speaking.

"Allow me just to read the words of Rabbi Judah Halevi to the people," he requested. The president agreed.

Avraham Yochanan walked up to the lectern and began quoting Rabbi Judah Halevi. "Zion, will you not seek the welfare of your prisoners?!" The piercing words were spoken with emphasis on the passages most pertinent to his message, and the audience was held spellbound by his words. Many contributed generously to the cause.

SPIRITUAL STRAITS

Traveling the length and breadth of the United States, Avraham Yochanan became aware of the immense lack of Jewish knowledge in the country. Adhering to his personal standards of kashrut, he was careful not to consume any chicken or meat without personally checking the knife of the *shochet*, ritual slaughterer, and ascertaining that he was well-versed in the pertinent laws. As a result, his diet was mostly vegetarian for much of his stay in the United States.

Upon his return to Palestine, he was asked about the spiritual state of Jews in America. He gave a deep sigh and answered simply, "*Shlecht* (not good)."

Avraham Yochanan was terribly pained by the spiritual straits of his brethren in America. Upon his return to Jerusalem, he established an institute whose goal was to teach young men the art of public speaking to enable them to disseminate Torah in the Diaspora.[5]

In addition, Avraham Yochanan forged close bonds with many American rabbis who, when they later visited Israel, would often visit the orphanage.

---

5   See chapter 23.

CHAPTER 20

Business as Usual

For the three years that Avraham Yochanan was in America, the orphanage continued to run smoothly, thanks to his wife, his son-in-law, and the devoted counselors. New children were admitted, and several boys left to join a newly remarried parent or other relatives who had decided to take them in. The vast majority, however, remained in the orphanage for years, some even until they established their own homes.

Two new orphans who arrived at this time were Mordechai and Aryeh Kalinsky of Petach Tikva. The Kalinskys were among the pioneering families of the fledgling settlement. When the father was murdered during the Arab uprisings of 1921, his sons were brought to the orphanage.

One day, as Mordechai Kalinsky strolled through the alleyways of the Old City on his way to the Western Wall, an Arab threw a large stone at him, hitting him squarely on the head. Bleeding profusely, he was carried back to the orphanage, where he was examined by a doctor. Miraculously, the wound was not deep, and the doctor quickly bandaged the boy's head and staunched the bleeding. Within a number of weeks, he had recovered completely.

LONG-LOST COUSIN

One day in 1921, an unfamiliar young woman knocked on the orphanage door, asking for Mrs. Blumenthal. After a short conversation, Mrs. Blumenthal discovered that the young woman was her first cousin Chana Krolovitsky from Poland, who had made aliyah to escape the rising anti-Semitism in Poland.

"Do you have a place to live?" Mrs. Blumenthal asked after a moment, intuiting the plea in the girl's eyes.

When the girl answered in the negative, Mrs. Blumenthal invited her to live with them. Young Chana grabbed at the

Mordechai Kalinsky, with his head bandaged

invitation like a life preserver. After a short while, she went to live with Mrs. Blumenthal's mother but continued to come to the orphanage every day, where she served as Mrs. Blumenthal's right hand. Eventually, the Blumenthals provided her with a dowry, and her marriage was celebrated in the orphanage.

Chana maintained her close connection to the Blumenthals for many years. She eventually repaid the debt of gratitude years later, when Mrs. Blumenthal was very ill. The doctor felt she needed surgery but feared that in her weakened state it could cost her life.

Hearing of the situation, Chana suggested another doctor that the family had never heard of. As Mrs. Blumenthal's doctor said there was nothing to lose by seeking another opinion, the family sought out the unfamiliar doctor. He prescribed a certain medicine, which healed Mrs. Blumenthal completely. She returned to her duties at the orphanage, living for another twenty-six years after this medical scare.

MIRACLE LIGHTS

On another occasion, a resident of Jerusalem who had traveled to America arrived home, bearing regards from Avraham Yochanan. After the Shabbat meal that week, Mrs. Blumenthal visited his home to hear how her husband was doing.

She was greeted warmly and seated with the rest of the family around the table. Suddenly, the lantern in the room began to emit black soot, filling the air with a cloud of smoke. This meant that the wick needed to be lowered via the screw on the side of the lantern. Since this act is forbidden on Shabbat, however, Jerusalemite Jews would call a non-Jew and hint, "Look, the lantern is black."

Local Arabs were familiar with the request and would fix the wick, receiving their payment in the form of cooked food. Occasionally, they would come by after Shabbat for monetary payment as well.

In the course of discussion, Mrs. Blumenthal's host exclaimed, "Do you know what they have in America? Wonder of wonders! There is a switch in the wall. You press it, and light fills the entire house without any soot or smoke!"

"Magic!" responded the others. They could not begin to fathom the electrical wonder he described.

TIGHT QUARTERS

The Palace had served the orphanage well for several years. However, in the early 1920s, Mr. Yehudayoff, the building's owner, arrived from Bukhara, notifying Mrs. Blumenthal that he wanted to move into his luxurious residence and requesting that she prepare a number of rooms for him and his family. Eventually, the Yehudayoffs occupied the entire second floor of the building.

After three years of living in spacious quarters, conditions in the orphanage were crowded once again. Mrs. Blumenthal was forced to rent an apartment for herself and her children across the street, while the boys and the staff crowded together in the first floor of the building.

To make matters worse, with the onset of winter, plumbing problems caused the building to flood. The children were forced to crowd together even more. The sun's weak rays barely filtered down into the first floor, so it took many days for the rooms to dry.

Yet neither her husband's prolonged absence nor the travails of winter could break Mrs. Blumenthal's spirit. She continued to care for her family and the orphans with strength and devotion.

FATHERLY GUIDANCE

After two years abroad, the Blumenthals' son Yisrael Chaim returned home to find a suitable match. Before he set out on the long journey, his father presented him with the following unusual letter:

> Now, my beloved, I ask that you read this letter every single day until you reach home, so you remember to do all the things I am commanding you to do on your travels, as follows:
> 1. Don't forget to recite the Traveler's Prayer each day and to ask God to guard you from all evil and bring you to your desired destination — in life, joy, and peace.
> 2. Be sure to pray the three daily prayers at their proper times.
> 3. Recite ten chapters of Psalms each day, from the beginning of the book, in order, until you finish the entire Psalms, and then start again from the beginning.
> 4. Set aside at least an hour for Torah study every day — Torah in its original form, rather than the books that are copied, for they often distort the words. Drink the living waters of Torah from their true and original wellsprings.
> 5. Associate with people who are loyal to God and His Torah.
> 6. My beloved son, avoid the company of women and young girls.
> 7. My beloved, do not forget your exalted roots. Take care not to put food into your mouth if there is any room to doubt [its kashrut]. Take pleasure in foods that are absolutely kosher without a shadow of a doubt. The Master of the Universe has placed in His world many things you can enjoy that are absolutely kosher.

8.   *My beloved, the apple of my eye, don't forget the Almighty*
      Who created you, He Who does not slumber or sleep, the
      Guardian of Israel.

I ask you, my beloved, to read this letter every single day on your
journey, immediately after morning prayers in the morning,
even before you eat. [Write and] inform me at each stop along
the way until you get home that you have fulfilled my request.
My blessings and prayers for you are that God send His angel
before you to guard you on your way and to save you from all
evil, and that He bring you to your desired destination, in life,
joy, and peace. Amen.

Your father who is hugging you and kissing you with warm
tears and true love, and who anticipates seeing you speedily in
the Holy City of Jerusalem,

                            Avraham Yochanan Blumenthal

P.S. Please, my beloved, safeguard this letter, which will
accompany you on your way, so that it be with you always.
Please [share] it also with your mother when you get home,
and perhaps it will comfort her in her pain, until I too merit to
embrace the holy stones of the Holy City once again.

HOMECOMING AND MARRIAGE

After twenty-four long months of separation, Mrs. Blumenthal prepared to greet her husband and son, assuming, due to the lack of clear
communication, that Avraham Yochanan was also on his way home. But
when the wagon stopped in front of their home, only Yisrael alighted.

Her heart dropped. Had tragedy, God forbid, befallen her husband
on the way?

"Father stayed in America," Yisrael explained. "He sent only me."

Avraham Yochanan did not even travel home for his son's marriage
to Esther Rivka Ordentlich, choosing to forgo his personal joy and to
continue establishing a financial base for the orphanage.

SAVED BY A MIRACLE

In 1923, a number of months before Avraham Yochanan's return, Mrs. Blumenthal witnessed an open revelation of the Divine Providence that embraced her and the children in her care.

The golden sun coaxed the children out of their rooms and out to the large yard in front of their building. A gentle wind brought a rosy hue to their faces as they ran around the yard. Suddenly, a strange figure aroused their interest. With a friendly smile, the Arab passerby invited the children to witness the miraculous feat he was about to perform. A circle of curious boys gathered around him, their attention riveted to the strange box that lay at his feet.

The Arab bent over the box, sprinkling white powder inside. Then he added a number of small stones to the mixture and stirred.

The children's interest electrified the air. What would happen next?

When the man finished stirring, he quickly left the area, leaving the children with his box. Their eyes widened as they saw a thin white cloud of smoke rising from it like a pillar and then evaporating into the air.

"Watch out! Move away!" someone cried out, noting the Arab's hasty escape. The children dispersed in all directions as a loud explosion rent the air.

The glass windows of the Palace were shattered, and a small crater formed in the place where the man had stood moments before. Hearing the boom, Mrs. Blumenthal ran out of the building in a panic, imagining the worst. To her vast relief, when the smoke evaporated, she saw only a dusty and confused group of children who were very much alive and well.

HOME AT LAST

After three and a half years of toil, Avraham Yochanan's work abroad was complete. He had established a committee that would continue working for the orphanage, as well as a firm base of donations that would enable him to maintain the institute and pay all the debts he had incurred since its opening. Finally, he was coming home to his beloved family and city.

The Blumenthal family stood excitedly on the platform a full hour before the train was slated to arrive. At last, the long-awaited train pulled in. Avraham Yochanan disembarked and walked toward the family, his warm smile melting away the loneliness of three and a half long years.

Shabbat evening came, and Yocheved turned to her father with a request. "Father, you once promised to buy me a watch..."

A momentary cloud settled over Avraham Yochanan's features as he considered the request. Then his face cleared and he declared, "You're right! I promised you a watch but was so busy attending to matters for the orphanage that I didn't manage to buy it. God willing, on Sunday we'll go and buy you a watch!"

On Sunday morning, the two went to select a watch. The simple watch was duly chosen as Yocheved's heart beat wildly with joy. A watch! Who had ever seen a young girl with a real watch on her wrist? In those days of poverty and want, watches were reserved for adults who needed them.

"And now you deserve another prize," announced Avraham Yochanan. He took Yocheved to the store next door, where he bought her an olive-wood pencil case. Yocheved floated home, thrilled at her father's loving attention. Yes, he was a father to one hundred fifty children, but he was her own father as well!

The watch remained on Yocheved's wrist until her engagement. Upon receiving a new watch from her future husband, she gave the old one to her niece, who used it until her own engagement. At that point, the watch was returned to Yocheved, who eventually gave it to a boy from the orphanage, Meir Berdugo, so he could gift it to his bride. Such was the perennial power of Rabbi Blumenthal's kindness.

CHAPTER 21

Planning Futures

D etermined to provide the children with the warmth of Jewish tradition, Avraham Yochanan walked the thin line of standing firm on his principles and maintaining close relationships with influential people in other ideological camps. He carefully guarded the orphanage's sterling reputation while maintaining cordial relationships with the government officials and others who oversaw the orphanages throughout the country.

Delegates from all Jewish backgrounds who visited the orphanage for regular inspections were forced to admit that the children under the Blumenthals' care exuded a calm sense of security. Watching the children at play, one delegate wondered out loud, "Where did Rabbi Blumenthal study pedagogy?"

GOAL-ORIENTED EDUCATION

Coming as he did from a religious background, Avraham Yochanan guided many of the boys to continue their Torah studies. At the same time, he recognized that they would have to eventually provide for their families and encouraged them to learn trades or professions as well.

Sometimes the orphanage boys found themselves in conflict with their parents, who, although unable to physically care for their children, continued to follow their development. As soon as the boys were deemed old enough to help support the family, the parents wanted them to learn a trade and return home rather than continue their studies. Avraham Yochanan grieved for these children, cut off from their Torah studies, and would not be comforted.

One mother who attempted to remove her son from the orphanage was persuaded to allow him to remain. He eventually grew into an accomplished Torah scholar, becoming the principal of a religious elementary school.

Other boys, whose skills lay in other directions, were apprenticed to carpenters, watchmakers, tailors, or shoemakers. Yet others continued with their Torah studies, acquiring skills that would enable them to earn a livelihood. Most important to Avraham Yochanan was that the children forge a lifelong love of Torah study and absorb its many life lessons.

An orphanage child, barefoot but unashamed

The orphanage's records document these trends:

Mordechai Palpel, age fourteen, was born in Safed and orphaned of his father. He stayed at the orphanage for two years and was then sent to work for Mr. Yechiel Werker, owner of a Hebrew printing house, who received five liras as a salary [for training the boy].

Ephraim Shimshilshvili, age thirteen, was born in Kutaisi, Georgia. Because of the violence in the city following its capture by the

Bolsheviks, Ephraim was separated from his parents. He arrived in this country and was accepted into the orphanage through the efforts of Mr. Chaim Elyashvili, who had accompanied him on his journey. After four years in the orphanage, he was sent to work as a secretary for Mr. Elimelech Zaks.

SAVED FROM MISSIONARIES

Yitzhak Douek's story is an appalling one.

On January 19, 1921, a father appeared at the orphanage with his young son. "Is the orphanage willing to take him in?" the father asked. "If not, I have another option."

Puzzled by this strange question, Rabbi Blumenthal's son-in-law Fischel Zaks inquired what the other option was. The man, who was from Tiberias, admitted that he was widowed and unable to provide for his three children, so he had placed two of them with Christian missionaries. For some reason, he had decided to try the Zion Orphanage for the third.

"If you can't take him, I'll place him with his brothers," he explained unapologetically. "They've already expressed their willingness to take him."

Fischel accepted the child into the orphanage on the spot. The doctor who examined him reported that the boy was starving, clearly in need of adequate nutrition.

Once Yitzhak settled in, the orphanage management decided to do everything in its power to remove his brothers from the missionaries as well. This was a complicated process, as the missionaries did not easily relinquish their prey. A number of influential individuals got involved, and with much effort, the two boys were released. One was placed in the Diskin Orphanage, established by the venerable Rabbi Yehoshua Leib Diskin in 1880, while the other was sent home to his father and provided for through the Sephardic community funds.[6]

---

6   The Diskin Orphanage building, while still in existence today, no longer functions as a home for children. Today, the building is rented by different schools. The Diskin Fund provides needy youngsters with clothing, dental care, hot meals, and educational guidance.

After four years at the orphanage, Yitzhak was apprenticed to a shoemaker in Jerusalem. Sometime later, he returned to Tiberias, where he opened a shoemaker's shop and began to earn a living.

SUCCESS FOR LIFE

Other children found their fulfillment in religious pursuits. Meir Berdugo, for example, arrived in the orphanage at age eight. His mother had died, and his father, who worked for the *beit din* (religious court) of

A grandfather from Baghdad with his orphaned grandson, who was placed in the orphanage

Jerusalem's Birkat Mamila neighborhood, had remarried. He registered his son in the orphanage on August 27, 1919.

Meir was a gifted child who excelled in his studies. After graduating elementary school in the Bukharian Quarter, he transferred to Yeshivat Porat Yosef. As he progressed in his studies, he studied ritual slaughter and became a certified *shochet* (slaughterer) and *mohel* (circumciser).

Dr. Moshe Wallach of Shaare Zedek Hospital honored young Meir with a certificate of excellence for his many accomplishments. Meir continued his Torah studies even after marriage, providing for his family through his work as a *shochet* and a *mohel*.

Rabbi Berdugo recalls his years in the orphanage and his beloved mentor in the following letter:

> To this day, there is a glow in my heart when I recall my years
> in this home [the orphanage]. For myself and many others like
> me, the years we spent in this house are our most treasured

memories, the guiding light of our lives. Central to these memories is the image of our beloved director and guiding light, our dear teacher, who found no rest neither by day nor night, for he was constantly looking out for us — his sons.

He invested much effort into feeding and dressing the orphanage boys in the very best way. If a child was sick, [Rabbi Blumenthal] found no rest. A cloud of sorrow rested on his face, and he prayed [for the child's recovery] constantly... He personally fed the sick child at his bedside until the boy recovered.

And how he exerted himself for our education! His was not a one-mold, unbending form of education. It was a fatherly education, one that recognized the unique qualities and abilities of each child and attempted to draw them out accordingly. Some would receive an exciting new toy for learning a Torah portion by heart, others received two shillings and a lira for learning a page or chapter of Talmud. For the gifted among us, his hopes were high, and he spared neither effort nor expense to hire expert private tutors and provide for all the necessary expenses with a generous hand, a smiling face, and pure pleasure. His main goal was that we become great in Torah and wisdom...

I recall the day I received my rabbinical ordination. When I arrived at the orphanage with the letter in hand, I rushed in a veritable storm of joy to the director. He held the letter in a hand that trembled with joy and thirstily drank in every word written on it. With indescribable excitement, he hugged me close. "I have not planted my seeds upon a barren stone, my beloved son! You have returned to me crowned by the crown of Torah. Fortunate are you and fortunate am I!"

His warm kisses rang on my cheeks as his eyes glistened with tears...

CHAPTER 22

Training for Life

Children steadily continued arriving at the orphanage, each one seeming to bear the weight of the world on his young shoulders, the sadness in his eyes telling its own tale of unspeakable tragedy. Avraham Yochanan compassionately called each of these new arrivals "*yatomale* (little orphan)," expressing a world of empathy along with a deep sense of responsibility for the child's welfare.

In the loving enclave of the orphanage, the children began to heal from their physical and emotional wounds. Slowly, they returned to the joy and innocence of childhood.

Mrs. Blumenthal kept a close watch on the new arrivals, often expressing her opinion to Avraham Yochanan about each one. "This child is a sweetheart," she would say. "You will see much success with him. Grab him with both hands!"

About another, she would offer, "He is sly as a fox. Be careful, for he is bright but crafty. If we guide him correctly, he will become somebody." Or "The little one is a good child, but extremely sad. We must try to make him happier... The other is stubborn and difficult. There will be much trouble from him."

"They're just children," Avraham Yochanan would object. "They can still change. And be-sides, how can you discern the nature of a child after one short meeting?"

Orphanage children studying together

Yet Chana Shaina's initial impressions often proved to be correct.

One of the orphans was a sweet child who connected with her immediately. Though she immediately sized him up as "a sly one," she showered him with warmth. From time to time she would send him on errands, and the fact that he tended to pilfer small items of value did not escape her notice. Nevertheless, she played dumb, hoping that the warmth and love she bestowed would empower him to leave his dishonest ways. The boy's behavioral problems worsened, however, and the Blumenthals were eventually forced to transfer him to a different institute.

This, however, was a rare occurrence. Most of the children lived up to their mentor's expectations and made the Blumenthals as proud as any parents could be.

A TALE OF TWO BROTHERS

Yisrael and Moshe Rubin entered the orphanage together in the spring of 1923. Their faces were frightened; their expressions spoke of endless sorrows and travails. Their father had died, and their mother had disappeared without a trace after the German attack on their hometown of Stanislav, Ukraine, during World War I.

Yisrael and Moshe were little more than toddlers when they were left completely on their own. They were sent from one place to the next, suffering hunger, poverty, and emotional neglect. Finally, they were brought to the orphanage by Yisrael Balkind, a Russian Jew who took many orphans under his wing.

For the next two years, the Rubin brothers reveled in the island of serenity they had found in a turbulent world. Avraham Yochanan became their father, Chana Shaina their mother. When Yisrael expressed an interest in farming, he was sent to study agriculture so he could gain the necessary skills.

Moshe, who was blessed with golden hands, was set on becoming an electrician. Electricity was still in its developing stages at the time, and the typical Jerusalemite family still made do with its old-fashioned stove, kerosene lanterns, and charcoal iron.

An expert electrician was located who was happy to take Moshe Rubin as an apprentice. Once he began to receive a salary, he decided to leave the orphanage and rent himself a small room to live in. Avraham Yochanan encouraged him to set out on his own, even purchasing basic furniture for the apartment.[7]

THE BOY FROM SAFED

Avraham Wilner, a child of unusual purity and innocence, had been born in the city of Safed. His grandfather, recognizing his sweet nature, requested that Avraham be entrusted with saying Kaddish for him following his death.

During World War I, a typhus epidemic raged through Safed. Avraham's father unfortunately contracted the dreaded disease and passed away, leaving behind a widow and five young children. A broken Mrs. Wilner decided to return to her hometown in Russia, where she

---

7   Later, Moshe traveled to Vienna, where he furthered his education in electricity, yet strayed from the traditions he had imbibed in the orphanage. Eventually, he returned to his roots and became a dedicated member of the synagogue near his home in the Kiryat Moshe neighborhood of Jerusalem. He would rise early to unlock the synagogue and pass the time until morning prayers by reciting Psalms. "I returned to Torah observance because of the education I received from Rabbi Blumenthal," he would often say. He maintained a strong connection with the Blumenthal family until the end of his life, attributing all his achievements to "the saintly Rabbi Blumenthal."

hoped relatives would come to her aid. But there too tragedy dogged the family. Several of her children passed away, and she and Avraham both fell ill as well.

One night, her husband appeared to her in a dream, holding a large red apple in his hand.

"Is the apple for me?" Mrs. Wilner asked, hoping to hear good news.

"No," her husband responded. "Avremale [a nickname for Avraham] will receive the apple."

A short while later, Mrs. Wilner too succumbed to her illness. Avraham recovered, left bereft of both parents and responsible for the care of his two surviving sisters.

One night, Rabbi Elimelech of Lizhensk, author of the holy book *Noam Elimelech*, appeared to Avraham in a dream and instructed him to recite Kaddish for his grandfather in Safed. Several days later, the news reached the boy that his grandfather had passed away on the day he had begun reciting Kaddish.

The orphaned Wilner children returned to Jerusalem with a group of Russian immigrants. The girls were accepted in the Weingarten Orphanage, while sixteen-year-old Avraham found a home with the Blumenthals.

A refined young man, he became known for his devotion to his studies, attending Yeshivat Chayei Olam, located in the Old City of Jerusalem. While the orphanage boys received money for transportation, Avraham preferred to make the long trip to yeshiva on foot and save his money to buy treats for his sisters when he visited them in Weingarten's.

The Blumenthals married off Avraham as if he was their own son, assisting him in every way as he established his home. He became a well-known Torah scholar who served as a lecturer in Yeshivat Chayei Olam, his close ties to Avraham Yochanan remaining strong over the passage of time.

A RISING STAR

On August 13, 1923, thirteen-year-old Aryeh Geiger arrived at the orphanage after two years in an orphanage in Safed. His father Nota had died of starvation, and his sickly mother was unable to care for her children.

Aryeh was registered in the Etz Chaim school, where his abilities quickly became evident. When he completed seventh grade, the principal decided to skip him to ninth grade due to his superior abilities.

An orphanage graduate sends his wedding picture to his beloved mentor, Rabbi Blumenthal

After four years in the orphanage, Avraham Yochanan presented Aryeh with the princely sum of six lirot and, as per his wishes, sent him off to the United States to learn in Yeshivat Rabbeinu Yitzhak Elchanan. Aryeh eventually married and settled in the United States, where he served in a distinguished rabbinic position.

ACCIDENT AT THE PRINTER

Avraham Yochanan closely followed his charges' development on all levels — physical, emotional, and psychological. He was pained when one of his boys was in pain. His discerning eye saw every wound, bruise, or scratch. Whenever he felt a medical situation was serious, he made sure to arrange the best care possible.

Fifteen-year-old Reuveni arrived from Poland after his father's passing. Once he had settled into the orphanage, he was apprenticed to a printer to learn a trade.

One day, Reuveni's finger got jammed in a heavy metal machine at the printing press. Most of the finger was severed. Reuveni was rushed to the hospital, where the doctors operated immediately.

Reuveni returned to the orphanage, yet his bandaged finger was in excruciating pain. Various painkillers did nothing to alleviate the pain. Days passed, then weeks, and Reuveni continued to suffer. At night, his screams would rent the air as the pain became overwhelming.

Avraham Yochanan brought the boy back to Hadassah Hospital, where he insisted that the wound be examined and the cause of the pain be determined. The doctors decided to operate on the finger again. During the surgery, it was discovered that several nerves in the boy's finger had been left exposed.

After this second surgery, Reuveni fully recovered and was soon happily interacting with the other boys and going about his usual routines.

MONEY NO OBJECT

Twelve-year-old Aharon Shapira arrived in the orphanage from the Ukraine with his brothers following Passover of 1923. Although he was a sturdily built boy, he walked with a pronounced limp. Avraham Yochanan was determined to cure Aharon of the limp. He tried various treatments suggested by the doctors at Hadassah Hospital, to no avail.

Three years passed, during which Aharon finished his studies and was apprenticed to a bookbinder. But the boy still had an unsightly limp. Perhaps, thought Avraham Yochanan, Aharon's cure could be found elsewhere. He arranged a consultation with the top doctors at Hadassah Hospital, who suggested taking Aharon to the medical center in Vienna, but the cost of travel and medical care would be exorbitant.

"Money is no object," Avraham Yochanan declared. "Aharon must be able to walk normally!"

Without further ado, Aharon was dispatched to Europe with a guardian who would attend to his needs and care for him during the treatment. When the pair arrived in Vienna after a long trip by boat and train, they settled into the lodgings Avraham Yochanan had arranged. Following several weeks of examinations, the doctors operated on Aharon's leg.

Aharon and his guardian returned to Palestine after a prolonged recovery period, but it soon became obvious that the boy needed a second operation. The following year, Avraham Yochanan sent the boy back to Vienna for further treatment. Fortunately, the second operation was a success. Avraham Yochanan's hands shook with emotion when he read the letter saying that all was well.

Following his recovery, Aharon decided to remain in Europe, where he found work. Avraham Yochanan continued to support him for a full year afterwards, as if he was his own son.[8]

---

8   After several years, Aharon returned to Israel to study optics, which would provide a better income than bookbinding. Once he had finished his studies, he married and moved to Tel Aviv.

CHAPTER 23

One Big Family

On the eve of Passover 1925 (14 Nissan 5685), the sun came full orbit, a rare occurrence that takes place once in twenty-eight years. A special blessing is recited on this occasion, referred to as *Birkat Hachamah*. A great deal of excitement accompanies the recital of this blessing, as it occurs so rarely.

A week before the big event, Avraham Yochanan announced to the children, "Next week, we will gather before sunrise to recite *Birkat Hachamah*!"

After the search for *chametz* on the night of April 7, Avraham Yochanan reminded the children of the great event to take place the next day. His joy was infectious, and the boys retired to their rooms excitedly calculating how old they would be at the next opportunity to recite this blessing.

By three o'clock in the morning, the first boys had awoken, sleepily peering out the window to ascertain they hadn't missed the great event. Before long, the counselors entered the rooms to rouse them. Everyone dressed hurriedly, gulping in the chilly night air and quivering with excitement.

Soon, the wide roof of the Palace was crowded with the boys and their counselors. In the distance, night began to fade. The children whispered among themselves, afraid to raise their voices.

From the roof of the orphanage, the entire city spread before their eyes. To the east stood the Temple Mount, the Mount of Olives, and Mount Scopus. To the west lay silent barren fields and beyond them, in the distance, the tomb of Samuel the Prophet. Soon, figures became visible on the other nearby rooftops, all awaiting the sunrise.

The sky grew clearer and all eyes turned eastward, where the dawn was breaking over the horizon. As the blazing ball of fire revealed itself, the blessing burst forth from hundreds of lips. It carried over the distance and seemed to dance through the morning air in praise of the Creator: "Blessed are You, God...who creates the works of Creation."

A cool wind accompanied the caressing rays of the sun as the young voices lifted in song from the orphanage roof. The children formed a circle and danced joyfully, creating memories that would last for years to come.

THE SPEECH CENTER

That same year, Avraham Yochanan had a novel idea to raise the pedagogic skills of Torah students. Having met countless families whose children had abandoned their heritage in favor of financial success, he hoped to stem the tide of assimilation taking place around the world. The Speech Center was essentially a religious youth movement, training boys to speak eloquently and engagingly on Torah topics. Membership was not limited to the boys from Zion Orphanage; it was open to boys from all backgrounds and religious affiliations.

Participants learned how to draft an organized and cohesive speech, which they then delivered to their friends. At each meeting, one boy would speak while the others listened attentively and took notes on the content and delivery. These exercises proved to be an excellent training ground, and many of the young men later took on rabbinic positions around the world. In addition to gaining public speaking skills, they also spent their free time constructively, hearing thoughts on the weekly Torah portion and other topics.

From time to time, the Speech Center organized trips for its members as well. On one of these trips, the boys visited Kfar Ivri, known today as Neve Yaakov, a bustling suburb of Jerusalem. At the time, it was a small farm on the outskirts of the city.

Rabbi Meir Orenstein, who visited the Speech Center that winter, penned his impressions:

> I was once invited on a public holiday to a place where a huge crowd had gathered. Everyone was standing, and some stood on the podium to speak about the significance of the day. The speakers were greeted with a round of applause, yet as far as I can recall, their words were meaningless and their method of delivery lacking...
>
> Sometime later, I chanced to be in the Bukharian Quarter on a Saturday night. As I strolled through the quiet streets, my ears picked up the sounds of pleasant voices. I was lured up the steps and into the Zion Orphanage, from where the pleasant sounds emanated. I saw the boys sitting around the tables and escorting the Shabbat Queen away with sweet and holy tunes. Their voices merged, distinguished by a deep sense of yearning for the holy Shabbat, which had made way for the coming week. The boys, the director, and the counselors seemed like one big family, as though the director were a father of many children. There were no signs of misfortune or orphanhood.
>
> When the singing had ended and I rose from my seat to leave, the director gestured for me to stay on. One of the young men stood and walked up to the podium. I wanted to turn on my heels and leave. Would this young man give a speech? I so detest speeches...
>
> The boy began to speak. He related in vivid detail the concepts and commentaries on the giving of the Torah. Each sentence was masterfully crafted and resonated with truth. His speech was rich in content and replete with knowledge.
>
> I turned to the director and asked, "Where did this come from?" He explained that they had established a Speech

Center where young men could acquire public speaking skills alongside rich spiritual content for their speeches. Instead of the counselors dictating the contents of the speech, the young men were encouraged to draw their sources from our holy Torah themselves.

"Job well done!" I told him.

I returned the next week, and following the rousing round of melodies, another boy rose to speak. He spoke about the contents of that week's Torah portion, stringing his words together like pearls as he recounted the laws regarding guardians and damages in perfect detail. The young man was well-versed in [Talmudic] tractates, and his words were seasoned with nuggets of wisdom.

This speech took place in a more public and festive setting. Many Jerusalemite notables were invited, and they were stunned by Rabbi Blumenthal's innovation.

After two years of successful activity, a pamphlet was published about the innovative movement and its successes. Unfortunately, however, during the Arab uprisings of 1929, the difficult political situation and lack of proper funding forced the Speech Center to close.

CHAPTER 24

Household Duties

R unning the Zion Orphanage was a complex endeavor. With few resources at their disposal, most of the work fell on the shoulders of Mrs. Blumenthal and her daughters.

All the boys' clothing was sewn at the orphanage. A woman in charge of the laundry room sorted, folded, and made alterations when necessary. When she was forced to leave due to the orphanage's tight financial straits, Nechama Blumenthal took over — sewing buttons, cutting material for new clothing, and sorting the laundry. The ironing was done with a heavy iron that constantly had to be filled with hot coals.

Twice a year, for the holidays of Passover and Sukkot, Avraham Yochanan went to great efforts to ensure that the boys had new clothing. For weeks beforehand, the children would come to the workrooms to be measured. The sewing machines worked nonstop, spitting out dozens of white shirts. Suits for the older boys were sewn by a tailor who worked out of his own home. Finally, Mrs. Blumenthal and her girls distributed the new shirts and pants, delighting in the boys' joy upon receiving their new garments.

In 1929, the orphanage was drastically affected by the stock market crash in the United States. Overnight, previously wealthy supporters

had become virtually penniless, and donations ceased. Rabbi Blumenthal was forced to cut back on many of the orphanage expenses, and new clothing was no longer an option. Instead, Nechama would sit with several other employees, patiently sorting through piles of used clothing sent from America through the efforts of Avraham Yochanan's brother Simcha. They painstakingly

The cloakroom, with a cubbyhole for each child

opened the stitches, ironed the material, and turned it into new clothing for the boys.

There was no mass production of socks in those days. Instead, a woman would come to the orphanage from time to time and take orders based on the children's sizes. At home, using a special machine, she deftly knitted thick black cotton socks for everyone in need. When the socks needed repair, the Blumenthal girls would mend them.

In order not to confuse the items while laundering, each sock was labeled with a number and stitched to its pair. Outer garments, underwear, and towels were numbered as well. Workers laboriously laundered the clothing in the large washtub placed over a stovetop. Once everything was dried, it was sorted out and placed into each child's cubbyhole with a matching number.

CARING FOR THE NEIGHBORS

Even while they cared for the orphans in their home, the Blumenthals did not neglect their neighbors' welfare.

Cheftziba Levinsky, who grew up near the orphanage, recalls:

When I was young, my closet did not boast an abundance of dresses or nice clothing. One day, Rabbi Blumenthal's daughter invited me to the orphanage's seamstress, who took my measurements. A few days later, I received a new dress. I cannot describe the pride and joy that filled my heart! I was floating! Someone had noticed me! Someone had sewn a dress especially for me! Unbelievable!

NABLUS SOAP

"The Arab has brought his *reine* (sand used for washing dishes)," Nechama reported to her mother as she stepped outside to purchase the cleaning agents the orphanage needed.

The Arab peddler tied his donkey to a post and loosened the ties on his sacks, which were filled with sand and Nablus soap. The soap, so called because it was produced in the city of Nablus, had a sharp and offensive odor and resembled a beige-colored lump. Its sole redeeming quality was its unquestionable ability to remove stains from soiled clothing.

Although there was a local woman who produced fragrant, flower-scented soap, the price was too high for the average Jerusalemite, and the orphanage had to make do with Nablus sand. With this primitive cleaning agent, the Blumenthal staff tackled piles of dirty dishes and mountains of soiled laundry.

FRUITS AND VEGETABLES

Shopping for foodstuffs was another gargantuan task. On summer days, Mrs. Blumenthal and her daughters would shop in the *shuk*, Jerusalem's open-air market, where prices were significantly cheaper than the stores. Mrs. Blumenthal would personally select the fruit to ascertain its quality, haggling with the merchants and occasionally shooing away the hordes of flies that had gathered. An Arab porter would carry the produce to the orphanage on his back.

During the winter, few fresh fruits and vegetables were available.

Potatoes, cabbages, and carrots were the only vegetables to be had, as to-matoes, cucumbers, and peppers could be purchased only in the summer.

During these months, Mrs. Blumenthal would purchase a huge quan-tity of cucumbers, which were abundant and cheap. They were packed into a special container, and water, garlic, and salt was added. The con-tainer was hermetically sealed and placed outside in the sun to pickle.

Summertime plums were cooked into jelly, then carefully trans-ferred to jars and stored alongside other fruit jams for use throughout the year. Mrs. Blumenthal supervised the orphanage cook, tasting and testing until the results were satisfactory.

SPECIAL TREATS

Without refrigeration, fresh meals had to be cooked daily. It was almost impossible to keep food from one day to the next, especially in the summer. Only foods that did not spoil easily were placed in the "air closet" (a closet riddled with holes), located in the northern part of the house to enable cooler air to penetrate.

One of Mrs. Blumenthal's famous delicacies was chicken patties, which she made not only for the orphanage boys but also distributed to needy neighbors. Because of the scarcity of food, she formed the patties from chicken necks and gizzards, yet they were seasoned with such love that they became a well-known and beloved treat.

Olives, like cucumbers, were pickled at home. "Today we are grind-ing olives," Mrs. Blumenthal announced one day. The Arab woman who had come around with her little son on her shoulders had offered olives for a reasonable price. Mrs. Blumenthal grabbed at the opportunity and purchased a full sack. In the afternoon, the boys could be found enthusiastically hitting the olives with stones so they could be cured.

Once the olives were sufficiently crushed, Mrs. Blumenthal trans-ferred them to large tin cans and covered them in coarse salt. The tin-smith was then called to weld the cans shut. For long weeks, the olives sat until they had fermented, acquiring their unique flavor.

The pickles and olives were considered special treats, leaving the children with lifelong memories of love and care.

CHAPTER 25

Earthquake!

I n the orphanage laundry room, a woman stood by the huge washtub of boiling water, scraping dirt off the children's clothes. Suddenly, the room seemed to tilt and the washtub spilled out hot, sudsy water like waves on a stormy sea. The woman screamed and backed away as the water sloshed onto the stovetop, extinguishing the fire beneath it.

The other people in the room trembled in fear. Would the entire building collapse over their heads?

The Jericho earthquake of 1927, as it became known, had devastating consequences on the cities of Jerusalem, Ramla, Tiberias, and Nablus. An estimated 500 people were killed and many more injured.

Avraham Yochanan, fearing that more tremors would follow, ordered the dorm counselor to make sure the children were all accounted for and unharmed. As the children gathered in the synagogue to recite Psalms, a huge stone dislodged itself from the wall in a building across the street and fell inches away from a bassinet where a small baby slept. Miraculously, the baby was unharmed.

In Chaya Sima's home nearby, the ceiling had cracked, and the steps leading to her apartment collapsed. She couldn't return home until it was repaired. Fortunately, however, no one in the Blumenthal family or the orphanage sustained injury.

TORAH LESSONS AND READING MATERIAL

The orphanage children had a set routine for Shabbat, which included studying Torah and reciting Psalms. Shabbat meals were enhanced by words of Torah and songs, which uplifted all those present.

At the Blumenthal family's table, Avraham Yochanan would share with his children chapters from the Prophets and Writings, raising intriguing questions and listening to their thoughts. They would sit enthralled as he related stories from the Talmud. Often, when he wanted to give them gentle rebuke, he would do it by relating a story about the character trait that needed improvement.

Avraham Yochanan also kept a close eye on his daughters' friends and on how they spent their leisure time. Books that were deemed inappropriate were banned. Although there was a dearth of suitable reading material in those days, Avraham Yochanan made sure to buy his children books that enriched their inner world.

One of Yocheved's close friends as a teenager was Zelda Schneersohn (Mishkovsky), who became an award-winning poet. While Zelda wrote poetry even as a teen, Yocheved enjoyed writing prose. She would listen to the boys' stories and recount them in her diary along with her personal impressions.

After one holiday vacation, for example, she wrote the following:

> There is chaos in the courtyard. Everyone is running and calling: "Menashe Mizrahi has arrived!" Menashe has returned from Tiberias. This is grand news, for Menashe is clever and beloved by all. Some boys have even nicknamed him "Zahav" (Gold).
> Here he is: short and thin, with an olive-brown complexion and a pair of bright, inquisitive black eyes. He is inundated by his friends' queries, asking all about his holiday in Tiberias.

Right now, however, he seems oblivious. He asks about Rabbi and Mrs. Blumenthal and how the holiday has passed for them all. Tired from his long journey, he wants to go unpack his things, but the children don't allow him to leave. "Unpack later," they insist. Eventually, he begins to share his adventures.

"Yesterday, on Shabbat, I went for a walk with my friends," he says. "We went to the grave of Maimonides. We wanted to visit the graves of other righteous people as well, but we knew it was dangerous, so instead we went to a park, where we saw a Jewish boy with a cigarette in his mouth.

"I approached him and asked, 'Are you a Jew?'

"The boy looked at me and said, 'Of course I'm a Jew. Why do you ask?'

" 'Because you're smoking on Shabbat,' I answered him. 'Don't you know that it's forbidden?'

"The boy smiled and asked my name, where I live, and which school I attend... I told him that I have been living in the Blumenthal Orphanage for five years, and that I come to spend the holidays with my grandmother in Tiberias.

"The boy threw his cigarette away and continued to question me: 'When are you returning to Jerusalem? I have many friends there... Recently they wrote to me about the valuable stamps they had found for their collections. Here in Tiberias,' he continued, 'I wasn't able to find even one valuable stamp.'

"I told him that at the orphanage we also collect stamps, and the boy took out an envelope filled with stamps and began to grill me about the value of each stamp. The two that I was unable to identify, he gave me as a present. Here they are!"

Menashe pulled out his wallet and removed the two carefully wrapped stamps. One was a triangular stamp from Peru, and the other an antique Turkish stamp. The children jostled each other excitedly to see them. After they had been passed around and everyone agreed they were valuable indeed, Menashe returned them to his wallet.

"I would have given him my address so he'd send me additional stamps," said Dovid.

"Of course I did that," responded Menashe.

Bothered by the details in the story, little Mordechai piped up, "But when did he write down your address?"

Children from Morocco, Iraq, Egypt, and Hungary all came together in the orphanage

"After Shabbat was over," Menashe said at once. "What do you think?"

The other children took out their stamp collections and began showing them to each other. Little Mordechai also took out his stamps, and the other boys mocked him: "Those are worthless American stamps."

Mordechai lowered his eyes, flushed with embarrassment. Reuven rebuked his friends: "Why did you embarrass the little one? For him these stamps are valuable!"

Everyone was quiet, realizing their mistake.

Looking at Menashe, I recalled the day that his grandmother brought him to us, five years ago.

She was a woman in her forties whose face was as black as a charred pot and lined with wrinkles. Prematurely gray hair peeked out from beneath her worn headscarf. Her body was thin and bent over. She looked like the burned remains of a beautiful palace, the rubble testifying to lost grandeur.

Two little boys clung to her skirt, one about four years old and the other six. The young one looked very much like his grandmother. His face had charm, but his expression was dull, without a hint of youthful exuberance. The older one was

Menashe. He looked first at his grandmother's face, which was wet with tears, and then took in everyone around him. One of his shoulders was exposed due to a tear in his shirt, and thick bangs came down low over his forehead.

The woman began to tell her story, occasionally bursting out in choked sobs.

"I had two sons and two daughters before I was widowed and left with my four children, three of whom were deaf-mutes from birth. Only one, these children's mother, was in good health. I raised all my children at home and earned a living

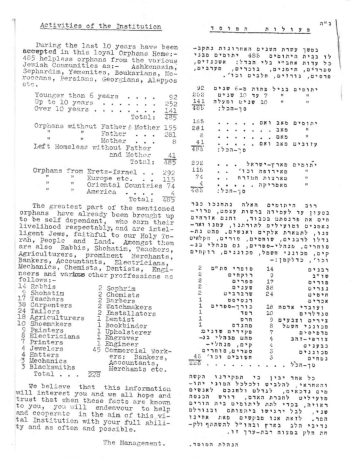

A summary of the orphanage's activities in the first ten years after its founding, in both Hebrew and English

through my own hands. Once the children had grown, they began to earn money as well, and my healthy daughter married and bore these two children. Menashe was healthy like his mother, but the younger one was deaf and mute like his aunt and uncles.

"Suddenly my healthy daughter got sick and passed away... The Master of the Universe gave me a precious treasure, a wonderful daughter, but only for a short while... and He took her."

The woman covered her eyes with her fingers and then kissed them — as is customary among Sephardic Jews — as a sign of acceptance of the Heavenly decree.

"And now," she continued, "their father does not want to know of them any longer. He sent them to me and disappeared. I have no idea where he is. Have pity on us! Have pity on me and the children! Menashe needs to recite Kaddish for his mother. You will teach him. He is a good and clever boy!"

The woman's last words, spoken from her broken heart, still ring in my ears. Father accepted Menashe, of course, and also arranged a home for the younger deaf-mute brother.

This is the story of one boy among many, who was mercifully and lovingly taken into the orphanage and became part of our large and exciting family...

CHAPTER 26

Celebrations

n the mid-1920s, the famed Slabodka Yeshiva of Europe, headed by Rabbi Moshe Mordechai Epstein, relocated to Mandatory Palestine, settling in the ancient city of Hebron. While many of the Old Yishuv Jews viewed the yeshiva students with suspicion, since they dressed in a modern European fashion, Rabbi Yosef Chaim Sonnenfeld welcomed them warmly, as did his devoted disciple, Avraham Yochanan Blumenthal, who went so far as to visit the yeshiva and inspect it.

Several years later, one of the top students of the yeshiva, Michel Dovid Shlapovarsky, became engaged to the Blumenthals' daughter Nechama. On June 8, 1928, Michel Dovid and Nechama stood under the chuppah in the courtyard of the Palace, surrounded by their families, the orphanage children, and many of the Slabodka yeshiva students.

On Saturday night, a festive *sheva berachot* celebration took place. A group of yeshiva students arrived from Hebron to gladden the young couple. The bride wore her wedding gown again, and the celebrations lasted until late into the night. The students piled several tables on top

of each other in front of the winding staircase of the Palace, and one
student climbed on top of the tower and began to dance.

The young couple lived in Hebron for the first month of their marriage and then moved to a rented room in Jerusalem, where the groom
continued his studies.[9]

A NEW HOME

Meanwhile, the huge Palace, once so spacious, had become too small
for the orphanage's needs. With the building's owners occupying its
second floor and the children crowded into the first floor, Avraham
Yochanan realized that the time had come, once again, to seek out a
new location for his "family."

Together with Rabbi Zeidel Hollander, who was also looking to purchase a plot of land in Israel, Avraham Yochanan set out for Bethlehem,
where he had heard of a suitable property for sale. The large, two-story
building, situated right near Rachel's Tomb, was owned by a Greek
monastery. It was surrounded by one hundred thirty dunams of land
that could easily be transformed into a beautiful campus.

Avraham Yochanan, anticipating an idyllic countryside setting for
his boys, began negotiations for the building, but things did not go
as smoothly as anticipated. With neither side willing to compromise,
the settlement dragged out. Then, the peaceful summer erupted with
violence, as the Hebron Massacre wreaked its havoc on the city's centu-
ries-old Jewish community, with ripple effects throughout the country.
The plan of relocating the orphanage to Bethlehem, whose population
was largely Arab, became untenable.

Avraham Yochanan realized with relief that the delays in the negotiation process had served to shield his boys from harm. Yet he still
needed to find a new location for the orphanage. He soon discovered
that a building on nearby Ezra Street, Yissacharoff House, was available.

9   A year later, when the Slabodka Yeshiva was devastated by the 1929 Hebron Massacre, the
     yeshiva relocated to Jerusalem. The administration decided to open a yeshiva for younger
     boys, and Michel Shlapovarsky, only twenty-nine at the time, was chosen to stand at its
     helm.

A four-year lease was signed, and the children adjusted quickly to their new surroundings.

HANUKKAH CELEBRATIONS

Despite frequent upheavals in the tiny country, the orphanage provided the children with joyful memories of each holiday. Hanukkah was always accompanied by the smell of donuts and latkes, a week of celebration that lit up the dark winter nights.

When the menorahs were placed on the windowsill, it seemed that a special light descended upon the entire house. Rabbi Blumenthal lit his menorah, surrounded by his family and his boys. Afterward, the older boys lit their own menorahs as well.

The children enjoyed parties, performances, and special games throughout the week of the holiday, including a huge annual Hanukkah party.

Preparations for the party began weeks in advance. Because the winter nights were rainy and public transportation was disorganized, the Kesher taxi company was hired to transport guests of honor to the party, while the Hamekasher (later to become Egged) bus company sent a special bus to transport the many guests from around the city to the party and later bring them home.

The party was always graced by an important guest of honor who would speak to the boys and bless them. One year, this guest was Sephardic Chief Rabbi Ben Zion Uziel, a childhood friend of Avraham Yochanan from the Old City.

A band stood on a decorated stage playing bugles and cymbals. Nearby, a choir led by a professional cantor sang Hanukkah songs. The famous cantor Shlomo Zalman Rivlin, son of Yosef Rivlin, a leader of the Jewish community in Jerusalem, ran this choir for many years.

The children, dressed in Shabbat clothing for the occasion, cast sidelong glances at the huge pile of presents — which had been either purchased or donated by manufacturers — that seemed to wink at them in festive anticipation from the side of the room. No matter how difficult the orphanage's financial situation, Avraham Yochanan did everything he could to make the holiday special.

During one of these parties, young Shemarya Nuri stood onstage and described his dream about Matityahu the High Priest. "I saw Matityahu the High Priest standing outside the Holy Temple dressed in his priestly garments, with a long white beard and piercing eyes. I approached to ask him when the Messiah will come, but he disappeared, and I was left alone, waiting for a response."

Young Shemarya turned to the crowd and raised his hands in the air, asking plaintively, "When will the Messiah come already?"

A thunderous round of applause erupted as he returned to his seat.

The program continued with contests and games. No child walked away without a prize. Hanukkah gelt was distributed by the visitors, and there were treats in abundance.

PURIM PLAY

After Hanukkah, the countdown to Purim began. Following evening prayers and the reading of the Megillah on Purim night, the boys would hurry to finish their dinner and change into costumes that they had been planning for weeks. Then they lined up in anticipation outside the director's office.

As they entered the office one at a time, Avraham Yochanan's task was to identify each costume-clad boy. Pretending not to recognize the children, he would peer at each boy's mask and guess a number of wrong names. The children laughed uproariously, pleased at the "success" of their costumes. Finally, in mock despair, Avraham Yochanan would ask the costume-clad boy to speak so that he could identify him, and then hand him a small bag of treats from the pile he had prepared.

In later years, the Blumenthal grandchildren would participate in the ritual as well. This often went on for hours, as Avraham Yochanan knew the long-term value of these precious memories.

The orphanage Purim play was legendary. Neighbors would pile into the building and join the audience, glued in fascination. The audience followed with bated breath the schemes of the cunning Haman who planned on destroying all the Jews, jeered at the weakness of the king who gave in to his minister's vices, and cried along with Queen Esther as she prayed for her nation.

At the end of the play, the boys would burst into song. The joy and merriment spilled out into the streets, uplifting the entire neighborhood.

Yosef Gafni recalls his experiences on Purim night:

> *I was chosen to be one of Achashveirosh's guards. I remember the rehearsals each night in the dining room, the excitement of preparing costumes and props, and the tall, black cylindrical hat that my counselor helped me prepare from oak tag. I even remember the lines I had to say: "Here he comes, here he comes, the big dog.[10] Oops, sorry! King Achashveirosh and all of his ministers..."*
>
> *Preparations for the show and the holiday gripped everyone in the institute — children and adults. [For weeks beforehand] you could hear children rehearsing their parts or singing songs from the play in the dining room, in the courtyard, and in the bedrooms.*
>
> *The play on Purim night was the climax of all the excitement. Guests were*

The children putting on a Purim play

Original Purim costumes

---

10   A reference to Psalms 22.

invited and sat in the front rows, as the orphanage boys looked on in eager anticipation. They all knew the script by heart, and a more enthusiastic and supportive audience would be hard to find! At the end of the play, our dear director approached us with a shining face and thumped us on the back.

The next day, the costumes used in the play were worn by boys sent to deliver Purim packages on behalf of the orphanage.

CHAPTER 27

Every Child Counts

Avraham Yochanan would often say with a smile, "All the people in the world — young and old, the distinguished and the plain folks — have one collective name: they are all human beings. When we look at a young child, we also need to see a human being!"

This attitude was in marked contrast to the prevalent attitude of the day, which often viewed young children as objects to be manipulated at will. As a result, the boys knew they could always approach Rabbi Blumenthal regarding any matter, large or small.

When he went out to the yard when the children were playing, they would

A child in the orphanage

stand at attention to listen to him. His conversations with the boys were his way of imparting the proper outlook and the depth of Jewish identity. Every story had a lesson, every act had significance.

His personal standards were very high as well. With all the warmth that he showered on the boys, he was constantly aware of his responsibility for their future and of the need to guide them to become God-fearing individuals.

On Yom Kippur, he always told the children, "We are like a bank that's making an accounting of its funds. We need to evaluate the number of our mistakes and good deeds, to see where there's room for improvement." In addition, while he never hesitated to rebuke a boy who needed it, he was also careful not to do so when he felt a rebuke would bring more harm than good. He once explained: "When Moses descended from the celestial spheres of Mount Sinai, we don't find him describing the things he had seen, the likes of which no human eye had ever seen before. Moses was called by God 'the faithful one of My home.' One who wants to be faithful must know how to remain silent as well."

TANGIBLE TREASURES

Avraham Yochanan believed that Torah study held the key to emotional and spiritual well-being. Once, when one of the boys decided to go out to work instead of utilizing his talents for Torah study, Avraham Yochanan told him, "The prophet bemoans two types of people: he who desires [to study] and is incapable, and he who is capable but does not desire."

Yet his approach was to encourage but not insist on Torah study. He praised the boys who succeeded in their studies and rewarded their achievements and efforts. When Yosef Appel left the orphanage and moved back home to his widowed mother in Rehovot, he was presented with a set of the Malbim's commentary on Torah, a complete set of *Ein Yaakov*, and a silver wine goblet — a veritable treasure for a young boy at the time.

"The director very much encouraged the boys to study," relates David Aharoni, who lived in the orphanage from 1933 to 1939. "I was sent to study in the Porat Yosef Yeshiva in the Old City. Sometimes, the director would ask me to study with the weaker boys and even paid me for my efforts."

Avraham Yochanan carefully selected the counselors who supervised the boys, hiring only young men that he felt would serve as positive role models. During the evening hours, the boys would do their homework under the counselors' watchful eyes. They provided help and guidance when necessary and reviewed the boys' notebooks.

THE MOTHER BIRD

One day, a widowed mother arrived at the orphanage with her two sons to entrust them in Rabbi Blumenthal's care. When she had left, Mrs. Blumenthal, who had heard the exchange between them, lifted her eyes from her sewing and looked at Avraham Yochanan, knowing exactly what his next words would be. He did not disappoint her.

"I'm simply carrying out the Torah's injunctions," he said with a smile. "Does it not say, 'Send away the mother [bird], and take the offspring for yourself?'"[11]

Yet Avraham Yochanan often went beyond the particular commandment he was so fond of quoting. He would take in the sons, and rather than "sending away" the mother, he would find her work or lend a listening ear to her troubles.

When the cleaning woman, a widow who had served the orphanage for many years, fell ill, Avraham Yochanan accepted her sons into the orphanage and arranged for her daughter to be accepted to the Weingarten Orphanage. Later, he helped the girl train to become a professional seamstress, and she eventually married one of the boys from the orphanage.

In the days before any concept of pension existed, Avraham Yochanan would send his previous employees monthly stipends.

---

11   A quote from Deuteronomy 22:7, referring to the commandment to send away a mother bird before taking her offspring.

COMING OF AGE

It was not unusual for a mother to bring her children to the orphanage as soon as they "came of age." David and Nissim Cohen's mother arrived at Avraham Yochanan's door one day with her five-year-old, Shlomo, explaining, "I want to enroll Shlomo in your institution. He was too young until now, but this week he turned five, and I am unable to provide for him."

Mrs. Cohen and Shlomo were sent to Hadassah Hospital for a medical examination, and as soon as Avraham Yochanan received a note that the child was healthy, the boy was admitted into the orphanage.

The orphanage nurse who weighed little Shlomo was beside herself. "How can you take responsibility for a child who is so pale and emaciated?" she demanded of Yocheved, who was in the room at the time.

"The doctors said he's in good health," Yocheved responded. "He'll be fed properly here, and he'll gain weight."

Her prediction proved true. After three months of devoted care, the little boy's cheeks had filled out, and his face had a healthy glow.[12]

SLEEPING LIKE ANGELS

Avraham Yochanan was not content with caring for the children within certain limits, but rather made himself available whenever they needed it. His main concern was always the children's welfare, their education, and their well-being.

Often, when he returned from his rounds in the sleeping boys' rooms, he would sigh with pleasure and comment, "If I have any merit due to my work with the boys, who knows how much of it is detracted for the utter bliss I experience when watching them sleep like angels?"

---

12   Shlomo developed into a broad and well-built young man. As a teen, he worked as a counselor in the orphanage.

CHAPTER 28

Arab Uprisings

Y et all was not quiet in the little country. The summer of 1929 was a tense one in Mandatory Palestine, as relations between the Jews and the Arabs began to deteriorate. A week after Tisha B'Av, on Friday, August 23, tensions escalated, with cries of incitement heard from the mosques where hundreds of Arabs had gathered for prayer. The rousing speeches spewed hatred and venom against the Jews, whom the Arabs viewed with deep suspicion, fearing they would overtake the country.

At midday, an excited rabble burst out of the Al-Aqsa Mosque on the Temple Mount, waving knives and clubs as they charged toward the Jewish neighborhoods. Some headed toward Jaffa Street, while others set out in the direction of Talpiot and Mekor Chaim, to the east. The vast majority, however, marched toward Beit Yisrael and Meah Shearim, hatred in their eyes. Cries of "*Atbach el Yahud* (Butcher the Jews)" and "*Il dula maana* (The [British] government is on our side)" echoed through the streets, which quickly emptied of people.

The terrified Jewish residents bolted their doors. The men armed themselves with saws and kitchen knives in the event they'd be forced into hand-to-hand combat with the Arab mob. In the Bukharian Quarter, all the gates and doors of the orphanage were locked and bolted. Garbage pails — some filled with rocks to serve as ammunition and others filled with drinking water — lined the porches. The Arab guard abandoned his post at the gate. Heavy tables, piled atop one another, blocked the doorways.

The children prayed together as the Arab horde came down Shivtei Yisrael Street. In a widely reported incident, an Arab sheikh led the crowd, waving his sword in the air and stirring the crowd to jihad against the Jews. The British guards had vanished; there was no one to stop the imminent pogrom.

Suddenly, a young man emerged from a flour mill located at the southern tip of Meah Shearim and shot in the sheikh's direction, killing him.

In panic, the crowd began to retreat, escaping for their lives. A grenade thrown by members of the Haganah killed another three rioters, turning the mob on its head. The Arabs' bloodlust was momentarily forgotten as they fled.

The Jews of Jerusalem remained holed up in their homes for several long hours, fearing the crowd's return. Seventeen Jews were killed and thirty-eight badly injured on that fateful Friday and Shabbat that followed.

HEBRON MASSACRE

Meanwhile, in Hebron, where Jews and Arabs had lived peacefully side by side for many years, the situation was not as easily diffused. Although the Arab sheikhs had sworn that no harm would befall the Jews, their promises evaporated when violence erupted in the ancient city. Two yeshiva students were murdered in their study hall close to the onset of Shabbat, and the Jews were warned to remain in their homes as the British officers dispersed the Arab mob.

By morning, Arabs from the neighboring villages began streaming toward Hebron. Once again, the Jews were warned to remain in their homes. Many of them crowded into the home of the community leader, Rabbi Yaakov Slonim, hoping to be protected there, but to no avail.

As the Arabs went from house to house, murdering their Jewish neighbors in cold blood, they burst into the Slonim home as well, killing anyone in their path. Next, they approached the home of the head of the yeshiva, Rabbi Moshe Mordechai Epstein, where several families had congregated, and attempted to break down the door. Thankfully the inhabitants of this home were spared when the wife of the governor, who lived across the street, asked the Arabs to spare them, and the governor himself dispersed the crowd by shooting several bullets into the air.

By the end of that fateful Shabbat, sixty-seven Jews had been killed in Hebron, among them twenty-four yeshiva students, with many more injured. The surviving Jews were evacuated to Jerusalem, along with what remained of the yeshiva.

A COMMUNITY IN MOURNING

Michel Dovid Shlapovarsky, the Blumenthals' son-in-law, lost many of his close friends from the Hebron Yeshiva. Some of them had been frequent guests at the Blumenthal home, their smiles and refined spirits infusing the home with warmth. Now they were gone. A deep mourning cast its pall over the orphanage.

Gradually, the chaos passed. The children returned to their daily routines and forgot the fear of death that had been hanging over their heads. In the weeks that followed, however, the orphanage witnessed the devastating effects of the riots that had swept the country. Several new orphans whose lives had suddenly been overturned by the tragic death of one or both parents joined the orphanage.

The Chevronis, for example, were a Sephardic family that resided in Hebron. They had enjoyed friendly relations with their Arab neighbors, and when the riots began, their neighbors suggested that they hide in the branches of the large tree in their front yard. Most of the family survived, but the trauma took its toll on the boys' mother, who fell ill and passed away shortly thereafter. Her two sons, Avraham and Emanuel, came to the orphanage, where they remained for several years.[13]

THE VISITOR FROM PEKI'IN

Overnight, every Arab became suspect of murderous intent. One day, a young man dressed in full Arab garb and speaking fluent Hebrew entered the orphanage and asked to speak to Avraham Yochanan.

"He'll be here shortly," the boys told him, wondering who he could be.

When Avraham Yochanan arrived, one of the boys informed him that an Arab was here to see him.

"An Arab?!" the young man cried out. "You're calling me an Arab?!" Deeply hurt, he asserted, "I am a Jew, just like you!"

It turned out that the young man had been raised in the village of Peki'in in the Galilee, a descendant of the single Jewish family who had remained in the village since the destruction of the Second Temple. He had simply come to talk to Avraham Yochanan about the possibility of accepting an acquaintance of his into the orphanage.

---

13   Even after they had grown and married, the boys maintained a close connection to the Blumenthals and visited often, recalling their experiences in the orphanage.

CHAPTER 29

Meeting with the Bishop

O ther historical events unfolded in the neighborhood in the early '30s as well. Today, the religious neighborhood of Geulah is famous for its narrow, winding streets and alleyways lined with small stores and flanked by residential apartment buildings on all sides. Streets signs sporting names of the prophets such as Zephaniah, Amos, Haggai, and Malachi grace the bustling neighborhood, which older residents still refer to by its original name, "Kerem Avraham."

In 1930, however, as the nearby neighborhood of Achva thrived, Kerem Avraham was still a grassy field bordered by a forest on one side. In the middle of the field stood a lone building, called Kerem Avraham Avinu (Our Patriarch Abraham's Orchard, or *Karm Al-Khalil* in Arabic), which had been purchased by a devout Christian couple, James and Elizabeth Anne Finn. Finn was the British consul in Jerusalem from 1846 to 1863, and though he belonged to a Christian missionary society, during his years in Jerusalem he focused on providing jobs and vocational training for the impoverished Jewish community.

After his death, Mrs. Finn continued her husband's efforts, developing the plot of land into a thriving estate, complete with an olive press, winery, soap factory, and quarry. The entrance to the estate was marked by a stone archway that stood directly behind the Palace on what is today Zephaniah Street.

Mrs. Finn died in 1921, at the age of 96. After her death, various Christian groups set their eyes on the spacious property of Kerem Avraham Avinu, making plans to build several churches on the site, which bordered several Jewish neighborhoods.

Collective cries of protest arose from the Jewish residents of Jerusalem. While the unnerving presence of solitary missionaries was a fact they'd grown accustomed to, allowing them to establish an entire neighborhood in the capital of the ancient Jewish homeland was unthinkable.

Hearing of the tumult, Avraham Yochanan decided to inspect the plot of land himself and perhaps attempt to purchase it. His daughter Yocheved accompanied him to the sleepy grove, where foxes could be seen darting to and fro. Shepherds would often bring their flocks to graze in Kerem Avraham, as there was plenty of grass for the sheep to eat. Although the grove was a pleasant and quiet spot, the children dared not enter it, even in broad daylight. At night, it was even more frightening, with the howls of jackals echoing through the fields.

Investigations led Avraham Yochanan to the person behind the alleged plans to turn the estate into a Christian complex, a bishop from Cambridge who lived in Jerusalem. Avraham Yochanan arranged a meeting to ascertain his intentions and try to negotiate a purchase.

On the appointed Friday morning, Avraham Yochanan arrived at the bishop's house. When he introduced himself as Rabbi Blumenthal, recognition flickered in the other man's eyes.

"Is your first name Simcha?" the bishop asked.

"Simcha is my older brother," Avraham Yochanan responded in surprise.

The bishop flushed. After a pause, he ordered the others present to leave the room, and, once he had ascertained that the door was locked, addressed Avraham Yochanan in fluent Jerusalemite Yiddish.

"I studied with your brother Simcha in elementary school, and later in yeshiva..." he said haltingly, relating his previous name.

Slowly the puzzle came together. Avraham Yochanan recalled his brother's childhood friend, who had left Judaism as a teenager, eventually making his way to Cambridge, England. He had converted to Christianity and over the years rose to the rank of bishop.

Now facing Avraham Yochanan, the wayward Jew was overcome by nostalgia. He asked about acquaintances from his youth and recalled experiences he had shared with the Blumenthal boys.

The two men decided to meet again to discuss Kerem Avraham. As the meeting drew to a close, the bishop told Avraham Yochanan that he had a sudden longing to taste Yerushalmi kugel.[14] "Could I come to your home tomorrow at noon to partake of a *shtikel* (piece of) kugel?"

Avraham Yochanan hesitated. "Tomorrow? On Shabbat?" he stalled, wondering how to prevent this desecration of Shabbat.

"Are you afraid I'll come by car?" replied the bishop, understanding the concern. "I assure you that I will come on foot, without my black cloak. And I won't discuss business matters. You see, I still remember some of the lessons of my youth."

Avraham Yochanan hurried home, where the Shabbat preparations were underway, and asked Chana Shaina to prepare a larger kugel, as he was expecting guests the next day.

The following day at noon, the bishop duly arrived at the orphanage, accompanied by another man. The two were ushered into a room with Avraham Yochanan and his family — and the requisite kugel.

Conversation flowed. The bishop mentioned his plans to visit the cave of Elijah the Prophet on Mount Carmel (now Haifa), insisting that the cave belonged to Christians. Yet it was obvious he was not fully comfortable with his new faith.

"Money and honor are not things to be laughed at," he commented in an attempt to excuse his life choices.

---

14   A sweet pudding made of noodles and caramelized sugar, traditionally served by Jerusalemite Jews on Shabbat.

At their next meeting, Avraham Yochanan once more attempted to reach an agreement about the plot of land, but to no avail. Eventually he decided not to pursue the matter, turning his attention to the orphanage and other public needs.

With great blessing, in 1933, a committee of dedicated Jewish activists finally succeeded in purchasing Kerem Avraham. The ground was razed, the barren trees uprooted, and residential buildings sprouted — becoming part of the nearby neighborhood of Geulah and the rest of the developing holy city.

CHAPTER 30

Noble Visitors

"A carriage is coming!" called out someone looking out the second floor window. "Rabbi Yosef Chaim Sonnenfeld is arriving at the orphanage!"

The venerable Rabbi Sonnenfeld, the undisputed leader of Old Yishuv Jewry for nearly half a century, was a captivating personality in Jerusalem as well as Avraham Yochanan's mentor and teacher. Quickly, Avraham Yochanan hurried out to greet his distinguished guest. "To what may we accord this honor?" he asked, as Rabbi Sonnenfeld stepped down from the carriage. A group of children gathered around, straining their necks to get a glimpse of the holy rabbi.

Rabbi Sonnenfeld entered the orphanage building with Avraham Yochanan. The two closeted themselves in an office, leaving the rest of the building's inhabitants wondering. If the elderly Rabbi Sonnenfeld needed to speak to Avraham Yochanan, why didn't he simply ask the younger man to come to him instead of the other way around?

When the two emerged an hour later, Rabbi Sonnenfeld gazed lovingly at the crowd of boys that had gathered and blessed them before returning to the waiting carriage. His surprise visit and noble visage left a lasting impression on the entire household, though the reason for his coming was never revealed.

The Solimonov brothers, immigrants from Georgia who arrived at the orphanage

Several other distinguished visitors graced the orphanage with their presence throughout the years, including Rabbi Ben Zion Alfas, a well-known author of Torah works, with whom Avraham Yochanan had formed close ties during his time in the United States, and the famous Dr. Wallach, founder of Shaare Zedek Hospital and close friend of Avraham Yochanan's.

Yet even while Avraham Yochanan was deeply engrossed in conversation with one of his distinguished guests, if one of the boys approached to ask something, Avraham Yochanan immediately turned his attention to the child; only once the issue was resolved would he return to his conversation. The children always took priority.

COMMUNAL RESPONSIBILITY

The orphanage also extended its hospitality to others by hosting communal meetings and even weddings in its dining room. Needy couples without the means to cover the cost of a wedding hall knew they could use the orphanage's large dining room for free.

Avraham Yochanan often took responsibility for families in distress even when they could not be serviced by the orphanage. One irreligious young woman arrived in the orphanage by the instruction of Rabbi Avraham Yitzhak Kook, the Ashkenazic Chief Rabbi. She related that she had worked as a secretary for the British commission, and met and married a British officer.

Unfortunately, her husband began drinking regularly and beating and cursing his wife. The couple had a son and a daughter before the husband's commanding officer arranged for a legal divorce and deported him back to England. Left alone and unable to cope, the young woman had turned to Rabbi Kook for help, who sent her to Avraham Yochanan.

Avraham Yochanan assured the forlorn young woman, who had no family to come to her aid, that he would find someone to provide her with the support she needed. After consulting with Rabbi Kook, he succeeded in placing the girl in an orphanage. The boy, only a toddler, was placed in a temporary home.

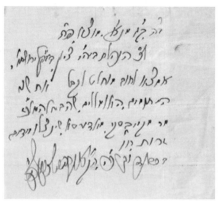

A request from Rabbi Avraham Yitzhak Kook to accept a child into the orphanage

Then a well-to-do childless couple from the town of Atarot, just north of Jerusalem, heard about the children. They approached Avraham Yochanan, begging to adopt the little boy. "He has no home!" they said. "Give him to us and we'll provide him with everything a child could want."

The couple searched for the children's mother to authorize the adoption, but she had disappeared. In the ensuing weeks, the husband began making daily appearances at the orphanage to entreat Avraham Yochanan, who now had legal guardianship of both children, to give them the child. When Avraham Yochanan mentioned the boy's sister, the couple unhesitatingly agreed to adopt her as well.

Avraham Yochanan deferred the matter to Rabbi Kook, with whom he'd had several dealings in the past. When Rabbi Kook confirmed that the couple would provide the two children with a proper Jewish education, the children were given over to their new adoptive parents, filling their previously empty home with the sounds of joy and laughter.

Shortly thereafter, the couple and their neighbors began to donate milk from their agricultural settlement to the orphanage. Since
the Tnuva milk company bought milk from Atarot, the residents of
the town signed a document authorizing the donation of a specified
amount of milk to Zion Orphanage. People in the neighboring Kfar Ivri,
now known as the northern Jerusalem neighborhood of Neve Yaakov,
donated milk to the orphanage in the same way, and the orphanage
received Tnuva milk for free for many years.[15]

LAND PURCHASE

Once again, the crowded conditions in the orphanage led Avraham
Yochanan to look to new horizons. His dream was to purchase a plot of
land surrounded by fields where the children could grow and flourish.
In 1932, he purchased a large plot near Shuafat, north of Jerusalem.

At the time, he couldn't have chosen a more secure location. Unlike
the western side of the city, which was surrounded by hostile Arabs, the
northern area of Jerusalem was mostly empty land. However, fortune
did not smile upon this particular plot. It was purchased as smaller plots
through two Jewish agents who had foreign passports, since British law
prohibited local Jewish residents from purchasing land, and then divided
among a number of partners without clear boundaries being delineated.

When the War of Independence broke out, Arabs settled in the area,
and the land was sold to Palestinian settlers, with Avraham Yochanan's
investment lost.

ANOTHER NEW HOME

With the four-year lease on the building on Ezra Street expired,
the orphanage was forced to move again. Avraham Yochanan rented
a building for a year from another Mr. Yehudayoff, nephew of the
owner of the Palace, called Yehudayoff House. This building too was

---

15   Eventually, the isolated village of Atarot became a target for Arab violence. In 1948, the
      Israeli government decided to evacuate the village, and its inhabitants moved to other
      locations across the country.

located in the Bukharian Quarter, on the corner of David and Aaron Fischel Streets.

During its year in Yehudayoff House, the orphanage hosted the renowned chazzan Yossele Rosenblatt, who was visiting the country at the time. Jerusalem's citizens flocked to the orphanage to hear the famed cantor's mellifluous voice. Other cantors of

Avraham Yochanan holding a Torah scroll as it is escorted to its new home, 1929

note who held prayer services in the orphanage included David Reznick and Samuel Vigoda. People flocked to the orphanage to hear them pray, and the profits from the tickets sold for these performances were a welcome addition to the orphanage's always tight budget.

תפלת יוסלה רוזנבלאט

A newspaper clipping relating that world-renowned cantor Yossele Rosenblatt performed in Zion Orphanage, May 5, 1933

CHAPTER 31

The Farming Orphanage

Yet another crisis was about to unfold for the orphanage. Before each holiday, Avraham Yochanan sent letters to his many generous donors in the United States, penning his greetings and best wishes together with a reminder of the orphanage's need for ongoing monetary support. The funds that arrived in response were the economic base of the entire institution.

One year, although the letters were sent out as usual, not a single response was forthcoming. In an isolated occurrence, Avraham Yochanan might have chalked it up to personal difficulties or forgetfulness. Yet, suddenly, dozens of regular donations from the United States had ceased abruptly. There was no economic disaster or war that might explain the situation. What had happened?

The orphanage, depending solely on the generosity of Jews from abroad, was suddenly in peril. Having no means of paying salaries, the Blumenthals were forced to let go most of the domestic help. Mrs. Blumenthal became the cook; her daughters supervised the table setting, cleanup, laundry, and sewing repairs.

Debts piled up. Orders of repossession arrived, with no relief in sight.

After intensive inquiry, Avraham Yochanan uncovered the terrible truth. A man who had worked for the orphanage during the chaotic days of World War I, when new orphans were arriving daily, had kept up his connection to the Blumenthals for many years. He would often stop in to study with various boys and walked around the building as though he were a regular member of the staff.

This unscrupulous man had somehow gained access to the list of donors who supported the institution. He wrote solicitations of his own representing the orphanage and mailed them off, adding his own name to Avraham Yochanan's on the stationery and changing the post office box address, thus pocketing all the generous sums sent by unsuspecting donors in America.

When a new telephone directory was distributed in Jerusalem, someone noticed that the orphanage's post office box address had changed, and the story came to light.

Once discovered, the man brazenly insisted that it was his right to receive some of the funds allocated to the orphanage. In a bizarre twist of logic, he convinced himself that he was Avraham Yochanan's partner and was the victim rather than the perpetrator!

The pain of this betrayal broke Avraham Yochanan's heart. He collapsed one day, and Dr. Weitz, summoned to examine him, determined that he'd suffered a heart attack.

The doctor ordered total rest for six full weeks. After a few days, he returned to check on his patient. During the course of his examination, the legendary Rabbi Aryeh Levin, known as "the Tzaddik of Jerusalem" and a friend of Avraham Yochanan's, appeared in the orphanage, having come to perform the mitzvah of visiting the sick.

When the doctor was ready to leave, Mrs. Blumenthal went to look for money with which to pay him. There was not a penny to be found in the entire house. Rabbi Levin, witnessing the scene, immediately grasped the matter at hand.

"Perhaps you are lacking a few pennies with which to pay the doctor?"

he asked gently. "Here, I happen to have a little money on me." He promptly paid the twenty *grushim* for the doctor's home visit, leaving the Blumenthals immensely relieved and grateful.

THE ORPHANAGE IN MOTZA

As soon as he'd recovered somewhat from the ordeal, Avraham Yochanan began to agonize over how to address the tremendous financial damage to the orphanage. How would he divert the donations back to the orphanage without causing harm to the orphanage's good name back in the States?

The orphanage in Motza

Planting trees in Motza

Finally, he hit upon a creative plan. He would establish a new branch of the orphanage in Motza, a Jewish settlement on the road to Jerusalem, where boys who enjoyed working with the land would be taught farming skills. A house with three spacious rooms and a surrounding plot of land was promptly rented, and several children from the orphanage moved in along with a young couple who served as surrogate parents. (To this day, the remains of the house are visible from the Jerusalem–Tel Aviv Highway.)

The boys continued their regular Torah studies with the husband, and for several hours a day would work in the garden, digging and weeding. The Blumenthals' daughter Yocheved became their gardening teacher, after taking a speedy course in gardening by reading a book on the subject. In the serene Judean Mountains, the children learned to fertilize, weed, and keep the insects away from their garden. Soon, the garden boasted flowers and vegetables, and the boys took much pleasure in this success.

Yet running a branch of the orphanage far from the city was not a simple undertaking. The children's clothing was sent to the city once a week to be laundered. After being washed, ironed, and folded, the clean laundry was returned to Motza. Food and other essentials had to be delivered from the city. Nonetheless, the children's development and the lovely garden made all the difficulties worth it.

Most importantly, under the new name "The Farming Orphanage," Avraham Yochanan was able to send out letters to his longtime supporters, together with a new post office box number for donations. Slowly, donations began to arrive and the orphanage started to recover from the damage caused by the larceny.

EVACUATION

In 1936, after several years in operation, the orphanage branch in Motza was forced to close when a delegation of Palmach officers (the elite fighting force of the Haganah, the main underground Jewish militia) arrived with an order that it be evacuated immediately. The nearby Arab village of Qalunya had become a danger zone, and with the deteriorating security situation, the Palmach needed the house as a lookout station. That very day, the children and the young couple packed up their belongings and returned to Jerusalem.

Avraham Yochanan, however, refused to give up on his idea of teaching the boys farming. He searched for a local plot of land where the Farming Orphanage could continue its activities, soon locating a farm called Gan Hamelech (the King's Garden), situated on a spacious plot of land in the Sanhedria area of Jerusalem. The farm was run by a man named Mr. Gruman, who cultivated vegetables, fruit trees, and beehives.

Mr. Gruman agreed to teach the children basic farming and botanical skills. Boys who were interested would go to Gan Hamelech twice a week for farming lessons, an arrangement which lasted four years. In 1940, with World War II raging, farming became a pleasant but distant memory.[16]

---

16   After the War of Independence, Gan Hamelech was uprooted and the Sanhedria Cemetery was built in its place. The Farming Orphanage was officially closed, and the orphanage's name once again reverted to the Zion Blumenthal Orphanage.

CHAPTER 32

Close Ties

espite these tumultuous events, the orphanage children continued to thrive. Chaim, for example, was a sweet, blond, blue-eyed boy who had been born in Russia. He was orphaned of both parents during a pogrom and arrived in Israel in 1930 with his uncle. The orphanage became his home, replacing the love and warmth so brutally snatched away.

Little Chaim devoted himself to his studies, yet his social adjustment was less smooth. One day, the sound of crying coming from the yard aroused Avraham Yochanan's attention. He hurried outside, his eyes landing on a forlorn figure huddled in a corner, his small shoulders shaking with sobs.

The children stopped their game and grew silent. Avraham Yochanan turned to them. "A Torah scroll is lying on the ground and you are playing nearby, yet you do nothing to pick it up?"

The children looked around in confusion. Where was the Torah scroll?

Avraham Yochanan lifted Chaim up and continued, "A boy who

studies Torah is a living Torah scroll! How could you leave him lying on the floor crying?"

The children lowered their heads in shame. From then on, Chaim was included in the group and its games.

A child from Caucasia, who arrived in the orphanage after losing contact with his father

Chaim remained in the orphanage for eleven years. He completed his studies with honors and went on to study in Hebron Yeshiva. When he married, his bride found it hard to believe there were no blood ties between him and the Blumenthals; they treated him like a son. Yocheved and her husband walked him down to his chuppah.

Avraham Yochanan underwrote the expenses for the entire wedding and purchased a small apartment for the young couple, enabling Chaim to continue his Torah studies. He and his family lived in this apartment until the end of his life.[17]

STUBBORN CHILD, STUBBORN COUNSELOR

Yisrael Hirschler and his brother moved into the orphanage after their father was murdered by Arabs near the Old City of Jerusalem in 1934. The two acclimated well, and Yisrael was known as a talented and generally obedient boy.

---

17   Chaim later received a position in a yeshiva. He maintained close and loving ties with the Blumenthal family all his life.

"My father was a Torah scholar, a talented speaker, a paragon of loving-kindness, and a chazzan," writes Chaim's daughter. "He was very sensitive to the pain of others. These characteristics are usually developed in childhood, nurtured by the warmth and security of a loving home. My father, however, was orphaned at a young age and grew up in an orphanage. But the orphanage and the Blumenthal family provided him with the warm home and devoted care that helped develop his unique personality.

"Throughout his life, my father felt that the Blumenthals were his own close and supportive family. His many descendants are forever indebted to the Blumenthal family."

Yet ten-year-old Yisrael had a stubborn streak as well. When he announced plans to fast on Yom Kippur, his counselor didn't think much of it. Ten-year-olds often view fasting as a sign of bravado, but as soon as hunger pangs set in, they quickly change their minds.

Yom Kippur arrived. The children gathered in the synagogue. From time to time, the counselor's eyes wandered to thin little Yisrael. Slowly, other young boys left to break their fasts. Yisrael, however, touched not a morsel of food.

"You look exhausted," the counselor told him. "It's time for you to eat."

"No!" insisted Yisrael.

At noon, the counselor decided to exert his authority. He placed a plate of food in front of the boy and commanded him to eat.

Yisrael, usually obedient, kept his mouth firmly shut.

Fearing for his health, the counselor forced the food into his mouth.

Wounded to the depths of his soul, Yisrael ran out of the room, crying bitterly, "I'll make up this fast, you'll see!"

The next day, little Yisrael did not appear at the breakfast table. When he didn't show up for lunch either, the counselors began to worry. They decided to wait a while longer, in the hope that the child would return on his own.

At dinnertime, Yisrael finally showed up. A victorious glow illuminated his exhausted face.

"Where have you been all day?" the concerned counselor demanded.

"I hid so you wouldn't force me to eat," Yisrael responded.

When Mrs. Blumenthal heard the story, she became very concerned over the frail child and spent the next several days fussing over him to be sure that the fast had no negative effects.

AN ADOPTED GRANDFATHER

The elderly gentleman who arrived at the Blumenthal home impressed Avraham Yochanan with his dignity and kind features. He had one "small" request. Would Avraham Yochanan allow him to move into the orphanage, where he could spend his remaining years in the cheerful company of youth?

Avraham Yochanan was at a loss for how to respond to this strange request. Upon investigation, he discovered that the gentleman, whose name was Yosef Levine, had been born in Poland and moved to Mexico with his parents at a young age. As an adult, he went into business and married, but he and his wife were never blessed with children. He had made aliyah after his wife passed away, leaving him alone in the world.

"I have a small amount of money saved up, but it's not enough to pay for an old age home," Mr. Levine explained. "Even if I could afford it, though, I prefer to spend my time in the presence of young, happy children rather than with the elderly."

After weighing the matter carefully and ascertaining that the man would indeed be an asset to the orphanage, Avraham Yochanan agreed to the request. The two wrote up a legal contract, and Mr. Levine moved into a small room in the orphanage building. His presence lent a special flavor to the home, and he embraced the children with warmth and love.

When Mr. Levine passed away several years later, he left behind a pamphlet of original Torah thoughts as well as fond memories in the minds of his adopted grandchildren. His *yahrtzeit* was always recalled in the orphanage, and many of the boys recited Kaddish for him.

ANOTHER NEW PATRON

One day, Rachamim Mizrahi entered the orphanage with a treasure in his hands: a brand new pair of pants, the likes of which none of the children had seen in years. Within moments, Rachamim was surrounded by a group of curious boys, begging to hear where the pants had come from.

"An old man gave them to me," he said, carefully guarding his treasure.

"That's impossible," his friends countered. "No one gives presents like that to people in the street!"

When news of the mysterious pair of pants reached Avraham Yochanan's ears, he summoned the boy to his office. "Rachamim, my child, where did you get these pants?"

"An old man from America is distributing clothing to the needy,"

Rachamim divulged, as though he were a seasoned businessman sharing the secrets of his trade.

"If that is the case, maybe we should tell him about the other boys in the orphanage too?" Avraham Yochanan inquired gently.

"I didn't think of that," Rachamim acknowledged sheepishly.

One of the counselors was dispatched to accompany Rachamim to the elderly man's home. A short while later, the two returned, the counselor confirming the boy's story.

"His name is Binyamin Cohen," he related. "He's originally from Europe but arrived here from America with his wife several days ago. Their son has a clothing factory in America and they brought two cartons of excess winter clothing to distribute to the needy in Jerusalem."

Soon, many more children in the orphanage had received new pants from the generous Mr. Cohen. The next day, a messenger was dispatched to thank the elderly man for his contribution. Impressed by what he heard about the orphanage and its activities, Mr. Cohen immediately promised to donate additional supplies like sugar and rice.

Shortly thereafter, however, a messenger arrived from Mr. Cohen, asking Avraham Yochanan to pray for him, as he was unwell. The children gathered into groups and recited Psalms for the recovery of their patron. But it was not to be. A few days later, a messenger arrived to inform Avraham Yochanan that Mr. Cohen had departed from this world.

Avraham Yochanan immediately sent a group of boys to sit with the deceased and recite Psalms, according to the Jerusalem custom. The newly widowed Mrs. Cohen greeted them gratefully, struggling to maintain her composure.

During the seven-day mourning period that followed, the orphanage sent a quorum of boys to pray in the house three times a day. Afterwards, the widow made good on her husband's promise to Avraham Yochanan, giving a donation to the orphanage. Although she soon returned to her family in the United States, she never forgot Avraham Yochanan's kindness in her time of need.

CHAPTER 33

Angel of Mercy

T he high holidays of 1933 were approaching, and with every passing day the orphanage's debts mounted. In addition to the atmosphere of joy and elevation, the upcoming holidays heralded an added heap of expenses as well as demands to pay the long overdue rent on the orphanage building.

Avraham Yochanan refused to give in to despair, sending out letters to philanthropists, arranging loans, and saving and scrimping wherever he could, relying on the Father of Orphans to bring his salvation.

Mere days before Rosh Hashanah, a visitor appeared in Avraham Yochanan's office. "My name is Mullah Menashe Aminoff," he introduced himself, "and I live nearby.[18] As your neighbor, I see the wonderful work you do with the boys and the pure Jewish education you give them. I would like to become a partner in your holy endeavors." Without pausing for breath, Mr. Aminoff began to list off the many foods he planned

---

18 The term "mullah" is used in the Muslim world to denote respect for an educated religious man. In some Sephardic Jewish communities it is used to refer to community leadership.

to contribute to the orphanage: meat, flour, rice, beans, watermelon, and more.

Avraham Yochanan pressed Chacham Menashe's hand warmly in gratitude, his face lighting up with relief at this welcome news.

But Chacham Menashe was yet not finished. "I have been working on a new building for your orphanage," he said matter-of-factly, as though offering another sack of potatoes. "You'll rent it out in exchange for three lirot a year [a negligible sum], with a three-year contract."

"But not every building is suitable for an orphanage," protested Avraham Yochanan. "I have to check the premises first."

"Of course," Chacham Menashe agreed.

Avraham Yochanan immediately went to see the building. The impressive structure at 40 Yechezkel Street was no illusion. (Today, the building houses an elementary school.) After Avraham Yochanan inspected the building, he suggested several improvements to benefit the children. Chacham Menashe immediately agreed to the changes.

Who was this angel from Heaven who saved the orphanage in its time of need?

The Aminoffs were descended from Jewish families from the city of Mashhad, Iran, near the border of Afghanistan. Until 1839, Jews had lived in this city peacefully. Then, a pogrom broke out, with the Arab population turning against the Jews. The hapless Jews begged the local imam for protection. He agreed to spare their lives only if they converted to Islam. Left with little choice, much of the community converted, becoming known as *Jedid Al-Islam* ("the New Muslims").

To all appearances, the New Muslims were successful merchants and faithful to their new religion. Secretly, however, they remained faithful to Jewish law and traditions, like the Marranos of Spain before them. Each bore a Persian name by which he was known amongst his Persian neighbors, and a Jewish name by which he was known in his own community. The children gathered in hidden synagogues after school to learn Hebrew, prayers, and Chumash.

While most of the community's holy books had been confiscated by zealous Muslims, a small number of Torah scrolls were salvaged. To prevent assimilation, the community members married only amongst themselves, and at the earliest possible opportunity.

The community observed Shabbat and holidays. Guards were stationed outside the synagogues to alert the worshippers in case of danger. In order not to arouse suspicion, stores were kept open on Shabbat, with young children instructed to tell customers that their father was not in, or that he was ill and would return another day.

In 1889, one of the leaders of the community, Benjamin Kordevani, was seized by a tremendous longing to set foot in the Holy Land. He announced that he was embarking upon pilgrimage to Mecca. Once in Mecca, he joined a caravan headed for Israel.

He purchased a large plot of land in Jerusalem, and upon his return to Mashhad, informed his family that "when we move to the Holy Land, please God, we will donate the land to the poor and to Torah scholars."

In the early twentieth century, some of the "New Muslims" of Mashhad began to immigrate to the Holy Land, where they were accepted back into the fold of mainstream Judaism. When Kordevani passed away in 1918, his children changed their last name to Aminoff ("son of Benjamin"), to honor their patriarch. True to their heritage, they gave generously to the poor. The entire extended family made aliyah, settling in Jerusalem along with others from their former community. Chacham Menashe Aminoff, one of Kordevani's sons, and his brothers had decided to donate their father's plot of land to Zion Orphanage.

The wealthy Aminoff brothers were famous for their generosity — marrying off orphans, paying rent for countless struggling families, and distributing vast amounts of fabric to poor families to be sewn into clothing before Passover each year. Seeing Avraham Yochanan's efforts in establishing an orphanage, they supported these initiatives grandly. In return, the Blumenthals invited the family to join in various parties and occasions at the orphanage, forming a bond between the two families that lasted many years.

Before long, the building on Yechezkel Street was ready, and a festive dedication ceremony took place in the spring of 1934. Many prominent figures attended, including Rabbi Kook, Rabbi Uziel, Rabbi Nissim Elyashar (head of the Jerusalem Sephardic Council), and Rabbi Isser Zalman Meltzer (head of the Etz Chaim Yeshiva).

Throughout the years, the negligible rent payments were always returned to the orphanage through various donations and gifts. The children would reciprocate by visiting the Aminoff family on Passover and Sukkot. During these visits, they would recite Psalms out loud, as family members listened with pleasure and plied them with goodies.

The Aminoffs became the orphanage's adoptive family. The three-year

The dormitory in Aminoff House

rental contract ultimately lasted for two and a half decades. Throughout the years, the Aminoff family made improvements and renovations to the building whenever necessary, always with a smile and a generous hand.[19]

SCRIMPING AND SAVING

Despite the Aminoffs' generosity, the orphanage's debts were growing, and the minimal donations that came in could barely cover the astronomical cost of running the institution, especially as the economy faltered. When the holidays arrived and there was no money to hire a professional tailor, the Blumenthals would buy a bolt of material at a bargain price and sew the children pants themselves, taking apart an old pair to use as a pattern. The joy in the children's eyes upon receiving their new clothing made all the efforts worthwhile.

---

19   With Chacham Menashe's passing in 1938, a pamphlet was published by the orphanage in his memory. His many charitable activities were enumerated in great detail, along with words of Torah and eulogies by Rabbi Uziel, Avraham Yochanan, and several orphanage alumni.

The Blumenthals would also go out to collect contributions from different store owners in the city, who would pledge small donations such as a few pounds of sugar or rice each month. Sometimes, all they received was a single bottle of oil. With these random donations, they managed to scrape by, day to day.

A certain Mr. Chaviliv, a religious Jew of Middle Eastern descent who owned a candy factory, contributed a kilogram of halvah each month. Mr. Skolnik, who owned a store of building materials on Luntz Street, contributed a set sum of money each month. The Blumenthals welcomed every contribution, no matter how small.

These years were marked by poverty throughout the Old Yishuv. Yocheved remembers a neighbor who once entered her sister's house and loudly complained, "I don't understand today's children! Yesterday I made them an omelet with half an egg for each, and today they're demanding another one!"

In the midst of this difficult period, the cleaning staff went on strike, demanding higher wages. Avraham Yochanan explained this was simply impossible, as the orphanage debts were high already. In response, the staff left, and the older children began taking responsibility for the smooth running of the orphanage.

Yocheved's role was to ensure that tasks were allocated fairly, hanging a chart at the entrance to the dining room listing chores for each day of the week. The chores included setting and clearing the tables, cleaning the dorm rooms and shower rooms, and straightening up the synagogue. There were also "briefcase supervisors" in charge of school supplies; a "towel supervisor" to ensure a supply of clean, dry towels; and other positions of responsibility.

These tasks did not embitter the children; rather, they viewed it as a privilege to contribute to the upkeep. Many recalled this period as a time marked by unity and joy, as the youngsters pitched in together to help out.

A SUCCESSFUL MATCH

As much as Avraham Yochanan's fundraising efforts were focused on the orphanage, his vision extended to many other institutions as well. During the period before World War II, the Porat Yosef Yeshiva suffered an economic crisis. Located in the heart of the Old City, Porat Yosef was a yeshiva for students of Middle Eastern descent, and many of the orphanage's Sephardic boys studied there. Hearing of the institution's dire straits, Avraham Yochanan took upon himself to come to its aid, attending many emergency meetings to help it get back on its feet.

During one meeting, the name of a potential donor was mentioned, a Lebanese Jew named Rabbi Avraham Shalom. Rabbi Shalom lived in Mexico but was visiting Israel at the time. Arrangements were made for him to visit the yeshiva.

Impressed by the sounds of Torah emanating from the building located across from the Western Wall, Rabbi Avraham Shalom immediately offered the institution a donation of $25,000, a huge sum in those days. The money was invested as an endowment fund, with the dividends earmarked for the yeshiva's ongoing maintenance.[20]

Avraham Yochanan rejoiced at this connection as if the yeshiva were his own institution.

ANOTHER WEDDING

Happy occasions marked the 1930s as well. In 1939, Yocheved celebrated her marriage to the scholarly Chaim Natan Solomon, a student in Hebron Yeshiva and son of Rabbi Avraham Yisrael Moshe of Kharkiv, Ukraine, author of a commentary on the Jerusalem Talmud. The Solomon family had made aliyah in 1936. Yocheved continued to work in the orphanage after her marriage, and her husband later established a yeshiva high school for the orphanage boys, which was very successful.

Rabbi Chaim Solomon, Rabbi Blumenthal's son-in-law

---

20 After the War of Independence, with the Old City in Jordanian hands, Yeshivat Porat Yosef moved to the new city. Rabbi Shalom's endowment fund enabled the administrators to rebuild the yeshiva in its new location.

With Europe on the brink of war, Rabbi Shmuel Wosner, a first cousin of Avraham Yochanan, and his wife also made the hazardous journey to Mandatory Palestine. Avraham Yochanan rented an apartment in Jerusalem for the couple and their young son. Soon after, the Wosner family moved to the newly-established city of Bnei Brak, where Rabbi Wosner became a well-known Torah leader.[21]

---

21   In Bnei Brak, Rabbi Wosner established a yeshiva that he led for over half a century until his passing in 2015. He was also known as a renowned halachic authority, yet he never forgot the debt of gratitude to his cousin.

CHAPTER 34

A Childhood in the Orphanage

No matter what else was happening in the world at the time, orphanage alumni recall their years in the orphanage with fondness and appreciation. Yosef (Weiner) Gafni relates:

Half a century has passed since my years in the orphanage, where I lived from 1940 to 1947.

If I close my eyes, images immediately appear in my mind's eye, and the lilting tunes of the orphanage's synagogue echo in my ears. Above all, the image of my beloved spiritual guide, Rabbi Avraham Yochanan Blumenthal, remains with me.

I arrived at the orphanage as a young boy of six, a child whose entire world had been destroyed. Rabbi Blumenthal and his daughter Yocheved remained my role models for the rest of my life. In their merit, I chose all that is good and important.

In my time, the Zion Orphanage was located on the corner of Yechezkel Street, near the Turkish bathhouse and the Bukharian marketplace. The building was built of white

Jerusalem stone, a one-floor horseshoe-shaped building with an enclosed yard in the middle. The building's gate was made of two imposing iron doors that closed with iron bars. Over the entrance was a metal archway bearing the words "Zion Orphanage."

American visitors: Rabbi Avraham Shlomo Borwick from Massachusetts, Rabbi Gedalya Silverstone from Washington, Rabbi Blumenthal, Rabbi Elchanan Tzvi Gutterman from Scranton, PA, and Rabbi Dov Ber Baruchov from Malden, Massachusetts

Adjacent to the courtyard was a huge empty lot where we played adventure games. One exciting game lasted for several days. We gathered barbed wire left by the British and created a "fortress." Acting out events of the time, we would pretend to be underground fighters who "attacked" the fortress by entering it secretly. A few real injuries occurred as a result of the barbed wire, but these only added to the excitement of the game.

In the courtyard of Aminoff House. Rabbi Kook is speaking. Beside him is Avraham Yochanan.

The most dominant figure in the orphanage was its director, Rabbi Avraham Yochanan Blumenthal. He wore a white shirt, a dark vest with a round pocket watch, and a long black coat. A large black skullcap graced his white hair. His eyes were kind and caressing...

Rabbi Blumenthal became my father, in the deepest sense of the word. When my biological parents abandoned me, he adopted me as a son. He was with us day and night, winter, spring, summer, and fall. He would walk among us, supporting and encouraging us. When necessary, he would sit beside the bed of a sick child, stroke his forehead, and reassure him with soft, kind words. I loved this wonderful man.

He was like a prophet of old who instructed us in the word of God. He was with us during prayers, meals, playtime in the yard, and in the dorm rooms before lights-out. Very infrequently did he punish a child — only when all other choices had been exhausted.

His family stood at his side, helping him raise the children in the orphanage. Mrs. Blumenthal attended to all the meals — a significant undertaking, especially during those difficult days of World War II. The menu was basic but filling. For breakfast, we had bread, jam, a square of margarine, and tea; for lunch, beans, potatoes, and sometimes borscht; and for dinner, bread, vegetables, soup, and cheese. I do not recall ever leaving the dining room hungry.

The orphanage children in the courtyard of Aminoff House with their American visitors. Standing on the right is Avraham Yochanan; seated are Rabbis Silverstone and Baruchov. Standing on the left is Mr. Saliman, a counselor; seated are Rabbis Borwick and Gutterman.

The Blumenthals' youngest daughter, Yocheved, was like a mother to me. She fussed over us with maternal warmth, caring for the sick children and making the orphanage feel like home.

Every Friday, we would head to the Turkish bathhouse adjacent to the orphanage. I can still picture the steam, the wooden boards upon which we placed our clothing, the mikveh, and the adjacent hot water pool.

Afterward, we would cut our nails and dress for Shabbat and head to the dining room. Rabbi Blumenthal would sit in the corner of the room, and each child would file past and stretch out his hands to show his trimmed fingernails. Then, Rabbi Blumenthal would lay his hands on the child's head and bless him. This ceremony took place with utmost solemnity, a beautiful prelude to the arrival of Shabbat.

I'll never forget walking to the Western Wall at the age of eight. I somehow became separated from the rest of our group and suddenly found myself wandering the streets of the Old City. My heart filled with fear. Not knowing how to reach the Western Wall, I turned right at every juncture.

Suddenly, an Arab youth appeared and began to hit me with a stick. I escaped and continued turning until, miraculously, I reached a Jewish area. I went down the narrow steps between the walls of the city and Batei Machseh. On the steps sat dozens of beggars shaking their tin cans.

I was pulled along by the throngs into a narrow alleyway with a small British guard booth at its edge. I passed the British guard and suddenly found myself standing in the small narrow courtyard before the Western Wall. Dozens of Jews wrapped in prayer shawls stood and lifted their voices in tearful prayer. I could not believe that little me was standing at this tangible reminder of our nation's glorious past.

I recall the Solomon family, relatives of Yocheved's husband, hosting me in the village of Kfar Avraham, near Petach Tikva,

*for Passover. The Blumenthals and Solomons had arranged
this visit so I could experience a holiday with a family rather
than in an institution. The Seder was delightful, and the joyous
atmosphere in the room contagious.*

*I especially recall the scent of the citrus orchards in the village
and how delightful it was to eat oranges right off the trees.
I recall climbing to the top of a hill and looking out over the
greenery, experiencing a feeling of freedom and beauty I had
never felt in the city.*

*Now that I have children of my own, I appreciate Rabbi
Blumenthal's efforts on our behalf all the more. He dedicated his
entire life to giving needy children a warm home, an excellent
education, and endless love. He saved us from deteriorating
into a life of poverty and crime.*

May his memory be blessed.[22]

---

22   Yosef Gafni shared other memories as well, which can be found in other chapters of this book.

CHAPTER 35

World War II

R ather than encouraging the formation of a "national home for the Jews," as originally promised, the British issued the famous White Paper of 1939 in response to the 1936–1939 Arab Revolt. This severely limited Jewish aliyah to the country, leaving thousands of Jews trapped overseas during the perilous years of World War II. Illegal immigration became commonplace, with the British sending violators to prison camps in Mauritius.

Occasionally, Jews who wanted to make aliyah but could not obtain a coveted immigration certificate would arrive as tourists instead. If they could prove to be financially secure, they could receive a permanent resident's certificate.

A retiree named Mr. Slafter arrived in Avraham Yochanan's office one day with a request. "My wife and I are in the country as tourists," he explained, "and would like to settle here permanently. In order to prove my financial security, I'd like the orphanage to hire me as a clerk. I'm an accountant by profession, and I'm happy to work here free of charge."

The orphanage had always managed without an accountant, but

Avraham Yochanan agreed to the arrangement, which turned out to be satisfactory on all sides.

Several years later, Mrs. Slafter, feeling that she owed the orphanage a tremendous debt of gratitude, decided to solicit donations from her affluent friends on behalf of the orphanage. One of the families she approached was a childless couple named Mr. and Mrs. Makal, who were very impressed by the home's happy children and its clean, orderly rooms.

Mr. Makal approached Avraham Yochanan. "My wife and I are no longer youngsters, and there's no one to recite Kaddish for us when we die. We would like to have one of the children from the orphanage come and visit us once a week. This child will pray for us after we pass on. In exchange, we will donate part of a building we own to the orphanage."

Avraham Yochanan selected a boy, orphaned of both parents, whom he felt was a good match. The boy began to visit the couple's home each week, and after they'd passed on, he recited Kaddish for both husband and wife.

RUMORS AND REFUGEES

Unconfirmed rumors about the war in Europe trickled into the Land of Israel. Refugees who had managed to escape the conflagration and make their way to Israel brought many difficult tidings. However, unlike World War I, the Middle East did not play a major role in the fighting, and the citizens of the Mandatory Palestine were generally in no immediate danger.

When Italy joined the Axis Powers in 1940, declaring war on France and Britain, the cities of Haifa and Tel Aviv were bombed, resulting in many civilian casualties. Later, battles took place in Egypt and other parts of North Africa, but with no direct attacks on Jerusalem.

As the war dragged on, sad-eyed children, accompanied by a sorrowful-looking parent, relative, or guardian, continued to plead acceptance to the orphanage. There was always a saga of pain behind the child's arrival: sick or deceased parents, entrapment by missionaries, or weeks of wandering and hunger.

One such boy was Daniel Waldi, who arrived at the orphanage with his recently widowed mother. He was a charming boy of Greek descent with a quiet and pleasant demeanor. Once Daniel settled into life in the orphanage, the boys discovered that he was gifted with a beautiful voice. He subsequently became one of the star soloists of the orphanage choir — enthralling listeners with his soulful performance.

MEMORIES

Dr. Aryeh Oded, who entered the orphanage in 1939 at the age of eight, recalls:

> Rabbi Blumenthal had a glowing visage and a long white beard, with thick brows under which his loving eyes shone. He would walk slowly; each step was measured and thought out. He never raised his voice, and his words were always pleasant. Even during World War II, when the orphanage was in difficult straits, the children received all their — albeit paltry — meals on time. Sometimes, breakfast consisted of two slices of bread, coffee, and two falafel balls, which I was sent to buy from a poor woman who lived across the road and sold falafel balls for a livelihood.
>
> Mrs. Blumenthal would enter the dining room each day during lunch. If she sensed that a child was still hungry, she would give him another portion of vegetables or beans.
>
> To enhance the Shabbat and holiday prayers, the orphanage hired a music teacher who would come several evenings a week to lead a choir. To this day, I can recall the songs I learned then. Another acquisition of my years in the orphanage was memorizing the Book of Proverbs. Rabbi Blumenthal had a special affinity for this book and encouraged the children to study it, as it is filled with lessons for life. For every chapter memorized, we received half a grush.[23] If we learned ten chapters, we received an additional grush, and for learning the entire book, we received another few grushim — a not-insignificant sum in those days.

---

23   The smallest denomination of Israeli money at the time, worth one-hundredth of a lira.

After learning the entire book, if we were able to give Rabbi Blumenthal the chapter and verse of a specific quote, we would receive yet another few grushim. During after-school hours, my friends and I would sit and review Proverbs and test each other. To this day, I quote verses from this book on different occasions.[24]

KOSHER MEAT

For many years Avraham Yochanan did not consume red meat. He took this stringency upon himself after returning from the United States, when he discovered that a heated dispute had erupted in Jerusalem in his absence regarding ritual slaughter. He maintained this stringency until the end of his days.

Yet this did not prevent him from doing his utmost to provide the orphanage children with meat, which they needed for its nutritional value. The fresh meat, purchased sparingly, was koshered by the cook, under Mrs. Blumenthal's close supervision.

One day, koshering salt had already been sprinkled over the pieces of raw meat when Avraham Yochanan entered the kitchen and asked, "Where was this meat purchased?"

When he heard the response, he rushed out, returning a short while later with a prominent rabbi from the neighborhood who carefully examined the meat before finally rendering a verdict: "Kosher!"

Later, Avraham Yochanan explained that he discovered that a question had come up regarding one of the cows slaughtered that day. "I had to ensure that this meat was one hundred percent kosher," he explained.

INSPECTION

During World War II, however, almost no meat was to be found in the country. Ritual slaughter took place only occasionally in Jerusalem,

---

24   Dr. Oded served as Israeli ambassador to several African countries and authored several books on African-Israeli relationships. Today, he is a professor of Asian and African studies at Hebrew University in Jerusalem.

and the small amount of meat available was often allocated to hotels or hospitals. Acquiring meat for the children for Shabbat was a prolonged process, one that required much negotiation with government authorities.

One Friday morning, when the kitchen workers were busily preparing for Shabbat, a group of policemen burst into the kitchen, accompanied by an official in charge of meat distribution.

"We're here for an inspection," they announced, hoping to catch the orphanage in a misappropriation.

One policeman grimly inquired of the orphanage staff how much meat they had received. After checking his list, he asked to weigh the raw meat, which was standing in a large bowl on the counter. The officers painstakingly weighed the meat on the large kitchen scale and compared its weight to what was written on their list. To their shock and dismay, the amounts were exactly equal.

HOSTING A TISCH

Two great leaders who miraculously escaped Europe during World War II were the Chassidic rebbes Rabbi Aharon Rokach of Belz, whose entire family was wiped out in the war, and his half-brother Rabbi Mordechai of Bilgoray, twenty-two years his junior. They received coveted Jewish Agency certificates early in 1944 and arrived in Jerusalem shortly before the Nazis began deporting Hungary's Jews.

There was much excitement among the residents of the Old Yishuv at the news of the rebbes' impending arrival. The question arose where they would spend their first Shabbat in Jerusalem. A huge crowd was expected to arrive for the *tisch*, the customary gathering held on festive occasions by Chassidic leaders, and it was imperative to find a building large enough to accommodate everyone.

The Zion Orphanage building was suggested, and Avraham Yochanan, with characteristic generosity, consented. The dining room was emptied, and the kitchen, synagogue, and an additional room were prepared in honor of the expected guests.

The *tisch* was an incredible experience for the orphanage boys. Together with the other attendees, they gazed in awe at the two rebbes with their shining faces, listening to their words of Torah and drinking in the sweet melodies that wafted out to the streets. The atmosphere of that Shabbat remained imprinted on their memories for years to come.

CHAPTER 36

New Life for the Needy

While the Aminoff brothers relieved the housing burden from Avraham Yochanan's shoulders,[25] the costs of food, payroll, and upkeep were staggering. By the mid-1940s, the offices he had established twenty-five years before in America had all but ceased to function, and it was no longer feasible to depend upon solid support from overseas. Thus, the developing city of Tel Aviv, with its thriving industries, became a critical source of aid. Avraham Yochanan would travel there on a regular basis to solicit funds for the orphans.

Sometimes, he would stay in Tel Aviv for several days. Since the kashrut in the city did not meet his high standards, he barely ate while there, and often returned to the orphanage weak and exhausted. Once, he was so weak that, upon his return to Jerusalem, instead of going home, he went straight to the hospital.

Whenever he traveled, the children eagerly awaited his return.

---

25   See chapter 33.

Frequently, others were waiting to unburden their problems to his ever-ready ear. Patiently, without taking a moment for himself, Avraham Yochanan would turn to the widow who awaited him with downcast eyes, to the man who sought his advice, or to the young boy who had come to pour out his heart.

REVIVING THE DEAD

One day, a middle-aged man from Tel Aviv, whom Avraham Yochanan knew from his trips to the city, arrived at the orphanage. He entered the director's office, sat down, and burst into tears.

"What's wrong, Mr. Wasserman?"[26] Avraham Yochanan asked in concern.

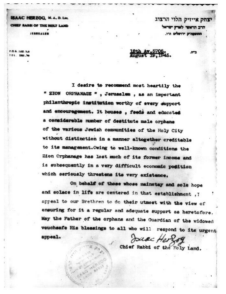

A letter of appeal on behalf of the orphanage from Chief Rabbi Yitzhak Isaac Herzog, dated August 1945

"My life...my possessions...all for nothing..." the man sobbed.

Avraham Yochanan waited quietly, allowing him to compose himself.

"Before World War II, I was a wealthy and respected citizen of the city of Danzig, where I ran a successful furniture business," Wasserman explained. "With the war approaching, I sold my possessions, liquidated the business, and arrived here with my wife, settling in Tel Aviv.

"We purchased a home that my wife decorated lovingly, though we never merited to fill it with children. I reestablished my business, selling expensive pieces from Europe, most of quality German wood. But there was little demand for the quality merchandise I imported. I tried my hand in other businesses, but nothing succeeded. I am now completely penniless. Nothing is left of my initial investments."

---

26   Name has been changed.

Heaving a deep sigh, he continued, "Dear rabbi, I have come to bid you farewell. After all our pain and disappointment, my wife and I have decided to end our lives."

"What?!" Avraham Yochanan jumped as though bitten by a snake. "How can you even contemplate such a terrible thing? You are a Jew, and Jewish law prohibits such an action!"

Taking the other man's hand in his, Avraham Yochanan sat and spoke to Mr. Wasserman at length about the meaning of life and each human being's special life mission. Then, realizing that lunchtime was approaching, he excused himself to the kitchen, asking Mrs. Blumenthal to please prepare a special meal for his guest of honor.

Once Mr. Wasserman was satiated and his nerves calmed, Avraham Yochanan said, "I just thought of an idea! I need a fundraiser for the orphanage. I'm sure that someone as kind and intelligent as you will be successful at the task!"

Avraham Yochanan described the children in dire need of support, and outlined how Mr. Wasserman would find satisfaction and fulfillment working for the orphanage. By garnering support for the orphanage, he explained, Mr. Wasserman would be saving these children and all their future generations.

The idea captured the pained man's heart, and a new light appeared in his eyes. Avraham Yochanan offered to prepare all the necessary documents so that he could begin the job immediately.

"No." Mr. Wasserman shook his head. "I must go home now. My wife will worry!" He left the orphanage a new man, his head high.

Two days later, Mr. Wasserman and his wife visited the orphanage to take a tour and speak with the children. At the end of the visit, they took the file of necessary documents and letters of recommendation in hand and set out to fulfill their new task. Traveling the length and breadth of the country, they succeeded in arousing people to share in the orphans' care.

As for the Wassermans, the pride and sense of accomplishment was palpable. "Rabbi Blumenthal's orphanage saves lives," Mr. Wasserman would often say. "Usually, he saves the lives of the orphans in his care, but sometimes he also saves those of adults..."

A LOVING GRANDFATHER

As when his children were young, Avraham Yochanan's many responsibilities to the orphanage and the community at large did not preclude his care for his family. His granddaughter Tziporah Zaks recalled how her grandfather saved her life when she was ill with typhus during World War II.

"I lay in the hospital for a number of weeks with a raging fever of over 106 degrees," she says. "Over thirteen thousand people in the country perished from typhus during the war, since there wasn't enough medicine available. After two months in the hospital, my strength began to ebb. My family was summoned to my bedside and the doctor said, 'We've done whatever we can. You can still hope and pray that God will help...'

"Grandfather was sitting near my bed. He whispered in my ear: 'Be strong and don't pay attention to the doctor's words. He doesn't really have faith in G-d's help, and he is causing you to despair...'

"With his rock-solid faith, he filled me with hope. He put a prayer book near my head and sat there praying and reciting Psalms until the morning.

"When the doctors arrived the next morning, they found me not only breathing but also smiling. They couldn't believe the miracle that had occurred. They took my temperature, which had gone down to 96.8 degrees. Only when Grandfather was sure I was out of danger did he go home to rest. His image was like that of an angel; it remains with me to this day."

Mrs. Chaya Schneerson, Avraham Yochanan's niece, was also hospitalized in critical condition during the war, and the doctors declared no hope for full recovery — she would have to be transferred to a long-term care facility. Avraham Yochanan refused to hear of this. He immediately moved her, at his own expense, to a private hospital in Jerusalem. Contrary to the dire predictions, Mrs. Schneerson recovered fully and returned home, where she continued to function for many more years.

FATHER OF ORPHANS

Avraham Yochanan's love and care for the orphans never diminished, even in the most extreme cases. Rabbi David Nisanoff, a rabbi in the Bukharian community, relates:

Escorting a bar mitzvah boy to the synagogue. In the foreground is Rabbi David Nisanoff, chairman of the Bukharian Committee

> In my work with the families that emigrated from Bukhara, I was involved in several cases of deep pain and suffering. In this way I had opportunity to become acquainted with the unique Rabbi Blumenthal, whom I secretly dubbed "the father of orphans." The orphans I brought to his office were always greeted warmly, with genuine love. I once entered the orphanage with a two- or three-year-old who looked like he hadn't been bathed in over two months. He was barefoot, and his shirt was so encrusted with filth that it was impossible to make out its original color.
>
> Rabbi Blumenthal took the child in his arms, kissed and hugged him, and soothed him, "Don't cry! I am your father!" Then he called his wife and asked her to heat some water to bathe the child.
>
> Once the water was heated, Rabbi Blumenthal himself scrubbed the boy of the accumulation of dirt. Then they brought out clothing in his size, and for the first time in months, the boy experienced the sensation of clean clothing.
>
> Rabbi Blumenthal hugged and kissed the child again, then brought him to the dining room and personally fed him a bowl of soup. All this took place before he even knew who the child was.
>
> If I ever stopped by the orphanage at bedtime, I would see Rabbi Blumenthal walk among the boys' beds, asking each one if he had enjoyed his dinner and if he had said the nighttime

Shema. He would lovingly stroke their heads. Many even called him "Father." Like a true father, he would accompany the children until their marriages. They would probe him for marriage advice, and he would pay their wedding expenses.

Once, I asked how he was able to devote himself to these children day and night, and he immediately responded: "The verse says, 'You shall not cause pain to a widow and an orphan...'27 While I am allowed to neglect myself, neglecting these orphans is completely forbidden!"

SPIRITUAL DEVELOPMENT

Over the years, the many financial setbacks never diverted Avraham Yochanan's attention from his primary mission: to educate and guide the children in his care. Despite worries over the orphanage's sustainability, the children's development took priority over everything else. Avraham Yochanan kept a close watch on their pastimes and occupations, often listening in to hear their games and conversations.

Twice a year, when the text of the Silent Prayer changes to correspond to the season, Avraham Yochanan would seat the children in a circle around him. Together, they would repeat the new text ninety times in order to become accustomed to it and avoid any mistakes.

When Rabbi Blumenthal witnessed immature behavior from one of the boys, he took it very seriously, yet his admonishments, as always, were warm and gentle. Smiling, he would say, "*Nu*, did your holy soul descend to earth from its exalted place beneath the Holy Throne for this?"

---

27   Exodus 22:21.

CHAPTER 37

Another Heavenly Angel

World War II devastated the international economy. Travel became dangerous, with fewer and fewer people braving the seas. The food packages and financial aid that regularly arrived on Israel's shores ceased almost completely. Once again, the orphanage was in crisis. Its limited income could not possibly cover the numerous expenses.

In discussing how to relieve the orphanage's crushing financial burden, Avraham Yochanan's son-in-law Chaim Solomon offered to speak with a wealthy relative, Mrs. Pearl Koltonsky, who lived in Tel Aviv and had connections to many successful businesspeople.

When he visited the following day, Mrs. Koltonsky indeed suggested a potential donor. "A relative of mine named Adina Levy is arriving soon for a visit from America," she said. "I'll speak with her and get back to you."

Mrs. Levy, it transpired, was a niece of the famed Rabbi Chaim Ozer Grodzinski, a leader of European religious Jewry in the early twentieth century. Her husband ran a successful silk factory in Egypt, where the family had lived before relocating to the United States. Adina was now planning to visit Mandatory Palestine. But as all civilian airlines had shut down due to World War II and she did not want to spend several weeks travel-ing by ship, the intrepid Mrs. Levy joined the US army as a hospital supervisor — travel-ing by military aircraft — and arrived in Jerusalem during the week of Sukkot.

Mrs. Koltonsky had told Mrs. Levy about the orphanage and she was interested in hearing more. After a preliminary meet-

The children in their pajamas, washing up before bedtime

ing with Rabbi Blumenthal, Mrs. Levy visited the orphanage, dressed in her army uniform. She arrived on the eve of Shemini Atzeret/Simchat Torah as the orphanage children were preparing for the holiday. Mrs. Levy expected to find an austere setting filled with sad-eyed children, darkened hallways, and a Spartan rule. Instead, however, song, dance, and warmth filled the orphanage, suffused as it was with a holiday atmosphere.

With great interest, Mrs. Levy toured the children's clean and order-ly rooms. At one point, she noticed a portrait hanging above a bed in the dormitory and asked Yocheved, her guide, "Who is that?"

"That's one of our donors," Yocheved explained. "When someone 'adopts' a child in the orphanage, we put his picture on the wall above the child's bed."

"How much does such an adoption cost?" Mrs. Levy asked with interest.

"Sixty lira," Yocheved said. (At the time, the average monthly salary in Jerusalem was a lira and a half.)

Mrs. Levy immediately assumed that sixty lira was an annual sum and calculated that adopting a child would cost five lira per month. When she mentioned this figure, Yocheved was astonished, given that a donation of sixty lira "bought" the privilege of "adoption" for many years to come!

"I would like to make a donation in memory of my nephew, who was killed in a car accident," Mrs. Levy announced. After some thought, she added, "I'll suggest this idea to some friends and acquaintances as well."

After evening prayers, the children danced enthusiastically in the orphanage synagogue, the traditional Simchat Torah songs filling the air. As the dancing stretched on, Yocheved offered to take her guest on a tour of the various synagogues and yeshivas in the neighborhood. Mrs. Levy accepted the invitation with great interest.

The two women, one a native Jerusalemite in her modest garb, the other a sophisticated European-born tourist in army uniform, entered the magnificent Bukharian synagogue, where beautiful crowns decorated the Torah scrolls and the community leaders wore traditional garments of silver and gold weave. Next they walked over to Hebron Yeshiva. Although the streets outside teemed with people, Mrs. Levy's military uniform seemed to have an impact and people cleared a path for the women to pass.

Mrs. Levy's air of authority and confidence dissolved in the tumultuous atmosphere of yeshiva students twirling around and singing their lively tunes. She stood as though hypnotized by the scene, dabbing the tears that welled in her eyes. "Let's stay a bit longer," she implored Yocheved.

The evening eventually drew to a close, but from that day forward, Mrs. Levy made it her personal mission to support the orphanage and ensure that the children were well cared for. Upon her return home, she began sending her friends and acquaintances to the orphanage to pledge donations in

The orphanage children in the courtyard. On the right is Adina Levy, on the left is Yocheved Solomon

memory of deceased family members. She also convinced her relative Yaakov Dori (who later became the first IDF Chief of Staff) to visit the orphanage.

Slowly but surely, the debts began to be paid off, and Rabbi Blumenthal was once again able to consider things like new shoes, replacing worn-out furniture, and enhancing the children's menu.

At one point, however, when Yocheved visited Mrs. Levy in her Tel Aviv apartment, Mrs. Levy received her very coolly. "I can no longer continue my work on behalf of the orphanage," she said.

Not knowing what had precipitated the sudden change of heart, Yocheved prayed for the right words. "What you have done for these children," she said slow-ly, "no one is able to do. With this strength you will be able to continue."

Mrs. Levy froze. Finally, she said quietly, "All right, you've con-vinced me."

In the ensuing

Bar mitzvah boys being called up to the Torah in the sanctuary named in Adina Levy's honor

weeks, she arranged for twenty-four families to underwrite the expens-es of a quarter of the children in the orphanage. This eased Avraham Yochanan's burden tremendously. Yet despite her continuous support and the time and energy invested, Mrs. Levy always shied away from the limelight, never taking the credit for her efforts.[28]

---

28   Yocheved and her husband maintained constant contact with Mrs. Levy through letters and visits. When Chaim Solomon traveled to America, he met with Mr. and Mrs. Levy and suggested they finance the building of a synagogue for the orphanage. Adina liked the idea and promised to make the donation. Sadly, however, she was unable to bring this plan to fruition, as she passed away suddenly in November 1963.

Her funeral took place in Jerusalem, with many friends and acquaintances in attendance. Afterwards, the Levys' daughter approached Yocheved and said, "We intend to fulfill every-thing that Mother promised." Mrs. Levy's sister sponsored the synagogue in the orphanage's current location, named "Ohel Adina" (Adina's Pavilion) in her honor.

CHAPTER 38

Danger on the Horizon

With the British Mandate disappointing its Jewish citizens, resentment against the government grew steadily, and underground military groups began training in the event of war. It was clear that the status quo would not last indefinitely. The entire country waited with increasing tension as political events unfolded before their eyes.

The Haganah, a paramilitary group formed to protect Jewish settlements against Arab violence, became a nationwide organization whose goal was to work politically to achieve its goals. Meanwhile, two splinter groups, the Etzel (also known as the Irgun) and the Lehi (the Stern Gang), employed more subversive strategies, including outright attacks against the British, to wrest control from what they perceived as an oppressive government.

Amidst a rash of anti-British operations carried out from 1944 to 1947, the British clamped down on Jewish citizens — forming military zones, imposing strict curfews, and conducting searches and arrests.

The Jewish community, meanwhile, was torn by internal strife, as members of the various groups sought to convert all able-bodied young men to their cause. Once, after a meeting in the Blumenthals' home, two Haganah members pounced on a young man named Avraham Roth, crying out, "Enough shirking of your responsibilities! Come help us fight the British!"

Hearing the commotion, Avraham Yochanan stepped outside, quickly sized up the situation, and quietly ordered the young men, "Release him immediately." Quailing in the face of his noble features, the Haganah members instantly made themselves scarce.

In another memorable incident, a group of Etzel members entered the orphanage courtyard one evening and spread across the yard, clearly planning some military activity. The children, watching from behind closed window shades, hurried to inform Avraham Yochanan, who was in his office conducting an important meeting with several rabbinic leaders.

The meeting continued, adjourning late into the night. Preoccupied by communal concerns, Avraham Yochanan had completely forgotten the information relayed to him earlier by the boys. He sat down to study, as he did every night, utilizing the rare silence to delve into the ancient words of the Talmud, and then went to sleep.

In the middle of the night, Avraham Yochanan awakened suddenly and recalled the children's report. *Why was the light on in the kitchen?* he wondered. He rose to investigate, but failed to notice a carton blocking his way. He fell over it, breaking two fingers and gashing his palm. With no telephone in the building and a curfew in effect, Avraham Yochanan had no choice but to return to bed. Not wanting to disturb his family, he slipped out of the house as soon as dawn broke and walked alone to Hadassah Hospital, then located in the center of town, to seek proper medical attention.

Several hours later, Yocheved arrived in the orphanage to begin her day's work. She discovered, to her astonishment, a group of armed young men sitting in the courtyard as though it belonged to them.

"This courtyard is private property, and you must leave immediately," she said sternly.

"Our business doesn't concern you," the young men growled. "Go inside!"

Yocheved stayed firm. "This is my house, and it is also an orphanage. If you want to carry out a military act, do it elsewhere. Not here!"

Yocheved's arrival, however, had come too late. At that moment, the militants, strategically hidden throughout the yard, threw their hand grenades at a passing army jeep. The jeep halted, and the Etzel members dispersed, escaping through the back entrance of the yard and disappearing into the convoluted alleyways of nearby Beit Yisrael.

As the drama unfolded outside, Yisrael Chaim Blumenthal, inside the building, noticed his father's blood-stained blanket. Finding Yocheved in the yard, he realized they had to act quickly. "Look at this," he told his sister hurriedly. "The British soldiers will soon be here in search of Etzel members. Their bloodhounds will smell this blood, and we will have to answer for it."

Without wasting a moment, Yocheved doused the blanket in water, sprinkling it with black pepper as an added precaution.

The street outside was strangely silent. Yocheved stepped out to survey the yard and discovered thick ropes left behind by the Etzel members, who had planned to hang a British soldier if he were to fall into their hands. She quickly coiled up the ropes and placed them in the storage room.

Just then, two army jeeps screeched to a halt in front of the gate. The stern-faced soldiers entered the orphanage grounds and began to search it systematically, looking for hidden weapons, clues of the perpetrators' identities, and ammunition.

After an hour-long search, the soldiers finally left the premises, finding nothing. A number of hours passed before Avraham Yochanan returned home, his hand bandaged and the broken fingers splinted.

CHAPTER 39

War Refugees

D espite the strict quotas, immigrants continued to arrive in Palestine, often via illegal means. With World War II finally over, several surviving relatives of the Blumenthal family emigrated from Hungary to Israel. Avraham Yochanan opened his door and his heart to these refugees, helping them to recover from the war trauma and to stand on their own two feet.

One of these relatives, Mr. Yitzhak Gal, describes: "After years of suffering in concentration camps, we came to Jerusalem, where we were lovingly welcomed by Rabbi Blumenthal, whose home was always open to those in need. Even after settling in our own homes, we would pray at the orphanage each Shabbat, witnessing Avraham Yochanan's incredible devotion to the boys. We will always remember his refined and loving smile."

Avraham Yochanan's nephew, Yisrael Blumenthal, son of his older brother Hershel who had relocated to Hungary due to a medical condition, was the lone survivor of his entire family. He made his way to the Holy Land after the war and went directly to his uncle's house, where he was greeted like a long-lost son. Yisrael lived with the Blumenthals until his marriage.

JOY AMIDST THE GRIEF

The orphanage dining room wore an air of festivity. The children tiptoed around, some of them arranging benches and helping out, others gazing curiously at the guests who had slowly begun arriving for the wedding.

Left to right: Rabbi Berel Soloveitchik, whose wedding took place in the orphanage dining room; Rabbi Yitzhak Zev Soloveitchik (the Brisker Rav); Rabbi Chaim Solomon; and Rabbi Meir Soloveitchik, youngest son of Rabbi Yitzhak Zev

Soon the Blumenthal family, dressed in their Shabbat finery, joined the throng. All waited in anticipation of the famed Brisker Rav, Rabbi Yitzhak Zev Soloveitchik, the father of the groom.

Avraham Yochanan's face wore an expression of unadulterated joy throughout the evening. It was a privilege for him to host this important event in his home and to greet the leaders of Jerusalem.

Rabbi Soloveitchik had arrived in the Land of Israel in 1941, at the height of World War II. As soon as the Jews of Jerusalem heard that the famed Torah scholar from Brisk, Lithuania (today known as Brest in Belarus), was on his way, an aura of excitement filled the city. The great rabbi initially stayed at the Zion Hotel, run by Rabbi Fischel Zaks and his wife Chaya Sima (née Blumenthal), as it was well-known for its exacting standards of kashrut.

Due to this family connection, Chaim Solomon formed a close bond with the Brisker Rav, which continued even after he moved into his own home. When Rabbi Soloveitchik's son Yosef Dov (known as Berel) became engaged, Chaim spoke to his father-in-law, who willingly offered the orphanage for the wedding celebration.

Hundreds of people participated in the joyous event, flooding the hall and its adjoining rooms, and spilling out into the courtyard. It seemed that all of Jerusalem came to celebrate this momentous evening at the Zion Orphanage.

UPROOTED CHILDREN

World War II had devastated Eastern and Western Europe alike, destroying families and leaving in its wake thousands of orphaned children and teens. Emaciated and homeless, they filled displaced persons camps and sought to rebuild their lives in the Holy Land.

Late one Friday afternoon, a group of thirty Hungarian yeshiva students arrived in Jerusalem, having reached Palestine in a rickety illegal immigration boat and docking without being caught by the British. They were slated to join a yeshiva in Jerusalem, but no beds were available.

With Shabbat quickly approaching, Hillel Schlesinger, secretary of the organization, ran to the orphanage and explained the situation to Avraham Yochanan.

"Rabbi Blumenthal put aside all his other affairs, as though it were obvious he needed to take responsibility for these boys," recalls Rabbi Schlesinger. "Within a short time, he had found a place for every one of the boys for Shabbat."[29]

THE IRATE UNCLE

When Purim arrived, everyone tried to forget the challenges of British rule and focus instead on the joyous holiday. Suddenly, a tall man with a grim expression appeared at the orphanage door, asking for Eliyahu. "Your uncle is here," someone whispered to the boy in question.

Eliyahu turned pale, unwilling to come forward.

Eliyahu was a refined young boy who had come from Morocco

---

29   In another version of the story, the yeshiva administration learned that Avraham Yochanan was planning to establish a home for refugees, and he had already rented a building in the Bukharian Quarter and had furnished it with everything necessary for a dormitory, which he gladly gave over to the refugee students until they could find more permanent accommodations.

following the death of his parents. While the earnest child clung to the traditions of his fathers, his uncle had tried on numerous occasions to convince Eliyahu to join him on a kibbutz.

"I don't want to go with him," Eliyahu moaned to his friends, as he hastened, trembling, to a hiding place.

"We don't know where Eliyahu is," one of the boys said.

"Where is the director?" the irate uncle demanded. He stormed into Avraham Yochanan's office, his face red with anger.

A few minutes passed, and loud shouts could be heard from behind the closed door. The man raged and screamed, pounding on the table and demanding access to his nephew. Avraham Yochanan, whose self-control was legendary, did not utter a single word in response.

After a full hour of verbal abuse, the man stormed out, promising Avraham Yochanan that he would yet return...

Avraham Yochanan emerged from his office greatly distressed by the incident. He refused to respond to any inquires about what had occurred. In order to protect the boy, Avraham Yochanan decided it was best to transfer him elsewhere. He arranged for Eliyahu to study in a yeshiva in Kfar Avraham, where the boy remained for several years. All the while, he maintained his close connection to Avraham Yochanan.[30]

---

30   A month after the Purim encounter, the orphanage heard that the boy's uncle had tragically stepped on a mine and was killed instantly. Eliyahu no longer had to fear him.

CHAPTER 40

Shalom's Story

The year 1947 found the orphanage in Aminoff House. Avraham Yochanan, already seventy years old but with the energy of a much younger man, was assisted in his duties by his devoted wife and his daughter Yocheved, who served as her father's right hand.

That year, a sweet and delicate seven-year-old named Shalom Babioff arrived at the orphanage. Shalom's memories afford a glimpse into his travails as a child and his subsequent adjustment to life in the orphanage. An excerpt from his writings follows.

> I was seven years old when my father died, leaving my pregnant mother, my elderly grandmother, and two small children — my older brother and me.
>
> Even before Father passed away, we struggled financially. People who didn't have a marketable skill often had to travel from place to place to buy old items and clothing and try to peddle them. Others worked for homeowners doing various

tasks. My father worked as a porter, transporting goods on a cart. Those who were able harnessed a donkey to the cart; others had to pull the cart themselves.

My father loved people and the Torah and those who studied it. He never complained to the Creator about his financial difficulties. He would pull a heavy two-wheeled cart from early morning until late at night, in the winter and summer, in order to support us... Although we lived in poverty, we were always happy and satisfied. My mother knew how to make use of every bit of food, and she would prepare good and satisfying meals for the family.

Suddenly, without prior warning, our lives turned upside down. I arrived home one day to see many neighbors and relatives outside our apartment. Inside, Mother was surrounded by women, her face streaked with tears. Why was she crying?

Slowly, I grasped that my father had collapsed in the street that morning and had been rushed to the hospital, where he was pronounced dead from a stroke. At first I did not believe my ears. I thought that Father would return that evening as he did every day. But following the funeral, I understood that Father would not be with us anymore.

The days passed. My mother was busy with different jobs in an attempt to provide for us. A neighborhood committee helped us as much as possible, and my grandfather did his utmost to assist. But our joy and lightheartedness was gone. When I returned from school each day, I would find Mother surrounded by her friends, mourning Father. I would go outside so as not to cry in her presence and increase her pain...

Soon after, Mother gave birth to a third son, who was named after my father. She could no longer care properly for my brother Raphael and me, and an interview was arranged at Zion Orphanage.

At the meeting, I studied Rabbi Blumenthal's face. In many ways he reminded me of Grandfather. He had a glowing visage and a long flowing beard that lent him the look of an angel. His face was smiling and quiet, his gaze fatherly. He looked at Raphael and me with a smile, and we immediately sensed that he liked us. The thought of living in the orphanage filled me with mixed emotions. On one hand, I wanted to stay with Mother, and I hoped that Rabbi Blumenthal would say there was no space for us. On the other hand, the beautiful synagogue, warm atmosphere, and cleanliness in the orphanage all appealed to me. I knew that I would receive a good education and would help ease my mother's financial burden.

Yet I was filled with doubts. Will I ever get used to this new life? To following rules laid out by a stranger?

At the end of the meeting, Rabbi Blumenthal accepted us into the orphanage. I knew it was for our good...

Raphael and I followed Rabbi Blumenthal into one of the rooms, where he pointed out two beds and said, "From now on, these are yours." Then we went to the clothes room, where a pleasant woman made room for our things in the closet and gave us a shelf number.

Every child in the or-phanage was assigned a cubby with a number. I was number ten, and my brother was number nine. Each time I needed a change of clothing, I would state my number and receive clean under-wear, shirt, and pants.

The younger boys' dorms

Everything was amazingly well-organized. In the dorm rooms, each boy had a shelf in the closet.

After Rabbi Blumenthal had given us a tour of the orphanage, he said that supper would be served at seven o'clock and left us on our own.

I lay on my bed and looked around. What am I doing here? I thought. At this hour, I was usually playing with my brother in the courtyard in front of our home. I could no longer come and go as I pleased.

I shared these thoughts with my brother, who said, "Let's try it for a few days and see what happens. Grandfather knows Rabbi Blumenthal and he wouldn't have put us in a place that isn't good for us. My friends in school say it is good here. We'll grow accustomed to it eventually."

"And if we don't?" I countered.

"All beginnings are difficult," my brother said earnestly. "In a few days we'll know better what lies ahead. Mother's burden is already too heavy… We'll be able to visit Mother whenever you want."

Tears filled my eyes. I sank into silence until sleep overtook me. Suddenly, I was awakened by the sound of boys entering the room. "Are you new here?" they asked. We nodded wordlessly.

Someone said, "You seem sad. That's how it is in the beginning. But you'll get used to it and you'll like the orphanage. It was hard for me in the beginning, too, but I got used to it."

We heard the counselor calling from the doorway. "Boys, it's time for afternoon prayers."

We joined the children in the synagogue, where we were assigned a place to sit. We recited afternoon prayers, and then we studied Mishnah.

Supper consisted of an egg, black bread, margarine, jelly, and a cup of tea. We sat with the other children at the long table and ate. All this time, the pain continued to weigh on my heart. I wanted to go home, but I didn't say anything aloud.

I could not fall asleep that first night. I twisted and turned from side to side, peeking at my brother, who was sound asleep. Eventually I fell into a deep sleep, only to be aroused by the counselor entering the room to wake the children. "Good morning, children. Time to get up!"

So early in the morning? "*What time is it?*" *I asked.*

"*Five a.m.,*" *someone answered.* "*We always get up at this hour.*"
*I rose reluctantly and followed the boys to the synagogue for
morning prayers. After breakfast, we walked to school.*

*In the afternoon, on my way home from school, I went to visit
my mother and tell her all about the orphanage. Half an hour
later, I returned to the orphanage, where I found everyone
sitting in the dining room and eating the midday meal.*

*Rabbi Blumenthal looked at me and smiled. He didn't ask where
I had been or why I was
late, yet I felt uncomfortable and quickly sat down.
Only afterward, when we
went out to the yard to
play, did he ask where I had
been. I told him I had gone
to visit my mother.*

A counselor serving the children soup

"*Next time you want to
visit Mother, let us know
first,*" *he said,* "*so we don't worry where you are.*"

*I accepted his gentle reprimand, embarrassed that I hadn't
thought of asking permission. I decided from then on to try to
succeed at the orphanage. I knew that with a spiritual guide
like Rabbi Blumenthal, things would be okay.*

CHAPTER 41

Life in the Orphanage, 1947–1952

S halom Babioff continues to relate:

Over time I got to know Rabbi Blumenthal better. One day when I was playing checkers with a friend, he entered the room. Without saying a word, he watched as I won one game and we started a new one. Suddenly, he moved one of my friend's pieces in a complicated move.

I looked at the board in surprise, trying to think of a way to salvage the game, when it dawned on me that Rabbi Blumenthal had taken pity on my friend and was trying to help him win the game. A

Doing homework in the dining room

few moves later, I lost the game, and my friend, thrilled at his victory, asked to play again.

The director did not call me Shalom, but rather "Shalomke." I was not the only one who had a loving nickname, yet there was never any preferential treat-ment in the orphanage. Whoever deserved reward received it, and whoever de-served reprimand received it as well. We were often warned that if we didn't be-have, we wouldn't be allowed to leave the premises on Friday, but I don't recall

Brothers Shalom (right) and Raphael Babioff

anyone ever actually receiving this punishment. All the children strove to follow the rules and get along with one another. We were like one family, and even the natural bickering of boys never developed into long-term fighting.

One day, Rabbi Blumenthal called me to his office. Such an invitation indicated either a pending reward or a reprimand. (He never rebuked a child in front of the others, so as not to embarrass him.)

I entered the room, and Rabbi Blumenthal invited me to sit. He asked how I was doing, then pulled a piece of paper out of his drawer. "Shalomke," he said, "I want you to learn these ten lines by heart. You have thirty days to practice. It's a short speech that you'll deliver before an honored guest from overseas who is coming to visit the orphanage."

I wondered why he had chosen me out of all the others. There were older and more experienced boys than I. But I didn't want to disappoint him. I understood that the visitor was an important person and I wanted to contribute to the success of his visit. "I will try, with God's help," I promised.

Later, I showed my brother Raphael the paper and told him: "I can do it, but I'm afraid I'll forget my lines out of nervousness," I said.

"Don't worry." Raphael thumped me on the back. "I'm sure you'll do a fine job. Just start practicing."

On the designated day, an air of festivity enveloped the orphanage. The special guest arrived, and a reception was held in his honor. I waited excitedly to be called up. When the moment arrived, I stood on a bench and recited the words I had memorized. I returned to my place quickly. A glance at my brother told me I had done a fine job.

For my efforts, I received a small but significant gift from Rabbi Blumenthal. He knew that my brother and I collected stamps, and he gave me three stamps from his own collection. I was floating on a cloud of joy! My brother was delighted, too.

On Friday, we would cut our nails, shine our shoes, bathe, and dress for Shabbat. After lunch, the director would check our nails and attire. The children who came from other cities used this time to walk around town; Raphael and I would go to visit our mother.

Toward sundown, we returned to the orphanage, where we prepared to greet Shabbat. Despite the difficult financial situation, our few and simple possessions, and overriding poverty, our lives were happy.

Shabbat day was dedicated to Torah and pleasure. After the meal, we would recite Psalms and then Rabbi Tzvi Michel Heller would arrive to teach us Mishnah, interspersed with stories of the sages and captivating parables. Then we would go out to play.

Slowly, my feelings of abandonment diminished, and my heart filled with joy. I felt tremendous gratitude to the orphanage for the wonderful education it gave me.

In the weekdays, during my spare time, I enjoyed helping the secretary, Mr. Patcho, open letters and peel the stamps off the envelopes. I loved the various colorful stamps through which I grew acquainted with faraway countries. Letters to the orphanage were written in a variety of languages, but the responses were always penned in English. Each response was carefully reread before being mailed out.

One Friday, I was playing with a friend in the courtyard when we suddenly felt a shadow descend upon us. We stepped outside the gate and could not believe our eyes. The street was filled with grasshoppers that had descended from the sky and covered everything. We covered our heads with our hands and scrambled back into the building.

I gathered my courage to examine the grasshoppers up close. They had saw-like teeth on the sides of their feet that they used to detach leaves from the branches before consuming them. One of the Yemenite boys in the orphanage recalled that his family would eat kosher grasshoppers. They would pickle and preserve them in salt or vinegar, and they were considered a delicacy. We could not imagine that people enjoyed eating those disgusting creatures! We prayed that they would disappear so we could resume our usual Friday routine. Our prayers were answered a few hours later, as the cloud of grasshoppers lifted up and disappeared.

One day after school, I grabbed my briefcase and hurried home to the orphanage. When I arrived, I waited for my friends, but it was half an hour before the first boys began arriving, their faces sad and downcast.

"A terrible accident occurred in the school," they told me. "Right after you left, a number of boys burst out of the building at once. The ramp leading from the building to the yard collapsed, and one boy was killed on the spot. Several others were injured and taken to the hospital."

Rabbi Blumenthal had already heard about the tragedy, and he was extremely worried as he waited for the rest of the children to return home. Fortunately, none of the orphanage children were hurt, but the death of our schoolmate caused us much pain. We recited Psalms for the elevation of his soul. Another boy in my class lost an eye in the accident and spent two weeks in the hospital.

*After the War of Independence, Mother remarried and moved
to Afula. Our connection to her continued through letters,
money, and treats that she sent us, but we did not see her
regularly anymore. During vacation, we would go to our
grandfather instead.*

*The Blumenthals' daughter, Mrs. Solomon, helped run the
orphanage. Her grace and nobility — inherited from her
father — lent her an aura of peace and serenity. She treated
each child with motherly sensitivity, without differentiating
any child from the others. Her stories left a deep impression
and remain with me forever.*

*In the freezing winter of 1950, a heavy snowfall descended
upon Jerusalem. For a week straight, the white flakes fell, and
over three feet of snow accumulated. The orphanage's heating
system broke down in the extreme cold, and we went about
wrapped in layers of clothing. For a full week we did not attend
school or go outdoors, since Rabbi Blumenthal was concerned
that we would get sick.*

*Eventually, the heating system was fixed and the house filled
with warmth again. At the end of the long and stormy week, we
finally went out to play in the snow and see the long icicles up
close. The streets were eerily silent, except for a delivery truck
that supplied the local groceries with fresh bread and milk, its
tires chained to prevent slipping.*

*The more adventurous children among us found a plank
of wood, sat on it, and went flying down the street on this
improvised "sled."*

*Our shoes and socks became soaked as we played. We had only
one change of socks, and we should have made sure they didn't
get wet, but we didn't think of that. At night, before going to
sleep, we put our socks under the sheets and slept on them. In
the morning, they were once again warm and dry...*

*That week I caught a virus. Rabbi Blumenthal kept close watch
on me, and after two days with no improvement, he called the*

doctor, who prescribed medication. Rabbi Blumenthal became my personal nurse — giving me medication and bringing me water to swallow the pill.

I drank almost half the water, but the pill would not go down. I gurgled a bit and pretending to swallow it, but Rabbi Blumenthal saw right through me. He told me to open my mouth and, to my embarrassment, the pill was still sitting on my tongue. Seeing how hard it was for me to swallow, he had me dissolve the pill in warm water and swallow it that way.

When I turned twelve, my grandfather decided to take me out of the orphanage. I was standing at the crossroads, and the future was uncertain. I was going to leave the home where I had spent some of the best years of my life.

I was saddened to no longer be spending my days in the orphanage. Rabbi Blumenthal's noble face, radiating warmth and fatherly love, would no longer be part of my daily life.

To this day, I cherish those wonderful years and the glowing image of Rabbi Blumenthal, who showered us with warmth, sensitivity, love, and patience.[31]

---

31   Shalom Babioff eventually grew into a Torah scholar who authored several books, in addition to publishing the writings of his grandfather, Rabbi Chizkiya Katanoff, on Chumash, in a two-volume work entitled *Midrash Chizkiya*.

CHAPTER 42

Battleground!

O
n November 29, 1947, after years of political unrest under
the British Mandate, the United Nations General Assembly
adopted a resolution recommending that the Mandate be replaced by an independent Arab state, an independent Jewish
state, and the city of Jerusalem under international rule. The
Arab nations strongly opposed this plan, and within days mobs began
attacking Jewish communities throughout the country. Jerusalem was
a primary target, with the Arab residents in the eastern part of the city
determined not to relinquish control of their homes.

The orphanage, located as it was in the Bukharian Quarter, was within
easy reach of snipers in Sheikh Jarrah, an East Jerusalem neighborhood
that led to Mount Scopus. The residents of the Bukharian Quarter and
the surrounding areas found their lives endangered long before the War
of Independence officially broke out in May 1948. Even going to collect
wild herbs from the fields near their homes was fraught with danger, as
the neighbors learned when a woman living across the street from the
orphanage was hit by a sniper's bullet on one of these forages.

As hostilities escalated, the Jews of Jerusalem found themselves besieged, with access to the city from the west blocked by the Arabs. As supplies dwindled day by day, water and basic foodstuffs were rationed. Electricity, powered by a British company, was provided minimally; residents received a half hour of electricity in the morning and an hour in the evening. Eventually, the British stopped providing electricity altogether, claiming there wasn't enough gasoline.

The Jewish Quarter of the Old City lay under siege for many months, its residents suffering from the heavy shelling and lack of basic supplies. They were eventually forced to evacuate, leaving heaps of rubble and devastation where there had once been glorious synagogues and a bustling, active community.

WAR BREAKS OUT

With the British departure on May 14, 1948, war broke out in earnest. The Jewish forces, having trained clandestinely for months, captured several strategic locations in Jerusalem, but Jordanian troops controlled the entire northern part of the city. The Jewish settlements in these areas were subjected to constant shelling before eventually being evacuated.

In Jerusalem proper, meanwhile, an estimated ten thousand shells fell on residential areas. Many lives were lost and dozens of civilians were wounded, the vast majority killed or injured while fetching water or bread for their families.

Shalom Babioff, whose story is recounted in the previous chapters, relates his experiences:

> *The War of Independence erupted one clear spring day. We sat in the designated shelter, the orphanage storage room, the director never leaving our side. He recited Psalms with us, spoke a little, and worried a lot as the sounds of gunshots and explosions reverberated from outside.*
>
> *During one of these rounds of shelling, the bitter news reached us that my teacher, Rabbi Yitzhak Zolpin, had been killed with*

his son-in-law as they stood in line for food outside the grocery store near his home. Before we could recover from this terrible tragedy, the father of one of my friends from school was killed by a sniper's bullet as he was walking toward a store that sold eggs, milk, and cheese — leaving behind his wife and five young children.

Horrific events passed before our eyes as though on film. A man was killed here, another was wounded there... The Jordanian snipers rarely missed their targets. In the city's northern neighborhoods, heavy sackcloth was draped over street entrances in an attempt to conceal passersby from the snipers' view. These makeshift curtains enabled us to occasionally run across the street.

During a brief ceasefire, the army decided to build a temporary stone barricade near the Turkish bathhouse on Yechezkel Street. The bathhouse was a weekly gathering place for people from different neighborhoods, who came to bathe and immerse in the mikvah. [Many Jerusalem homes at the time lacked indoor plumbing, making it difficult to bathe comfortably at home.]

The barricades built near the bathhouse were meant to stop the Arab legions from storming the city. They also protected us from the burning shells that flew in all directions, wounding anyone in their path.

Since we didn't have kerosene for heat or cooking, we used firewood instead. Cutting down trees for firewood, however, was no easy task, and even more difficult with bullets raining down. The Almighty took pity on us and a stray shell landed on a tall eucalyptus tree in our neighborhood. The huge tree fell to the ground, and we were able to chop off its branches for cooking fires.

We attempted to go about life as usual, but it was impossible to ignore the smell of fire and smoke that filled the air and the blood spilled in our midst. We children sat in the shelter, occasionally reciting Psalms. Although food staples were in short supply throughout the city, Rabbi Blumenthal succeeded in obtaining provisions for us. We subsisted on margarine, jelly, bread, eggs, and cheese, and occasionally falafel balls. In order to receive our vitamins, we swallowed a teaspoon of cod liver oil each morning. Twice a week, we received a small portion of meat.

Rabbi Blumenthal was everything to us: father, educator, psychologist. He would encourage and explain, stroke the heads of the frightened children, and sing songs with us, his gaze traveling from one child to the next. A pat on the head was enough to imbue us with a feeling of security and the knowledge that we were in good hands and had nothing to fear.

Water was rationed, so we had a supervisor in charge of water. Whenever necessary, he would fill a big barrel that stood in the corner of the bedroom. Each child received a cup of water in the evening, and we would drink it slowly, savoring the moisture on our lips. Some days we received only a quarter-cup of water and were left to dream about quenching our thirst with plentiful liquid.

We accepted the rationing of water as par for the course. Never did a child attempt to drink without permission, even when the others were asleep. If a child was overcome by thirst, he would request another cup from the supervisor, who would decide whether it could be granted. Usually they weren't strict with the younger children, but I was already eight years old and considered a big boy when it came to water.

More than once, the orphanage was targeted by snipers. During one round of shelling we heard a tremendous crash very close by. The entire building shook. We thought the ceiling would fall in on our heads. One of the younger children burst out crying, "Mother! Mother!"

After the shelling abated, silence reigned. The smell of smoke filled our nostrils. It seemed that this time the shell had landed directly on the orphanage.

One of the supervisors stepped outside to assess the damage. To his shock, he discovered that an anti-tank missile had pierced the kitchen wall into the synagogue and had stopped right in front of the Holy Ark. Miraculously, the Torah scrolls were unharmed. The damage to the building was minimal as well. The missile was a foot and a half long and very heavy. It could have caused the entire building to collapse, but Heaven had mercy on us.

At that point, Rabbi Blumenthal told me, my brother, and a few other boys to return home for several days. He did not explain why and did not tell us when to return — and we didn't ask questions. We understood that he only wanted our good. He armed us with cans of meat, peas, and carrots to take home and wished us well.

Hand in hand, my brother and I left the orphanage and headed home. On the way we stopped near the bathhouse to watch the soldiers building the barricade. Suddenly, heavy shelling began. We were terrified. Our dawdling could cost us our lives! We could no longer return to the orphanage. The gate was locked, and no one would hear us calling. We sprinted toward home. On the way we found shelter in the corridor of our school, where we rested for several moments. The shelling continued. Suddenly, a burning piece of shrapnel landed at our feet, sharp pieces flying in all directions. I took a piece of it with me as a memento. After several moments, which seemed like an eternity, silence reigned and we were able to continue home. Fortunately, we arrived home safe and sound, panting and frightened. We remained at home until things calmed down.

A TEMPORARY HOME

During the heaviest shelling, Aminoff House, which lacked a proper shelter, became too dangerous for habitation. The Blumenthals and the children remaining in the orphanage moved into the bomb shelter of Yeshivat Tiferet Tzvi.

Since the head counselor had gone home, Rabbi Blumenthal took over all his duties. The bomb shelter was unfinished, its floors untiled and its walls unplastered, yet it was safer than the orphanage building. Whenever there was a lull in the shooting, Avraham Yochanan would send someone to a nearby barn to bring back fresh milk for the children.

Nechama and Yocheved, both of whom lived nearby, cooked the daily meals for the children. Carrying the heavy pots of food to the shelter, however, was a real challenge. The street that ran between the buildings was exposed to gunfire. The Shlapovarsky and Solomon girls would run across the street clutching the heavy pots, their hearts pounding as they brought food for the children.

One day, Chaim Solomon realized that the orphanage Torah scrolls were still in the building, exposed to danger. In the haste to relocate, they had been left behind. Nothing else in the orphanage building compared to the priceless Torah scrolls. That night, Chaim and Rabbi Blumenthal set out under cover of darkness to remove the scrolls from the orphanage synagogue.

The night was pitch black. The sound of gunshots occasionally shattered the stillness. The two men advanced stealthily under the protection of darkness, hoping not to be sighted by snipers waiting in ambush. Several tension-filled moments passed until the key turned in the lock and they entered the synagogue, removed the Torah scrolls from the ark, and exited the building again, locking the gate behind them.

A sense of exile accompanied Avraham Yochanan and his son-in-law as they trudged back up Yechezkel Street, their treasures in hand. Who knew when the scrolls would return home?

PEACE AT LAST

After many weeks, peace descended on the battle-worn city. A ceasefire was announced on June 11, with Jewish forces holding the western part of Jerusalem and Jordanian forces holding the eastern part, including the Old City. Throwing off the fears of war, a parade of children once more made its way through the streets, headed for the orphanage building that had lain abandoned for weeks. Avraham

Yochanan and Chaim held the orphanage's Torah scrolls in one arm and kissed the mezuzah with the other, thanking God for allowing them to return whole in body and soul, and carrying in their hearts a prayer for peace and serenity.

The Aminoff building had suffered much damage during the weeks of shelling. The Holy Ark had been destroyed, having been hit by a shell. "What a miracle that we removed the Torah scrolls!" Chaim whispered in awe.

A shell that hadn't detonated rested on the floor near the synagogue door, casting its threatening glow over the room and preventing entry. The shell was removed by the army several days later.

The main building, too, had suffered several direct hits. The water cisterns on the roof had been pierced by shrapnel and water had leaked into the rooms. All the children's linens were soaked. There were puddles under the beds and the broken blinds were silent witnesses to the drama that had occurred within.

The Passover dishes stored in the attic were shattered to bits, as were the little boxes filled with earth from the Mount of Olives. Supporters of the orphanage from abroad would often request that this earth be placed in their graves when their time came.

Avraham Yochanan's first reaction to the damage was "Oy!" But immediately thereafter he stood up straight and declared, "Thank God we have returned safe and sound. Blessed is [God] and blessed is His name."

In the following days, repairs on the building began in earnest. A carpenter repaired the Holy Ark, and construction workers sealed the holes in the walls. The blinds were fixed, the walls repainted, the linens laundered.

The boys who had been sent home from the orphanage began to return. Everyone felt the loss suffered by many neighborhood families. A few children who had previously lived in the orphanage had been killed during the shelling as well. The memory of these innocent children and the pain of their untimely deaths remained with Rabbi Blumenthal constantly.

Each Shabbat, the orphanage children would visit the bereaved families and recite Psalms for the elevation of the victims' souls.

MORE WAR ORPHANS

New orphans arrived at Zion Orphanage during this time. Matityahu Niazoff relates:

> *On June 8, 1948, the terrible tragedy hit us. My father was killed on David Street, near Mr. Abuloff's store. In an instant, Mother became a widow, left to care for four children. For days we sat around her. I, the eldest, was seven, my brother Moshe was five, then came three-year-old Shmuel, and Sara, the baby.*
>
> *Mother was filled with worries and fears for the future. Left with no other choice, she placed me and my brothers in Zion Orphanage.*
>
> *Rabbi Blumenthal's serene and pleasant ways and his noble bearing cast an aura of tranquility upon us. He was a true fatherly presence. We became accustomed to the orphanage and became part of the expanded Blumenthal family.*

Matityahu (seven and a half) and Shmuel, whose father, a teacher in the Bukharian School, was killed during the War of Independence. After their father's death, the brothers came to the orphanage.

"Two memories have remained with me since I left the orphanage," shares Yaakov Muld, who lived in the orphanage for several years after the war. "One is of my name and picture, which hung over my bed, just like the names and pictures of each of the boys. This gave us a feeling of belonging and security. The other is Rabbi Blumenthal's

A child standing near his bed in the dormitory

strong handshake, which continues to warm my hands and my bones to this day."

LOSS OF THE WESTERN WALL

The War of Independence ended with a ceasefire agreement, leaving in its wake many widows and orphans, wounded citizens, and countless destroyed homes. A collective longing for the Western Wall, which remained under Jordanian control, filled the hearts of Jerusalem's Jews.

Avraham Yochanan would often express his longing for the Western Wall. He had grown up in the shadow of its presence and keenly felt its loss. Unfortunately, he would never see it again.

CHAPTER 43

The Fight for Food

"Soon a new oil delivery will be here," neighborhood women told each other as they washed their bottles in preparation for the arrival of the precious golden liquid.

Rationing had become an inseparable part of life in the fledgling country. Being alert to sudden deliveries, standing in long lines that snaked down the street, and hoarding ration slips were routine events.

Food rationing had begun during World War II, when travel was dangerous and few foodstuffs arrived from abroad. With all international resources directed toward the war effort, almost nothing was available in the open market. Under the supervision of the British Mandate, committees were formed to distribute basic food supplies. All products — domestic and imported — were strictly rationed.

Every resident in Jerusalem was acquainted with the distribution office on Mamilla Street. Each family had one member appointed to spend long hours waiting in line for the coupons allotted to each person. In exchange for these coupons, one could receive sugar, rice, oil,

234 HOME OF MIRACLES

beans, and other basic staples. Amidst the housewives, harried clerks, and others who waited impatiently in line, one could often spot a new father who had come straight from the hospital to the distribution office, holding the requisite forms that would give him a coupon for the purchase of ten cloth diapers, a blanket, and an undershirt for his newborn.

The news would buzz through the air. "White rice has arrived." "They say that in Tel Aviv one can get flowered cotton material." "At Tanchum's shop, you can buy laundry detergent." "Fish will be delivered this morning." "There's margarine in the stores."

These "luxuries" could only be purchased with the right coupon, in addition to money. Often, only those who reached the distribution office early enough and could convince the clerks that the item in question was a necessity in their home received the coveted item.

Time was of the essence in successful shopping. Sometimes, after hours of waiting for a coupon, people would rush to the store to purchase an item and, after waiting in line for hours yet again, discover it was sold out.

PROCURING PRODUCE AND MEAT

Imported vegetables spent days in moisture while in transport. They exuded an awful smell upon arrival and were all but unfit for consumption. Purchasing edible produce was nearly impossible. To buy material for clothing, people had to wait in line for hours — and then implore, convince, and demand from the clerk the coveted slip of paper that permitted purchase at a store.

At the orphanage, as in every household, food was received in exchange for coupons based on the number of children. Since institutions received their rations all at one time, the kitchen could operate more efficiently than a private home. Yocheved, responsible for acquiring the ration slips, made the trip to the distribution office on a regular basis.

Her exhausting job entailed putting pressure on the authorities, when necessary, to acquire everything from meat to fabric for bed linens. Even then, her efforts were not always met with success. No matter how much she pleaded, the clerk might announce with finality: "There is nothing to talk about. You will not receive eggs this week."

By word of mouth, Yocheved discovered that meat was available weekly for hospitals and other institutions. The orphanage children needed this meat, she decided, and after repeated entreaties to the proper authorities, she hurried to the butcher with ration slips in hand. There she waited in line

The orphanage dining room, with smaller tables than in previous years

for hours to purchase the small amount of meat the children were allowed for Shabbat.

AUSTERITY

While the variety of food available improved somewhat after the war, the channels of import were still disordered and costly. Local produce was meager and did not cover even half the demand. In addition, the young country doubled in population in its first few years, with seven hundred thousand new immigrants arriving from Arab countries and settling in temporary immigrant camps. Israel's fledging economy could not meet the demand for food and clothing necessary to absorb these immigrants.

In response to this crisis, the government established an official period of austerity in which food, and later furniture and shoes, was limited to strict quotas. By bringing down the cost of living to the minimum — while closely supervising prices — the government hoped to stabilize the economy and keep its citizens fed and clothed without prices soaring beyond normal means.

As Minister of Finance, Dr. Dov Joseph set rations for every citizen in the country and monitored the distribution of ration slips. Each individual was allowed a monthly ration of eight eggs, two hundred grams of white cheese, one hundred grams of farmer cheese, and half a kilogram of fish, with one bar of chocolate allotted to children. It was determined that sixteen hundred calories per day were sufficient for an adult, with more calories allocated for children, the elderly, and pregnant women. Each citizen was registered in a specific grocery, and food could not be purchased in any other store.

As in the days of the British Mandate, people were compelled to wait in distribution offices three or four times a week and employ all sorts of persuasive tactics to provide for their families.

"Did you bring your bag?" a grocer would ask each housewife who stood before him with the coveted ration slip for sugar in hand. She would hurry to present him with a clean cloth bag, which was then filled with sugar and carefully weighed. Oil was poured into a bottle brought from home. Paper bags were unheard of, let alone plastic bags or plastic bottles.

THE GIRLS OF THE GESTETNER HOME

The ration slips caused many difficulties for new immigrants and longtime residents alike. One group of twenty-one girls arrived in the country in the wake of World War II and was placed on various kibbutzim. Wanting to live in a religious environment, the girls established an apartment in Jerusalem known as the Gestetner Home.

Yet the girls faced a problem: Since the distribution office listed them as members of the kibbutzim, they could not obtain food. Learning that Yocheved was experienced in dealing with the distribution office, they turned to her for help.

Yocheved asked them to provide documents proving that they had lived on these kibbutzim. All the girls procured these documents, except for one whose kibbutz head categorically refused to acknowledge her request.

One afternoon, Yocheved strode into the distribution office with the documents in hand. She walked straight to the head clerk's office, presented him with the documents, and explained that every Jew had a right to live and survive in the Holy Land.

The clerk examined the documents and inquired about the missing one.

"You can confirm her registration by phone," Yocheved assured him.

The clerk called the kibbutz and received confirmation that the young lady in question had indeed resided there for a short while. He gave Yocheved the documents she needed, and she returned to the regular line to request ration slips for the girls.

The clerk frowned at the sight of her long list. "You again?" he asked. "Again you need ration slips?"

"Are you in charge of making decisions here?" Yocheved responded coolly. "You have written confirmation from the head clerk!"

Without another word, the clerk prepared the ration slips, and the girls had what they needed to survive.

BLACK MARKET

A thriving black market developed, with many grocers receiving products through unofficial channels. Some of the products came from America, others from local suppliers and even factory owners who had permits for manufacture and decided to sell their raw materials for a hefty profit.

The news would spread like wildfire: For a price, one could purchase eggs! A person who needed eggs for an ill family member or for a special occasion and could afford the cost would hurry to make his purchase, checking over his shoulder to ensure there were no supervisors in the area.

Those caught doing business on the black market were severely punished. Government inspectors would stop civilians on the street and conduct bodily searches for illegal goods. They often made inspections on buses returning from farming villages, even searching through houses when they had reason to suspect illegal purchases. With severe expressions on their faces, they would methodically check the contents of the icebox, and woe to the person who was found to have illegal food products in his possession.

Huge billboards featured a hand holding a snake with the caption, "Destroy the black market! If not, it will destroy you!" Yet to no avail.

People found other unconventional methods of increasing their food supply, including raising chickens for food. The sounds of roosters crowing from various porches filled the air each morning. Private vegetable gardens became common as well, with produce going straight from garden to table.

In 1951, Yocheved retired from her work in the orphanage to care for her growing family. Rabbi Betzalel Landau took over representing the orphanage at various government offices, which remained a full-time job even after the worst of the period of austerity came to an end in 1954.

CHAPTER 44

Communal Activities

The Holy Land was witness to numerous tumultuous events during the first half of the twentieth century as the tiny country survived two world wars, gained independence, and increased tenfold in population. The Old Yishuv experienced many growing pains during these years, and Avraham Yochanan emerged as a leader of the flock, giving the community the tools to withstand the winds of change. As a prominent community activist who was well-known among the Old Yishuv Jews, his was a voice of reason and calm, often addressing and creating awareness of issues of public import. When necessary, he would speak publically and frequently wrote essays that were published in monthly periodicals.

Under the Ottoman government, the Jewish inhabitants in the country were represented solely by the community's religious leaders. Rabbi Yosef Chaim Sonnenfeld, spiritual leader of the Old Yishuv, headed the delegation of officials who greeted Kaiser Wilhelm II, Emperor of Germany, upon his visit to Jerusalem in 1899, as he did many other political leaders.

After World War I, however, things changed. The British Mandate channeled most of its diplomatic relations to the various Zionist factions rather than to the Old Yishuv Jews. The 1917 Balfour Declaration, a letter from Foreign Secretary Arthur James Balfour detailing the British intent to establish Palestine as a national home for the Jewish people, was presented to Baron Walter Rothschild and Dr. Chaim Weitzman, Zionist leaders who were viewed as representatives of the Jewish population in the country.

These leaders made efforts to secularize the Jews of the Old Yishuv, attempting to revamp its educational system. In response, the leaders of the Old Yishuv fought their hardest to maintain their way of life.

Watching these events unfold, the leaders of the Old Yishuv, Rabbi Yosef Chaim Sonnenfeld and Rabbi Yitzhak Yerucham Diskin, called an emergency meeting of activists, where it was decided to form a system of religious legal courts, called "the Edah." This proved to be an uphill battle, and after prolonged deliberations, the British government agreed to recognize the community as an independent entity from the Zionist Movement.

Avraham Yochanan took a lead role in organizing the Old Yishuv into a legal entity. He met regularly with Rabbi Sonnenfeld to discuss ideas and plans for strengthening and protecting the community and its traditions. After Rabbi

Rabbi Blumenthal speaking at the ceremony celebrating the laying of a cornerstone of the Edah's office building

Yosef Chaim Sonnenfeld's passing on May 17, 1922, Rabbi Yosef Tzvi Dushinsky was appointed as his successor as president of the Edah. He led the Edah during the turbulent days of World War II, the War of Independence, and the establishment of the State.

With the dissolution of the British Mandate and the establishment of the State, the Edah fought to strengthen public Shabbat observance and kashrut supervision. Avraham Yochanan was involved in all of these activities. Alongside Avraham Roth, another prominent activist, he worked to establish an organized system of kashrut supervisors in accordance with the highest religious standards.[32]

Rabbi Dushinsky held Avraham Yochanan in high esteem, appointing him chairman of the organization. In this position, Avraham Yochanan participated in all its important meetings and was partner to the important decisions made, though always in his quiet and unassuming way. He worked diligently to moderate the more combative elements of the group, preferring instead his signature method of warmth and calm.

At Rabbi Dushinsky's funeral on October 17, 1948, Avraham Yochanan was the one to announce in the name of the leadership of the Edah that Rabbi Zelig Reuven Bengis, another prominent Jerusalem rabbi, would be Rabbi Dushinsky's successor. With Rabbi Bengis's passing in 1953, it was once again Avraham Yochanan who announced that the leadership would be passed to Rabbi Yoel Teitelbaum, the Satmar Rebbe.

---

32 To this day, the Edah's kashrut division, which supervises the production of the entire spectrum of food items throughout Israel, is considered among the highest standards available.

CHAPTER 45

The Home That Never Closed

One cool fall morning toward the end of 1946, a little boy named Aharon gazed curiously at the large building in front of him. It bore little similarity to the small home where he lived with his father and his younger brother. The sounds of children's voices raised in happy conversation, the pictures on the walls, and the impeccable order all stood in stark contrast to the silent and gloomy atmosphere in his home since his mother's death.

A father with his two sons at the entrance to the orphanage

"What's your name?" asked Avraham Yochanan, stroking the eight-year-old's cheek. The rabbi's face radiated goodwill and kindness.

242

Father left, and Aharon stayed, cautiously taking in his new surroundings. "Come," Rabbi Blumenthal gently prodded him. "I'll show
you your bedroom, the dining room, and the synagogue."

Within a few months, the initial shock wore off, and Aharon acclimated completely to his new surroundings. He recalls:

> *The orphanage remained active 365 days a year. Although many
> of the children spent the holidays with relatives, others had no
> place to go and were Rabbi Blumenthal's personal guests. These
> boys didn't feel the least bit deprived; on the contrary, it was a
> special experience to spend the holidays with the Blumenthals.
> Proximity fostered closeness to Rabbi Blumenthal, which was
> reward enough in itself!*
>
> *Rabbi Blumenthal's devotion was like that of a real father to
> his sons. I recall one time that a friend fell off a bench and hurt
> himself. After a few moments, he got up and resumed playing,
> and we assumed he was fine. Later that night, however, we
> heard him crying in bed, and we hurried to inform Rabbi
> Blumenthal. Although it was very late, he quickly helped the
> boy get dressed and took him to the emergency room.*
>
> *There were regular contests that challenged us to study
> and excel. Occasionally, Rabbi Blumenthal would hold an
> exciting and suspenseful Bible quiz. His favorite questions
> were: "Where do we find so-and-so in the Torah? When do we
> say such-and-such in our prayers? Where in the Bible is this
> mentioned?" We were challenged to search for answers and be
> the first to find them.*
>
> *Each Friday we were tested on what we had learned the
> previous week. Our score would be marked down, and whoever
> received a good grade would bring it to Rabbi Blumenthal and
> receive money to buy treats for Shabbat.*
>
> *Several months before each boy's bar mitzvah, Rabbi Blumenthal
> would ensure that he began learning the cantillation for the
> Torah reading. Sephardic children studied their pronunciation,
> and Ashkenazic children theirs. Thus, each of us came to our*

bar mitzvah knowing how to read the Torah according to our own family traditions.

Rabbi Blumenthal was a beloved, loving father, but he never asked the children to attend to his personal needs. He would not even ask a child to bring him a cup of water. Mrs. Blumenthal cared for us like a mother, worrying for our safety and urging us to eat. She supervised the kitchen, making sure the food was tasty and nutritious, and oversaw our clothing, bedrooms, and laundry.

I have a deep sense of gratitude to this wonderful couple who invested themselves completely in giving boys like me a warm home and an excellent education, so much so that I named my daughter "Chana" after Mrs. Blumenthal.

EVERYTHING TO US

Four years after Aharon's arrival at the orphanage, he was joined by his younger brother Raphael, who relates:

I transferred to Zion Orphanage from a similar institution. It too aimed at caring for orphans physically and spiritually, but that was where the similarities ended.

I felt the difference immediately upon my arrival. Here, all members of the staff and administration tried their hardest to give each child the best possible substitute for the home he was lacking. They showered us with love and affection and a sense of a warmth and homeyness — just what we needed.

The orphanage was everything to us. It was our home, our social network, our play area. It was the arena of memories that would accompany us for the rest of our lives. Here we grew and studied, here our personalities and identities were molded. Rabbi Blumenthal's warm and guiding hand was felt in everything related to the orphanage. He was the head of the family, a supportive and loving father who was personally acquainted with every single child, his praise and encouragement prodding us ever forward.

Each Friday we would be tested by Rabbi Tzvi Michel Heller. After the test, Rabbi Heller would give each child a note with his grade. We would take the note to Rabbi Blumenthal, who would read it carefully, encourage us, and take interest in our studies.

When a child received an excellent grade, Rabbi Blumenthal praised him elaborately, often bending down to kiss the child on his forehead. His enthusiastic praise imbued us with the desire to excel in our studies.

Once, one of the boys received the highest grade possible. Rabbi Blumenthal was elated! He called his son Yisrael Chaim and excitedly showed him the note. The boy-turned-celebrity looked on, his heart bursting with joy when he saw how his achievements had affected the director.

Rabbi Blumenthal educated and guided us just by being who he was. He was a living example of love for others, a paradigm of honesty and love of Torah. His visage accompanied us constantly, the standard that we strove to emulate.

One memory is of walking up Yechezkel Street in the direction of Yeshivat Porat Yosef one morning. Suddenly, I saw Rabbi Ezra Attiya, the head of the yeshiva, across the street. Rabbi Attiya called me over and said he was on his way to meet with Rabbi Blumenthal. He asked me to inform Rabbi Blumenthal that he would arrive momentarily.

Hearing that Rabbi Attiya was on his way, Rabbi Blumenthal donned his hat and jacket and went out to greet the saintly rabbi. The two returned to the orphanage together. At the gate, they

Rabbi Ezra Attiya, head of Yeshivat Porat Yosef

stopped, each wanting to honor the other by having him step through the gate first. Rabbi Attiya claimed that the honor of the host came first, while Rabbi Blumenthal claimed that the honor of Rabbi Attiya's Torah study took precedence. At Rabbi Blumenthal's insistence, Rabbi Attiya capitulated and entered first.

MILESTONES

Bar mitzvahs were celebrated at the orphanage with much fanfare. Every few months, a joint celebration was held for the boys who had turned thirteen, the head table graced by the presence of renowned rabbis who were invited to join the festivities. Rabbi Aharon Kotler, founder of Beth Medrash Gevoha of Lakewood, New Jersey, was present at one such celebration that took place during one of his visits to Jerusalem. Rabbi Blumenthal knew this was an important opportunity for the children to see this great Jewish leader up close.

As Raphael was a talented youngster, Avraham Yochanan prepared an especially lengthy speech for him to deliver at his bar mitzvah. On the big day, Raphael spoke with clarity and confidence. His father, relatives, and notables of the community were delighted, blessing him that he grow in Torah study and good deeds. Indeed, the boy excelled in his studies, remaining at Yeshivat Porat Yosef until his marriage.

Boys celebrating their bar mitzvahs

"Rabbi Blumenthal's joy upon walking me to the chuppah was like that of a father marrying off his son," Raphael recalls. "His exuberant dance with my bride's grandfather brought me much joy."[33]

AN AFTERNOON OF JOY

Other bar mitzvah celebrations were equally memorable. A visitor who frequented the orphanage writes:

Rabbi Aharon Kotler at a bar mitzvah celebration in the orphanage. To his right are Rabbi Tzvi Meltzer (son of Rabbi Isser Zalman Meltzer) and Rabbi Blumenthal

For the past twenty years, I have been participating in celebrations at the Zion Orphanage. From time to time, I receive a unique invitation with a photograph of boys from the orphanage, asking me to attend their bar mitzvah celebration, which would take place on such-and-such afternoon.

Something always urges me to come and see how the boys celebrate their big day despite their difficult lives. I arrive early to satisfy my curiosity, to see the preparations for the big event up close. The glimpses I get are enough to demonstrate the depth and breadth of the joy that fills the tender hearts of these boys and their guests...

The celebrants, dressed in new suits of superior quality despite the wartime shortage, are easy to pick out of the crowd. There is a glow on their faces, and their eyes shine with joy. Their lips move as they rehearse their speeches. Other children, dressed in matching shirts and pants, assist in arranging the tables and chairs in the large courtyard.

As the guests begin to arrive, the children take their seats with remarkable discipline and sing a welcome song. The crowd

---

33   After his marriage, Raphael continued his Torah studies for several years, later serving as a teacher and lecturer in Yeshivat Porat Yosef. His older brother, Aharon, became an educator as well.

swells and fills the entire courtyard. Rabbis, notables, and business leaders are present. The head table is beautifully set and filled with delicious food.

The bar mitzvah boys sit at the head table together with the city's chief rabbis. Nearby are Rabbi Isser Zalman Meltzer and Rabbi Yechiel Michel Tukachinsky, heads of the Etz Chaim Yeshiva; Rabbi Yosef Gershon Horowitz, head of the Meah Shearim

Another bar mitzvah celebration. From right: Rabbi Moshe Blau, Rabbi Yitzhak Meir Levin, Rabbi Zalman Sorotzkin, Rabbi Aharon Kotler, and Avraham Yochanan

A bar mitzvah in the courtyard of Aminoff House, attended by Chief Rabbi Yitzhak Isaac Herzog, Rabbi Isser Zalman Meltzer, Rabbi Yitzhak Nissim, Rabbi Ben Zion Uziel, Rabbi Yechiel Michel Tukatchinsky, and Rabbi Yechezkel Sarna

Yeshiva; Rabbi Yechezkel Sarna, head of Hebron Yeshiva; Rabbi Avraham Yitzhak Kook, head of the Merkaz Harav Yeshiva; Rabbi Chizkiya Shabtai, head of the Sephardic community; Rabbi Aryeh Chaimoff, rabbi of the Bukharian community; and many others.

Rabbi Avraham Yochanan Blumenthal accepts congratulatory wishes, his face wreathed with fatherly joy. One after the next, the boys confidently deliver their speeches in Jewish law and lore. They express their gratitude to the guests who have come to participate and to the orphanage staff for its unstinting dedication.

The crowd sits enthralled by their words. Joy and pain intermingle, and joy prevails. The other children delight in the celebration like true brothers. The unity between the boys is remarkable, an obvious result of the instruction they receive within the walls of the orphanage.

Presents are distributed, accompanied by written and oral congratulations, and telegrams sent by friends and relatives from afar are read aloud. First-time guests who have come from other towns and cities tour the premises and express their approval.

The joyous hours pass all too soon. As the sun begins its descent, all present rise to recite the afternoon prayers, with a sense of disappointment that the wonderful day cannot last longer.

CHAPTER 46

Inner Nobility

The summer of 1952 was a difficult one for the Blumenthal family. Avraham Yochanan's only son, Yisrael Chaim, lay critically ill following a sudden heart attack. He battled for his life for three weeks as heartfelt prayers were recited on his behalf, but the decree had been cast. On August 11, at the age of forty-nine, Yisrael Chaim passed away.

Yisrael Chaim Blumenthal

A humble and unassuming man, Yisrael Chaim left behind a series of important educational booklets on the Tabernacle, the priestly garments, and the laws of the offerings. The booklets were short but detailed, accompanied by precisely drawn diagrams, and Yisrael Chaim had often labored over them deep into the night. They became so well known that when his sister, Yocheved, showed one of them to Rabbi Eliyahu Essas, a prominent Russian refusenik who was instrumental in bringing Jews to Torah observance under the Soviet oppression, Rabbi Essas recognized it immediately.

Yisrael Chaim also authored a three-volume work on Jewish history, *Korei Hadorot*, as well as a commentary on the book of Ruth. His untimely demise left his family grief-stricken and bereft. His children, the youngest of whom was nine years old, would now experience firsthand the travails of orphanhood that they had witnessed in their grandparents' home.

While Avraham Yochanan's pain was deeply felt, he kept a tight rein on outward displays of emotion and continued his holy work with his typical staunch acceptance of Divine judgment. When he came upon his wife shedding tears after the prescribed thirty days of mourning had passed, he gently reprimanded her, "One must accept God's decree with love."

Avraham Yochanan also assumed responsibility for the education of his orphaned grandchildren. The next generation of Blumenthal children became very close to their venerated grandfather, who was their model for exemplary behavior in every facet of life.

Yisrael Chaim's son Asher, who was sixteen years old and studying in Hebron Yeshiva, developed an especially close connection to his grandfather. He recalls:

> As the days passed, I became aware that I was in the presence of a man who had generosity of spirit and boundless patience. Grandfather was a living example of the proper way to pray and speak, and of consistent and uncompromising adherence to the truth.
>
> Grandfather encouraged me to learn Mishnah by heart, to repeat verses from the book of Proverbs, and to become proficient in the Torah readings. Once, when a student spoke out of turn, I overheard a teacher ask Grandfather why he did not rebuke the young man. "The Creator is even more patient with us," he replied.
>
> Sometimes, when I erred, he would reprimand me with much wisdom, as it says, "Rebuke a wise person and he will love

*you" (Proverbs 9:8). In his unique way, he made me out to be
that wise man, as though I was perfectly fine but for the evil
inclination that had entrapped me. "Send your evil inclination
to me," Grandfather would tell me with a smile.*

*When he wanted to emphasize the importance of meticulous
Torah observance, he would do so through a parable about a
Torah scroll. Even if the entire scroll is written in accordance
with the details of Jewish law, if even one letter is missing, he
explained, the entire scroll is disqualified.*

*Once, he saw me reciting afternoon prayers after sunset. I tried
to defend myself by saying that many people did this. "If we
seek out all the leniencies," he responded, "we ultimately will
not perform the commandments at all."*

*Once, when we were sitting in the sukkah, a bee flew in and
landed on a bit of honey on the table. Grandfather used the
incident to arouse our hearts to the wonders of creation: "Who
let this little bee know that there was a drizzle of honey here?"
he asked in awe.*

*Grandfather aroused our intellectual curiosity with his
repertoire of challenges from the Bible and Midrash. He
posed riddles and initiated contests that propelled us to
look into the primary sources and deepen our knowledge and
awareness of Judaism.*

THE BATTLE FOR SHABBOS

Yet Avraham Yochanan's sphere of influence extended far beyond
his own family. As the country slowly became more prosperous in the
1950s and cars became more commonplace, the formerly quiet streets
of Jerusalem witnessed a veritable traffic explosion, disturbing the
religious residents' sensibilities. Yearning for the peace and tranquility
of yesteryear, religious Jews entreated city officials not to trample upon
the holy day in the Holy City — but to no avail. Demonstrations echoed
through the streets each week.

In 1966, the battle over Shivtei Yisrael Street, a busy thoroughfare that bordered the Meah Shearim neighborhood, reached new heights. Each week, local residents would go out to demonstrate against Shabbat desecration in their midst, with tensions rising steadily between various factions in the city.

Avraham Yochanan, eighty-nine years old at the time, was appointed by Prime Minister Levi Eshkol and Sephardic Chief Rabbi Yitzhak Nissim to make peace between the warring sides. He was given a car to aid him in his battle. Often, he would spend entire days traveling from one party to another without putting a morsel of food in his mouth.

Eventually he went to meet with Mayor Teddy Kollek to plead the community's case, and the mayor had the area closed off, finally leading to the coveted peace.

CHAPTER 47

Blessings, Prayers, and New Developments

O ver the years, countless people came to Avraham Yochanan's doorstep seeking advice, help, and blessings. In one such conversation, Moshe Feldman, a prominent Jerusalem community member who was a close friend of Avraham Yochanan's, turned to him and asked, "Please bless me to have a son. Until now, I have only been blessed with daughters."

Avraham Yochanan thought for a few moments, then said with a smile, "If you promise to give me the honor of *sandak* [holding the baby during the circumcision ceremony], I will give you a blessing." Feldman agreed.

A year passed, and Avraham Yochanan had all but forgotten the entire matter. One day, Moshe Feldman knocked on his door with the joyful news that his wife had given birth to a boy. Avraham Yochanan's delight nearly paralleled that of the overjoyed father, who had not forgotten his promise to give Avraham Yochanan the honor of *sandak*.

The day before the circumcision, however, Feldman returned to the orphanage, his face downcast.

"What's the matter?" asked Avraham Yochanan in concern. "Is the baby all right?"

"Yes, he's fine," Feldman responded slowly.

"Then what's wrong?" Avraham Yochanan probed.

"As you know, I am a disciple of Rabbi Dushinsky," the proud father explained hesitantly, "and it occurred to me that I should give him the honor of *sandak*. It's very difficult for me to ask because I gave you my word... but if you would release me from my promise, I will be able to honor Rabbi Dushinsky as *sandak* tomorrow..."

"No problem, no problem at all," Avraham Yochanan agreed with a smile. "Of course you must give the honor to Rabbi Dushinsky."

Several weeks later, Moshe Feldman's wife came to visit the orphanage with a donation of forty lira, a significant sum in those days.

"These forty lira," commented someone who was present, "parallel the first forty days after conception, during which the Talmud says that the gender of the embryo is determined..."

THE ANCHOR

Rabbi Avraham Mordechai Breitstein, secretary of the Edah from the 1950s to the 1970s, recalls:

> When an emergency committee was established to save the Edah from financial collapse, Rabbi Blumenthal helped ease the burden of debt and reduce the tremendous expenditures. I recall accompanying him to meetings with senior officials in which he sought to ensure the status quo regarding communal matters... His influence was vast. He was renowned for his many activities for the good of the Yishuv throughout the years. I recall an important meeting in the Beit Yisrael neighborhood where great rabbis spoke and participated. There were

vehement differences of opinion, and he was the anchor whose persuasive powers and wise words calmed all the sides and brought peace... It was a merit for me to be close to this great man; there was much to be learned from his deliberate and devoted ways, which earned him the love and respect of all factions of Jewry.

MEASURED WORDS

Rabbi Blumenthal was known for his humble, unassuming ways, even in the face of anger and disrespect. A prominent person once spoke to him derisively. Avraham Yochanan waited a few minutes before responding, then turned to the man and said quietly, "In my father's home, we did not hear people speaking in this manner."

Realizing he had erred, the man paled and immediately apologized.

When people gossiped or spoke contentious words in front of him, Avraham Yochanan refrained from responding. He would quote the words of the patriarch Jacob, "In their gathering, let my honor not be included" (Genesis 49:6).

"I would often go to Avraham Yochanan to ask his opinion on various issues," related Rabbi Yochanan Sofer, the Rebbe of Erlau, who built up a large following in Jerusalem after relocating from Hungary in 1950. "He had a clarity of vision; his eyes saw far into the distance and his advice was always correct and true."

All of Avraham Yochanan's activities were carried out quietly and without fanfare. "I learned this from Elijah the Prophet," he once told his family when they questioned his silence in the face of suffering. "When Elijah was in the desert, God commanded him to seek Him out. As the prophet relates, God was not to be found in the strong winds, nor in the booming of thunder, nor in the burning fire, but rather in the 'still, small voice' (I Kings 19:12).

"From there, I understood that the still, small voice," explained Avraham Yochanan, "is stronger than the winds, the thunder, and the fire."

LATE NIGHTS

"Father would go to sleep very late," Mrs. Blumenthal once told Yocheved in her later years.

Each night, Avraham Yochanan recited *Tikun Chatzot*, a Kabbalistic prayer recited at midnight. His wife, Chana Shaina, discovered this practice by accident when she awakened suddenly and saw a light in the kitchen. She hurriedly jumped out of bed to see who was there and discovered her husband pouring out his heart to his Maker.

He asked her not to reveal this custom to anyone. Many years later, Chana Shaina shared the secret with her children.

Rabbi Blumenthal would sometimes delve into the *Zohar* as well, and maintained a close bond to Rabbi Chaim Shaul Douek, the famed Jerusalem Kabbalist who was blind in his later years.

At the age of eighty, Avraham Yochanan published a book called *Arvut Hayeladim (Children as Guarantors)*, which elucidates verses and Midrashim on the connection between children and Mount Sinai.

IN SUPPORT OF THE SEPHARDIC COMMUNITY

An acquaintance stopped Avraham Yochanan in the street one day. "Rabbi Blumenthal, I have a question for you."

Avraham Yochanan leaned against the wall of a nearby building with a smile. The man lowered his voice. "Many of the children in your orphanage are of Middle Eastern descent, and you are heavily involved in the support of several Sephardic yeshivas. Why do you devote so much energy to the Sephardic community?"

This was not a new question. While the Sephardic and Ashkenazic communities in Jerusalem were often divided, Avraham Yochanan strongly believed that the mandate to pursue justice and kindness was not limited to those of his own community. He was committed to communal activism wherever he was needed.

If anyone speculated some hidden motivation behind Avraham Yochanan's involvement with the Sephardic community, he would often respond with a straight face: "I have a special bond with the

Sephardic community because my family's origins are Spanish. The name *Blumenthal* stems from the Portuguese town of Balamando."

The Sephardic rabbis of Jerusalem respected Avraham Yochanan and saw him as a noble and wise leader. He took a lead role in establishing a Sephardic rabbinic committee. Each Shabbat, he would pray in a different Sephardic synagogue and deliver a rousing lecture after the prayer service.

FRESH BLOOD

In 1951, Avraham Yochanan's granddaughter Rivka Shlapovarsky, Nechama's daughter, married Rabbi Eliezer Rakovsky, a student in Hebron Yeshiva. Like her siblings, Rivka spent many hours in the orphanage as a child. She had often been called upon to help out with various tasks and knew the orphanage intimately.

"I remember the big block of halvah that Grandmother asked me to cut up," Rivka recalls. "It was no simple task to divide the halvah into neat squares that would not crumble apart or stick together. Before there were bread-slicing machines, I was also asked to slice the bread. At one point, painful blisters developed on my hands, convincing Grandmother that I had done my share with the bread knife…"

After their marriage, the young Rakovsky couple moved to the city of Rehovot in central Israel, where Rabbi Rakovsky held a rabbinic post for several years. In 1961, Avraham Yochanan, feeling that the orphanage was in need of young leadership, sought them out. He believed that Eliezer's educational and administrative abilities made him the right candidate to step in.

Rivka initially had many hesitations about accepting the position, as she felt the responsibilities involved would be too much for her young family. But Grandfather refused to take no for an answer. Bowing to the inevitable, the young Rakovsky couple returned to Jerusalem, moving into the orphanage with the Blumenthals, and Eliezer Rakovsky soon became Avraham Yochanan's right hand.

CHAPTER 48

A Permanent Home at Last

vraham Yochanan's long-held dream was to erect a permanent home for the orphanage, one that would be designed from its inception to accommodate dozens of young children.

Prior efforts were squashed by the precarious security situation. His first attempt at fulfilling this dream was his trip to Bethlehem in 1928 to look at a plot of land for sale.[34] This plan did not come to fruition, as an outbreak of Arab hostility in the area rendered the region too dangerous for this purpose. A plot of land purchased in 1932 adjacent to Shuafat was similarly unsuitable for settlement.[35] And the orphanage's branch in Motza, slated to become a full-fledged institution, had to be evacuated in 1936.[36]

Despite repeated failures, Avraham Yochanan refused to despair. In his seventies, he renewed his efforts to purchase land and build a permanent building for the orphanage. An empty lot on the corner

---

34   See chapter 26.
35   See chapter 30.
36   See chapter 31.

of Yechezkel and Hoshea Streets seemed ideal for his needs. The land was still a cornfield when it was purchased in the 1940s, but Avraham Yochanan envisioned a large courtyard surrounded by several buildings, built to his specifications.

Yaakov Dori, an engineer by profession who was later to become Chief of Staff of the IDF, visited the orphanage at around this time (at

the encouragement of his relative, Adina Levy). When he heard of Avraham Yochanan's plans, he offered to design the building free of charge, on condition that it be built outside the city. Avraham Yochanan, however, decided that the orphanage would remain where it was.

The architectural design and construction were ultimately executed by Yosef Sheinberger, whose plans included a ground floor with a kitchen and dining room, and a second floor large enough to accommodate about one hundred

Rabbi Blumenthal at the laying of the cornerstone for the new building

children. After Avraham Yochanan carefully examined the blueprints and approved them, construction began.

The building was spacious, even grandiose, for the times. When questioned about this, Avraham Yochanan explained, "I don't want to

erect just another building. I want to build something that will grace the Holy City with its beauty."

After several years of construction, the main building was completed. The Aminoff family had graciously   hosted   the

The construction site on Hoshea Street

orphanage in its building on Yechezkel Street for twenty-five years. Finally, in 1961, the children would be relocating to a home of their own further up the street.

Throughout the many years of financial difficulty and challenges, Avraham Yochanan had experienced the hand of God supporting him in all his efforts. Standing across from the new building, he raised his eyes heavenward with a deep sense of gratitude, his lips murmuring, "I will exalt You, God, for You have uplifted me" (Psalms 30:2).

At the celebration in honor of the new building, Avraham Yochanan reminded those assembled that as long as Torah institutions exist, the Jewish nation lives on. "May it be God's will that this building be like Yavneh [the city of Torah scholars safeguarded by the first-century sage Rabbi Yochanan ben

The completed building on the corner of Yechezkel and Hoshea Streets

Zakkai]," he said, "and produce Torah scholars and those who safeguard the commandments, and may the Almighty protect them all."

"The first time I entered the new building," recalls Rabbi David Nisanoff, chairman of the Bukharian Committee, "I wondered why the sign on the building read 'children's home,' rather than 'orphanage.' I thought perhaps Rabbi Blumenthal had done this so as not to hurt the children's feelings.

"As the years passed, however, I was witness to the arrival of countless immigrant children from homes in difficult straits, whose parents were alive yet unable to care for them. At that point, I understood why Rabbi Blumenthal used the name 'children's home.'"

THE LOSS OF A MATRIARCH

Even when well into his eighties, Avraham Yochanan was distinguished by his upright posture, noble features, and piercing eyes. He continued to be the loving father and beloved role model of the orphanage children.

The death of his wife, Chana Shaina, on the last night of Hanukkah in 1963, was a devastating loss. Chana Shaina had been a true mother to the children of the orphanage. She stood by her husband's side for decades, her support and devotion upholding the entire institution.

She was the quintessential matriarch, the hidden cog that empowered the entire operation. Neither old age nor illness prevented her from providing "her" children with a warm and loving home.

Her passing left a gaping hole in the hearts of hundreds of orphanage alumni, many of whom were already parents themselves. They all came to pay their last respects to this great woman, accompanying her to her final resting place in the Har Hamenuchot cemetery in Jerusalem.

Yet even without his wife's staunch support, Avraham Yochanan, now eighty-six years old, continued his daily routine uninterrupted. He preferred to maintain independence and ate his meals with the children in the orphanage rather than at the homes of his children or grandchildren. When his daughters brought over hot meals, he insisted on paying them for the expense.

His granddaughter, Mrs. Rivka Rakovsky, recalls her memories of those years:

> *When Grandfather asked me to buy him something, he would not take the item from my hand until he had paid for it in full — even if it had as little value as half a lemon! Once he'd paid, he would say, "Now it's mine," and only then would he use it. He never wanted to be dependent on anyone else.*
>
> *He also never asked a child of the orphanage for a personal favor. No one understood why he could not request a cup of water or a chair from a child standing nearby, and why he would insist on asking his own grandchildren instead. Years later, we understood the deep educational significance of his actions.*

OLD AGE

By the time Avraham Yochanan was in his eighties, he had merited to see his life's dream — the new orphanage building — come true. His grandchildren and great-grandchildren lived exemplary lives devoted to Torah and good deeds, and many of the orphans he raised had developed into upstanding individuals who built homes of their own.

Chaim Sher, a resident of the orphanage who later became the orphanage's spiritual guide, recalls the bond that developed between Avraham Yochanan and the children:

> Rabbi Blumenthal's perfect vision surprised us each time anew. He would pray with the children, and we were always amazed at how he read from the Torah with no reading glasses!
>
> I loved him with all my heart and soul. I recall the twinge I would feel when I saw him covering his face with his hands, pained by the misbehavior of one of the boys. "You?!" he would ask incredulously. "How is it possible that you did something like this?" Often, his expressions and gestures spoke for themselves, and no further words were necessary...
>
> As a child, I had recurring instances of strep throat. Rabbi Blumenthal would come to my bedside and personally feed me lemon juice and sugar. He would also bring lunch to my bed — hot chicken soup, a Jewish mother's best remedy for all types of ailments. Each time I was touched anew by his devotion.
>
> When one of my peers accidentally swallowed a coin, Rabbi Blumenthal did not relax until he heard that the coin had emerged and the boy was fine.
>
> He never asked a personal favor of a child. If he needed someone to go to the grocery store, he would pay for the service.
>
> His attitude toward the orphanage, however, was very different. If he saw a piece of paper on the floor, he would immediately ask one of the children to pick it up. "This is your home, not mine," he would say.

CHAPTER 49

Final Days

Avraham Yochanan was extremely scrupulous in all his dealings with funds allocated for charity, making do with very little personally. "I'm not leaving you a penny!" he repeatedly told his children during his last days. He left instructions that his burial expenses be covered with money inherited from Mrs. Blumenthal's family, not with any funds donated to the orphanage.

Unfortunately, some assumed otherwise. Knowing that the orphanage survived on substantial contributions from abroad, these unscrupulous individuals erroneously concluded that Avraham Yochanan was hoarding money or other valuables. On the night of Yom Kippur 1966, when young and old alike were in the synagogue, thieves broke into Avraham Yochanan's home and ransacked it, looking for cash.

When he arrived home from synagogue, the aged Avraham Yochanan was crushed by the scene of destruction — broken dishes, clothes flung in every direction, and his beloved set of tefillin crushed. While the thieves came away with nothing of monetary value, they did succeed in robbing Avraham Yochanan of his health. The shock of the break-in left him so weak that he had to be hospitalized.

ON HIS SICKBED

In addition to the family members who took turns staying with Avraham Yochanan twenty-four hours a day, Binyamin Hausman, a former student who maintained a strong bond with the Blumenthals throughout the years, began to visit Avraham Yochanan daily.[37]

Despite physical weakness, Avraham Yochanan still possessed the same strength of spirit and character. Eliezer Rakovsky, Avraham Yochanan's grandson-in-law, wanted to prove that despite his haziness, Avraham Yochanan still remembered all the Torah he had studied. Approaching the sickbed, he asked, "Grandfather, is it true that in the book of Job it says so and so…?" He proceeded to quote a verse, deliberately changing some of the words.

Avraham Yochanan opened his eyes. "Why are you misquoting the verse?" He proceeded to quote the verse verbatim, continuing with the verses that followed it.

When he had recovered somewhat, Avraham Yochanan asked to be released from the hospital. The doctors allowed him to return home, where he spent his final five weeks of life.

Even during these last days, a love and care for the orphans was his central focus. In his final illness, his life ebbing away, Avraham Yochanan suddenly heard an unfamiliar voice outside his room. "Go see who it is," he urged Yocheved, who was attending him. "Perhaps someone wants us to admit a new orphan or is in need of help."

---

37   Binyamin was known for his exemplary respect for his elderly mother, Chasha the baker-woman. In her tiny home on Hayehudim Street in the Old City, she would bake sponge cake, which she then peddled from door to door. She was known to all as "Chasha the *lekach* (sponge cake) maker."

Chasha lived to a ripe old age. At 105, she was both blind and deaf. She lived with Binyamin, who refused to place her in an nursing home, lovingly attending to all her needs. When the elderly Chasha could no longer walk and there were no wheelchairs available, Binyamin thought nothing of carrying her on his shoulders. This same Binyamin saw it as his duty and privilege to visit Avraham Yochanan and be at his side in his old age and infirmity.

Two days before his passing, Avraham Yochanan turned to Yocheved and said, "Remind me to say a blessing!"

"What shall I bring you, Father?" she asked, wondering what he wanted to eat. Avraham Yochanan would often lay down his fork after eating only a few bites, maintaining, "Nu, for the worms [once I'm in the grave] it's enough!"

His answer came as no surprise. "I don't want to eat anything," he responded. "I simply want to thank God for the long life with which He has blessed me, for the ability to help others, and for all His kindness to me to this very day."

A THOUSAND ORPHANS

On November 30, 1966 (17 Kislev 5727), the ninety-year melody of Rabbi Avraham Yochanan Blumenthal's life came to an end. The pure notes, free of any personal agenda or desire for remuneration or bene-

fit, were silenced, leaving thousands of shocked orphans to reexperience the bitterly familiar taste of loss.

Avraham Yochanan's "children" came streaming to the funeral from all over the country, their eyes blurred with tears.

Rabbi Blumenthal's funeral in the courtyard of the orphanage

They had lost their beloved and loving father.

Bearded scholars and simple tradesmen, Ashkenazic Jews and Sephardic Jews, those of the Old Yishuv alongside those of the new, all crowded into the courtyard of the orphanage, spilling out into the streets, one large family in mourning.

Rabbi Pinchas Epstein, a prominent community member, sobbed as he delivered his eulogy. "Woe is to beauty that was swallowed by the earth! His deeds were beautiful, his character traits were beautiful, he was most beautiful in Torah and good deeds, and beautiful according to its simple meaning, for his visage was noble and his face was glowing, as it says, 'A man's wisdom will illuminate his face' (Ecclesiastes 8:1)."

Rabbi Shmuel Wosner, Avraham Yochanan's first cousin,[38] delivered one of the many eulogies. Then the procession made its tearful way through the streets of Jerusalem toward Har Hamenuchot, Jerusalem's largest cemetery.

Another view of the funeral, in a spot now known as Rabbi A. Y. Blumenthal Square, on the corner of Yechezkel and Hoshea Streets

LIKE SAPLINGS

During the week of shivah, the seven days of mourning, hundreds of people filed into the house to pay their respects to Avraham Yochanan's daughters. (His son, Yisrael Chaim, had passed away years earlier.[39]) Rabbi Aharon Katzenelbogen, a respected figure in Jerusalem, spoke at length, concluding with the words: "His greatness was that he did not speak much, but at rabbinic gatherings, everyone knew his opinion — and when the time came for a final decision, his opinion was accepted."

The tzaddik Rabbi Aryeh Levin also visited the house of mourning, telling the Blumenthal daughters, "The public thought they knew your father, but I am telling you that they did not truly know him or value him enough."

Yocheved summed up her father's life: "Father saw each disciple as a sapling to be nurtured and developed in his own way. When you see a recently planted sapling along the sidewalk, it's connected to a strong branch, and the two are enclosed by a gate that guards the sapling until it will grow strong. From time to time, the gardener checks to see how the new sapling is progressing, digging around it and fertilizing the surrounding earth.

38   See chapter 33.
39   See chapter 46.

"As King David says in Psalms (144:12), 'Our children are like saplings, to be raised in their youth.' When Father raised his boys, he made

The sign put up by the municipality, reading "Rabbi A. Y. Blumenthal Square," next to the orphanage

sure to develop them, to build them up, and to prepare them for their mission as Jews who safeguard the Torah and are proud of their Judaism.

"When we meet these children tens of years later and see the generations they have established, our hearts fill with delight and our

eyes with tears of joy. Father's legacy lives on and continues to bring forth new fruit."

CHAPTER 50

A New Era

Avraham Yochanan's lifework did not end with his passing. Rather, the orphanage continued to flourish, and in the decades to follow, many more children found within its walls the warmth and love they craved.

It was with a deep sense of mission that Rabbi Eliezer and Rivka Rakovsky assumed responsibility for the large family of children in the orphanage, gracefully accepting the challenges and uncertainties, the day-in, day-out, round-the-clock dedication required to supervise and care for the children.

EMBATTLED AGAIN

On the political map, the most immediate and critical conflict the Rakovskys faced was the 1967 Six Day War. For nineteen years, Jerusalem had been divided, its ancient holy sites inaccessible to the Jewish people. Barbed-wire fences and no-man's land separated the Israeli half of the city from the Jordanian half, with the Old City and the Western Wall in enemy hands. When the fledgling country faced war again, with simultaneous attacks from the north, south, and west, the country feared for its very existence.

Zion boys praying at the Western Wall

War broke out on Monday morning, June 5, 1967. The residents of Jerusalem were caught off guard, although the armed forces were not. For years, the border neighborhoods of Jerusalem — including the Bukharian Quarter — had grown accustomed to walking past the Jordanian legionnaires stationed on the other side of the barbed-wire fence dividing the city. Force of habit dulled their fears, and the gunfire that heralded the start of the war resulted in several fatalities.

Early on that fateful Monday, the Jordanians seized control of Government House (Armon Hanetziv) in the west of the city and planned to continue their attack. After fierce fighting, they were re-pelled by Israeli troops. To the north and west of the city, IDF troops gained control of Ammunition Hill and several other important stra-tegic spots. By the next day, June 7, the Old City had been returned to Jewish hands, with the Jordanians retreating to Jericho in the west.

Jews the world over rejoiced with the recapture of the Western Wall, the symbol of the eternal bond between God and His people. While Avraham

Yochanan, whose heart had so longed to pray at the Western Wall, did not merit to see it again, his children and his beloved orphans did.

During the war, an IDF commander took up residence in the orphanage building and used the director's apartment as her own. The children crowded into the bomb shelter, where the counselors attempted to keep them occupied, raise their spirits, and distract their fears. Unlike many others, who were forced to make do with almost nothing, the children were fortunate to receive hot meals alongside those provided for the army personnel stationed in the building. With the lightning-fast ceasefire, they, and the rest of the Jewish world, exulted in the trium-

phant victory — a swift turn-around that saw Israel expand its borders in all three directions and secure its military positions.

On Shavuot of that year, mere days after the ceasefire, the children and their new director walked to the Western Wall, the place they had heard about but had never seen before. The orphanage children marched alongside multitudes of Jews who converged on the holy site to pour out their hearts in gratitude, their hearts beating with joy.

Rabbi Eliezer Rakovsky with two bar mitzvah boys at the Western Wall

THE NEW DIRECTOR

Rabbi Rakovsky, too, was a child of Jerusalem, having grown up in a tiny apartment in the Knesset neighborhood (near Machaneh Yehuda) with eight siblings. Eliezer was the middle child, with four older siblings and four younger. Yet he grew and blossomed in his poverty-stricken home, where his father was occupied with Talmud study and his mother was a busy homemaker and mother.

"Eliezer was always extremely organized and meticulous," recalls his sister, Chasida Gevaryahu. "He liked to accompany Mother to the marketplace and help her carry the baskets home. He honored our parents greatly and utilized every opportunity to help them."

When he grew older, Eliezer studied in Rehovot under Rabbi Tzvi Yehuda Meltzer, son of the famed Rabbi Isser Zalman Meltzer. While there, he became close to the Torah leader Rabbi Elazar Shach, who at the time lectured in Rehovot's Yeshivat Hadarom.

After marrying, receiving rabbinic ordination, and serving as the rabbi of the Ekron settlement and Rehovot's Chavatzelet neighborhood, Rabbi Rakovsky returned to Jerusalem at Avraham Yochanan's behest. He willingly shouldered the task placed upon him and devoted his resources exclusively to this holy work, raising children whose parents were unable to do so themselves.

As Avraham Yochanan wrote in a letter to his grandson-in-law:

> *To my dear and wonderful grandson...*
> *I am hereby committing to writing that which I have told you several times since you have begun working for the Zion Blumenthal Orphanage.*
> *I am hereby giving over to you all the managerial tasks within the institute, which were my own responsibilities as director. All matters, both spiritual and physical, regarding both staff and children, will be managed by you. Nothing should be hidden from you or your knowledge.*
> *All this is on the condition that you take on no other job or position, paid or unpaid. I am certain that the Father of Orphans will accept my prayer to stand at your side so that you educate and raise the children to glory and a good name...*
> *Signed with a feeling of contentment and a blessing for your success,*
> *Avraham Yochanan Blumenthal*

RECOVERY AND REHABILITATION

Like his grandfather before him, Eliezer Rakovsky supervised every detail of the orphanage: the children's education, food, clothing, and extracurricular activities. Yet there were many hurdles to overcome. In his first years at the helm, Eliezer was thrust deep into a sea of debt that construction of the new building had generated, which only seemed to grow deeper with time.

Wanting to see the building completed, Avraham Yochanan had borrowed repeatedly to advance its construction. The country's difficult financial situation had reduced the flow of contributions to the orphanage, and interest rates threatened to sink the orphanage entirely. In addition, the government opposed the construction of the new building. Wanting to turn the orphanage into a government-run institution, various officials made regular inspections of the building, seeking out problems and pointing out supposed dangers.

Rabbi Rakovsky with a group of children in the orphanage courtyard

The young and energetic director immediately put a stop to this, focusing all his efforts on recovery and rehabilitation. Believing that one could not build on shaky foundations, Eliezer's first step was to halt all further construction until the institution's debts had been paid up. Taking upon himself the burden of repaying the massive debts, he spent the next year and a half raising money to return the orphanage to a state of equilibrium. Only once the debt had been cleared did he return his attention to putting the finishing touches on the beautiful building.

Another one of Eliezer's uncompromising principles was paying the staff on time. Although the salaries were not high, all staff members knew they would receive their checks on time, even if the institute was running a deficit. Eliezer ensured this was so, sometimes borrowing money in order to pay salaries rather than transgressing the Torah directive to pay a worker on time (Leviticus 19:13). His uprightness and integrity stood him in good stead, and the pile of debts slowly dwindled.

CHAPTER 51

New Children, New Challenges

I n the wake of the Six Day War, a new wave of Jews from Middle
Eastern countries arrived in the Holy Land, bringing a stream of
immigrant children to the orphanage. Chief among them were
Yemenite children with their piercing black eyes. Many had made
aliyah with their parents but for one reason or another were unable
to live at home.

These children, placed in the orphanage by struggling parents, newly
widowed fathers, or families that had disintegrated, were welcomed
into an organized, well-run home. They quickly grew accustomed to the
fixed routines, the story hour, and the various extracurricular activities,
allowing them the peace of mind to develop into happy, productive
members of society.

These children were also blessed with abundant tenacity. One
day, two brothers living in the orphanage decided to return to their
parents' home in Tel Aviv on foot. They were finally located near
Motza, a distance of about six miles, worn out and thirsty, and returned to the orphanage.

After the wave of Yemenite immigration, many children arrived from Morocco, then from Georgia, and later from Russia and Uzbekistan. Each time, the orphanage staff had to acquaint itself with a new culture and mentality, and all this entailed: different tastes in food, different Shabbat tunes, and different languages.

ABANDONED BABY

There were also children like Yossi, whose origins one could only guess.

Rabbi Rakovsky with a group of children in the orphanage courtyard, October 1984

The soft whimpers coming from the stairwell of her apartment building roused Mrs. S. from her thoughts. Investigating the source of the sound, she was shocked to see a small whimpering bundle — a tiny infant wrapped in a shabby blanket. A note attached to the blanket read: "Jewish, needs circumcision."

Mrs. S. lifted the little bundle into her arms. The baby's voice was hoarse from prolonged crying. After bringing him into her house and feeding him, Mrs. S. and her husband tried to locate the baby's family, but their efforts yielded no results. There was not a shred of evidence to lead them to the identity of the abandoned baby.

The baby was circumcised and remained in their home, spending the first years of his life in the bosom of the S. family. With time, however, the family's financial situation deteriorated considerably, and one morning, when Yossi was four years old, the S.'s decided that they had no choice but to give him up.

Following much turmoil and upheaval, a kind middle-aged couple was found who welcomed Yossi into their home and provided him with a warm and peaceful environment. But the abrupt severance from his adopted parents had turned the boy into a sensitive and easily wounded child. Yossi developed a stutter that rendered him often incoherent, and he withdrew into himself.

Several years passed. Yossi's adoptive parents aged, and he needed a suitable place to live. One day, he arrived at Eliezer's doorstep with his new adoptive father.

A short conversation revealed the depth of the tragedy of little Yossi's life. His dull eyes immediately captured Eliezer's heart. He stroked Yossi's hair, hugged him, and took him by the hand for a tour of the orphanage, just as Avraham Yochanan had done with new arrivals in previous decades.

From then on, the orphanage became Yossi's home, and Eliezer his father. During vacation times, Yossi visited his second set of adoptive parents, who were getting on in years. But more often than not, he preferred to stay with the Rakovskys.

As Yossi's peers began to leave the orphanage for various yeshivas and high schools, Yossi stayed on. He took on the role of a young counselor, a position that did wonders for his shattered self-esteem.

Yossi lived in the orphanage until his marriage. Eliezer helped him find a job and later a marriage partner, and he eventually built his own home.

LONG-TERM SUCCESS

Yossi, however, was one of the few children of this era with no family to call his own. Many of the children in the orphanage in the '70s and '80s had immigrant parents who were unable to care for them and thus handed them over to the orphanage for a number of years. Once the boys were in their teens, the parents often brought the boys home so they could help support the family.

This distressed Eliezer immensely, as he hoped that these children's futures would involve more than menial

Rabbi Rakovsky speaking at a bar mitzvah celebration

labor. The parents had often abandoned their heritage along the way, which meant that the boys, after being raised in the religious environs of the orphanage, would be returning to a very culturally different environment.

One bright and talented young boy had a great future ahead of him when his father, who had not shown his face in the orphanage for years, suddenly appeared. "I need the boy to help out in my restaurant," he announced.

Studying in the library

"We will cover his tuition and provide for all his needs. Please allow him to stay with us and study!" Eliezer begged. The child stood on the side of the room, tears streaming down his face.

The hot-headed father suddenly drew a knife from his pocket and waved it menacingly. Yet Eliezer did not bow to pressure. When the father left the orphanage, Eliezer sent the boy to a distant yeshiva in the southern town of Be'er Yaakov, hoping to buy him some time there. Two months later, however, the father arrived at the yeshiva and forcibly removed his son from the premises.

Many alumni of the orphanage did well in their studies, providing their director with much joy and pride. Eliezer assigned each of these boys a counselor, who played the role of a caring older brother, lending the boys a listening ear and assisting with their studies. They often found their futures in the study hall, becoming a pride to the director and to their alma mater.

A SPECIAL LEARNING PROGRAM

Some children arrived at the orphanage with limited abilities and skills. David, for example, was completely illiterate upon his arrival at age nine. The psychologist who evaluated him offered a grim prediction of his future, but Eliezer, impressed by the child's easygoing manner, accepted him, doing everything possible to ensure he would succeed in his studies.

One of the Rakovskys' daughters, Bracha Tauber, had a degree in special education. With her father's encouragement, she took David under her wing, investing countless hours teaching him the basics of reading and writing. Miraculously, the boy caught on and became a serious young scholar in an excellent yeshiva.

CHAPTER 52

Bar Mitzvahs, Surgeries, and Holiday Plans

T he thirty years of Eliezer's tenure saw many changes in the orphanage. The country emerged from its austerity period and became more prosperous; standards of living improved across the board. The Israeli Ministry of Social Welfare sent many children to the orphanage from dysfunctional homes, and the orphanage had to expand its services to rehabilitate these broken youngsters. The city, and the country, grew and developed, yet there were always new children who needed a loving home and parental guidance.

"Yitzhak is sitting and crying outside," the children reported to Rabbi Rakovsky. A tear glistened in Eliezer's eyes. He had done so much for Yitzhak, but to no avail.

Yitzhak had been brought to the orphanage by his widowed mother, who announced that she was planning to remarry and start her life anew and had no interest in seeing her son again. When the other children went home on a monthly basis for Shabbat, Yitzhak stayed in the orphanage. No care packages arrived for him and no letters appeared in the mail. He was orphaned in every practical sense of the word.

Six months after his arrival at Zion Orphanage, Yitzhak turned thirteen. His bar mitzvah celebration was to be a joint one, with two other

Nine boys celebrate their bar mitzvahs at the Western Wall

boys. Eliezer called Yitzhak's mother and reminded her of the upcoming momentous event in her son's life. He described the new suit, hat, and watch that the orphanage had purchased for the boy, and suggested that she present these items to Yitzhak as a personal gift. No one would know of the director's involvement.

"Three children are celebrating their bar mitzvahs together, and many guests will arrive for each of them. All I am asking is that you come and celebrate with your son," Eliezer begged. But the woman was deaf to his pleas. Not one guest arrived to share the joyous occasion with young Yitzhak.

With his new suit, crisp shirt, and shining shoes, Yitzhak sat down on the steps of the orphanage and cried unashamedly.

Sukkot arrived. The boys left, either to the homes of their biological parents, or to the homes of families that took them in. "Yitzhak will stay with us," Eliezer informed his family. "On Chol Hamoed [the intermediate days of the festival], I will take him to visit his mother."

When the anticipated day arrived, the director instructed the boy to dress in his new clothing for the trip to his mother's home. "I don't want to go," Yitzhak resisted. "She won't open the door for me."

"Perhaps if she sees you dressed so nicely, she will greet you warmly," Eliezer comforted the boy.

Yet his hopes were for naught. When the boy's mother saw them at the door, she burst into an angry tirade. "Didn't I tell you that I never want to see him again!? Leave!"

Eliezer managed to stop her from slamming the door. "Even a mother cat cares for her kittens! Will you not open the door for your son?"

The mother refused, and the two returned home, terribly pained. Tragically, the deep wound in Yitzhak's soul affected his stability, and he was eventually transferred to an institution that provided much more intensive psychiatric care.

Rabbi Yitzhak Kolitz, Chief Rabbi of Jerusalem, speaking to the orphanage boys

Many difficult cases were sent to the orphanage, requiring professional care and unlimited time and attention. The failures were stinging, but the successes imbued the staff with the strength to continue.

MEDICAL NEEDS

While Rivka Rakovsky devoted her energies to raising her children, four daughters and a son, her husband, Eliezer, had dozens of "sons" who required his love and care.

"Countless times, when the children were in need of medical attention, my brother would accompany them to the hospital," related Rabbi Yaakov Rakovsky, the director's brother, who served as rabbi of Hadassah Medical Centers for over fifty years. "Like a concerned father, he always sought the best possible care, with no thought to the expenses involved. Several times, he called and asked me to visit a boy who had been hospitalized, or to speak to a doctor about a child's treatment."

Once, three brothers arrived at the orphanage, appearing neglected and despondent. Eliezer was especially struck by one of them, whose head had a strange tendency to loll sideways, as though he had pulled his neck muscles.

Perhaps it is some temporary ailment, the director thought, as he arranged for proper clothing, beds, and everything else the children needed.

The coming days, however, proved that the condition was not a temporary one. The boy's teachers reported the strange misalignment as well, and his peers began to tease him. Eliezer decided to investigate. When he questioned the child's family, however, they were oblivious to the problem, claiming that they'd never noticed anything amiss.

Unable to let the matter rest, Eliezer did some research and made an appointment for the boy with an expert neurologist, accompanying the child to the doctor's office.

"It's not a neurological issue here," the doctor said, after a thorough examination. "I believe the problem stems from a weak eye muscle. Since he can't move one of his eyes, he compensates by turning his head to the side in order to see. Take him to an eye specialist." He recommended a certain specialist in Tel Aviv.

The specialist examined the child thoroughly and looked at Eliezer doubtfully. "You say he is in your orphanage? The weak muscle can be corrected through surgery, but it's a very expensive procedure, and I don't think you'll be able to cover the costs."

"The cost is immaterial," Eliezer answered immediately. "The child must receive the best possible treatment."

Soon after, the boy successfully underwent surgery. The doctor, impressed by Eliezer's devotion to his young charge, waived a significant portion of his fee.

The eye problem was corrected, and the boy returned to the orphanage with newfound vigor and confidence.

DOWN TO THE LAST DETAIL

On Friday nights, Eliezer would head to the orphanage dining room straight from the synagogue. He would greet each child with a smile and a *"Shabbat shalom."* In the winter, he never allowed a child to leave the building without a coat. He would often walk through the dormitory rooms to check what needed repair, and no unmade bed escaped his careful scrutiny.

Despite his attention to order and cleanliness, when the children returned from school and threw their knapsacks on the floor, Eliezer never said a word about it. Questioned by one of the counselors, David Uzan (currently director of Yeshivat Zohar HaTorah in Jerusalem), he responded that the day of learning was exhausting for the children. Throwing their knapsacks down was their way of releasing pent-up tension.

Eliezer's attention to detail extended to the smallest points. "Sometimes I would see him bending down to pick up a used pencil off the floor. He had a special drawer for pencil stubs," relates Rabbi Uzan. "He also encouraged us counselors not to spend our salaries on frivolities, but to save the money instead.

"He would recoil at the sight of food thrown in the garbage. 'It's like taking a wad of bills and throwing them out,' he would tell the children."

Holiday preparations create pressure in many households. In the orphanage, Eliezer would put all other matters aside and sit with the staff to plan the menu and the program for the holiday, down to the last detail. Everything was important to him; everything contributed to the special holiday atmosphere.

The children always received new clothing for each holiday. Unlike the early days of the orphanage, when the entire city lived in abject poverty and the orphanage children no less so, the standard of living had gone up and the children needed the

A Purim play in 1980

same self-respect that their classmates had. Understanding this, Eliezer never scrimped when it came to the children's clothing, devoting much time to dressing each child in the appropriate attire.

NOWHERE TO GO

Eliezer always noticed if a child was despondent or lacking in self-esteem. He would entrust the child with some important "task" in order to imbue him with a sense of worth, such as appointing him to be the dining room monitor or putting him in charge of distributing books.

Children with ADHD often arrived at the orphanage. In those years, there was little knowledge of this disorder or medication available, yet Eliezer never labeled a child as disruptive. Instead, he would encourage children who displayed hyperactive tendencies to release their energies. Following a short run or other such release, the child was able to sit with his friends and focus on homework or a story.

Programs, activities, and day camps were planned with precision, the overriding goal to provide the children with enjoyment.

"He had one unbending rule: He never threw a child out of the orphanage," says Rabbi Uzan. "Sometimes we counselors would complain about one child or another who was misbehaving or causing problems, but Rabbi Rakovsky always attended to the child and the situation, no matter how challenging. Never did he show a child the door. 'He has nowhere to go,' was his refrain. And we had nothing to answer."

The children responded to this love by maintaining a strong bond with the orphanage, even after returning to their families or moving on to institutions of higher learning. It was a common sight to see alumni returning to the orphanage for Rosh Hashanah, for example.

Eliezer would also invite the children to come and listen to the lecture he delivered at the Great Synagogue one Friday evening each year. He was visibly excited to see their faces among the audience.

CHAPTER 53

United in Its Cause

A s in the early years, the orphanage staff under Eliezer was completely dedicated to its cause. Their jobs entailed constant acts of loving ministrations. Mrs. Tziporah Meizlish, who served as the Zion Orphanage cook for thirty-six years, starting from 1967, was one such staff member. As she cooked, she would listen to the children's woes, give them motherly advice, stroke their heads, and sneak them a slice of cake.

"They need larger portions of meat and chicken," she told Eliezer at one point early in her tenure, when food was scarce.

"Buy whatever you think is necessary, I trust you," Eliezer told her.

When Purim approached, Mrs. Meizlish took on another task, outfitting all the children in costumes in honor of the holiday. Her home turned into a hub of activity as the children came and went, picking out costumes from the ensembles that the cook had created out of clothing packages sent by American relatives. The children's eyes shone when they left her home.

During the Six Day War, Mrs. Meizlish left her family and came to work, filling the children's bellies and showering them with warmth and love.

"CAN'T YOU BE MY MOTHER?"

"Just as a mother is sometimes called upon to do unpleasant or difficult tasks, we were also faced with such circumstances," recalls Mrs. Shoshana Egozi, who served as housemother in the 1970s. "One child was brought to the orphanage by the P'eylim organization, straight from the Carmel Market in Tel Aviv. He had been living for weeks among the vegetable stalls and was bruised, bleeding, and infested with lice.

"Rabbi Rakovsky's first response was to sigh in deep pain and close his eyes. But a mother cannot afford to close her eyes. I took the boy straight to the bathtub, washed him, and combed the lice out of his hair. Then I bandaged every wound on his body until he was almost entirely covered with bandages. When we returned to the office, he was transformed. His eyes shone, and a light seemed to radiate from his face as he asked me, 'Why can't you be my mother?' "

NEW SHOES

Other employees share stories of Eliezer's devotion to the children, which filtered down to them as well.

"Before every holiday, Rabbi Rakovsky would send me out with each child to purchase a pair of new shoes," recalls Mrs. Bella Sirota, who served as housemother in the 1990s. "Rather than ordering a stock of shoes to be distributed according to size in the orphanage, he felt a special trip to the shoe store was worth the extra effort.

Israeli Knesset Member Rabbi Menachem Porush speaking at a bar mitzvah celebration

"Every bar mitzvah was a personal celebration. A meal was served, speeches were given in honor of the bar mitzvah boy, and the child's relatives and other important guests joined the celebration.

"Rabbi Rakovsky ensured that total cleanliness reigned over the orphanage. In fact, the building was so immaculate that government inspectors decreed that it was possible to eat off the floors!"

DIAMONDS IN THE ROUGH

The counselors, as well, felt their patience tried at times, but Eliezer's example reminded them of their cause.

"We would often complain to Rabbi Rakovsky about a child who was wild or acting out," says Rabbi Chaim Sher, who lived in the orphanage as a child and later served as a counselor and then its spiritual guide. "'This is the purpose for which the orphanage was established,' he would respond. His face glowed as he explained, 'We are here to polish the diamonds in the rough.'"

Rabbi Sher recalls how, during his tenure as a counselor, one of the children who was sent home for Passover vacation a week after the others was greeted angrily at the door. "Why did you bring him so early?!" asked the irritable father. No wonder the child needed extra attention on his return after the holiday...

"Another child caused us endless worry when he disappeared on a trip to a Tel Aviv park. After a long search, we sent someone to his home in Bnei Brak,

Rabbi Yehuda Tzadka, head of Yeshivat Porat Yosef, speaking in the orphanage sanctuary. Seated, left to right: Rabbi Eliezer Rakovsky, Rabbi Fischel Zaks, Rabbi Shneur Zalman Reichman, and Rabbi Michel Shlapovarsky

where we discovered that the child had met some neighbors in the park and gone home for a visit..."

Other counselors recall how Eliezer was ever-aware of the sounds coming from the children's rooms, even late at night. Sometimes, he would stop in his tracks at the sound of a cough and go up to the dormitory to see who had caught a cold, offering the boy a hot cup of tea or cough syrup. In the morning, when he asked a counselor to look after the child in question, the counselor would often exclaim, "But I didn't hear a thing!"

"Young people sleep deeply," the director would respond, but in truth, it was the fatherly responsibility and concern that enabled him to hear more than others.

TASTING SUCCESS

Mrs. Basyah Barg, another devoted housemother and narrator of the book *Voices in the Silence*,[40] about her childhood behind the Iron Curtain, made aliyah with her husband in 1971. Not blessed with children of her own, she devoted herself to the children of the orphanage.

> *I arrived at the orphanage early every morning and would go to the dining room to check who had eaten and who hadn't, and why.*
>
> *When the children were prepared to leave for school, I would stand near the gate and not allow any child out until I looked him over carefully. Rabbi Rakovsky felt it was very important that the children look respectable, and I was in charge of ensuring that they did. If I noticed a button missing on a shirt, a dragging hem, or a worn-out shoelace, the child would be sent back to his room to change his clothing. I checked every knapsack to make sure there was lunch inside.*
>
> *"A child is not allowed to look unkempt," I told the children again and again. "If another child arrives in school looking untidy, his mother is blamed. If you arrive looking like a mess, they'll blame you! You must train yourself to be neat, so that in the future you'll be able to have a neat and organized home."*
>
> *I also worried for the children's self-respect, and many times I told them not to share details about themselves that would lead others to look down on them. "Do your homework and try to excel so everyone will know you don't come from just any home — but from a good home!"*

40   S.Z. Sonnenfeld, trans. Yaakov Lavon, Feldheim Publishers, 1992.

It was important to me that the children experience success, because someone who has never experienced success will never succeed.

APPENDIX ATTACK

A turning point in Mrs. Barg's years in the orphanage occurred during a major snowstorm.

There was no transportation in the city. The streets were silent and pristine. As housemother, I had to be with the children, so I set out in the morning on foot — from Talpiot, where I live, toward the orphanage [a distance of about four miles]. When I finally arrived at the orphanage, I saw that my presence was very much needed.

Some of the children, who had been sent to school in the morning, had returned upon discovering that school was closed for the day. Several younger ones, who had never seen snow before, were on the brink of hysteria. "The sky is falling down on us!" they cried out in fear as the storm progressed.

Others, who had been out in the snow without adequate clothing, were nearly frostbitten and required immediate care. I rolled up my sleeves and got to work, rubbing alcohol into their frozen feet and massaging frozen veins back to life. I took socks in all sizes and colors from the closet and clothed each child in five or six pairs of socks. When the alcohol was used up, we turned to the neighbors, and they lent whatever they had in their cupboards. Soon the boys' moods brightened.

Since the cook had been unable to reach the orphanage, the other staff members and I searched the pantry for food to cook for lunch. Soon, a huge pot of potatoes was bubbling on the stovetop. We opened canned vegetables and pulled soy hot dogs out of the freezer. Preparing the mashed potatoes was a joint project. Since the pot was impossibly heavy, the children

*excitedly helped out by moving a table near the stovetop. Then
we slowly maneuvered the pot onto the table...*

*Once their hunger was satiated and their bodies warmed, the
children could happily play in the dancing snowflakes outside.
Suddenly, eight-year-old Shimon began complaining of stomach
pains. Soon, he was crouched over and writhing in pain. As a
certified nurse, I realized that he was having an appendicitis
attack and required immediate medical care.*

*The roads were impassable, so I wrapped the boy in a blanket
and carried him outside. Together with one of the other boys, I
trudged slowly up the street toward Bikur Cholim Hospital [a
ten-minute walk uphill from the orphanage]. I arrived in the
emergency room completely winded. Once there, however, I
was dismayed to hear that the hospital had no surgical ward
and there was nothing they could do for him; I had to take him
to Shaare Zedek, then located on Jaffa Street.*

*Out we went again into the cold and piercing wind with
Shimon, moaning and crying, in my arms. The entire long
walk, I sang him songs and told stories to divert his attention
from the terrible pain in his stomach.*

*The emergency room at Shaare Zedek was packed to capacity
with people who had slipped on the ice and injured themselves.
I burst inside and placed Shimon on a bed.*

*A passing doctor began to yell at me, but I stated, "This child is
having a severe appendix attack."*

"How do you know?" he retorted. "Are you a doctor?"

*"I am a nurse and I work at Zion Orphanage. I carried him here
myself, as he is in need of immediate care."*

*Fortunately, the doctor was convinced by my words. He
examined the child, and after a blood test revealed a raging
infection, little Shimon was taken into surgery.*

*"You need to sign consent to the surgery," the doctor said. In the
orphanage I had been instructed to do whatever was necessary
for the boy's health since his mother lived in the north and there*

was no way to contact her [many Israeli homes in those years did not have telephones]. I signed the consent form, taking full responsibility for Shimon's welfare.

The surgery lasted five hours. All the while, I waited outside, my heart pounding and a prayer on my lips. Afterward, I learned that while Shimon was on the operating table, the infected appendix burst and the infection spread throughout his abdomen. We had arrived just in time.

A short time after this incident, the Ribnitzer Rebbe, Rabbi Chaim Zanvil Abramowitz, instructed Mrs. Barg to accept a position at a religious high school for Russian immigrant girls since she could speak to them in their native tongue and teach them a love for Judaism. When she left the orphanage, little Shimon told her, "You came here just to save my life."

CHAPTER 54

Love That Lasts a Lifetime

ike Avraham Yochanan before him, Eliezer lovingly nurtured the orphanage boys. These warm memories remained with the boys for years to come, as the following testimonies demonstrate.

RABBI MOSHE ABUTBUL, MAYOR OF BEIT SHEMESH

Late one Friday night, I walked through the empty streets, humming Shabbat tunes. It was a long walk, and much of it was yet before me. But I walked happily, feeling the holiness of Shabbat envelop me.

I was coming from Hadassah Ein Kerem Hospital, where I had accompanied a friend who had fallen on Friday. When it was decided to hospitalize him, the hospital staff suggested that I take a taxi back to the orphanage, but I informed them that I could not travel by car once Shabbat had begun. Thus I began the long trek back to the orphanage on foot [a distance of almost ten miles].

Moshe, whose parents were immigrants from Morocco and Tunisia, arrived in the orphanage from a nonobservant home. He had attended public school in his hometown of Beersheba, but even as a young boy, he had been drawn toward Jewish observance. At the end of fifth grade, his teacher asked if he would like to continue his Torah studies in a religious setting.

At first, Moshe's parents were hesitant, but in the end they allowed him to move into Zion Orphanage. The education he received at the orphanage infused him with a staunch commitment to Shabbat.

Beit Shemesh Mayor Moshe Abutbul speaking at the orphanage

All along the way, cars stopped and offered me rides, but I refused. I reached the orphanage at one in the morning and immediately knocked on Rabbi Rakovsky's door to report on my friend.

The director, who had assumed I would stay in the hospital over Shabbat, was shocked to see me. He quickly invited me in and asked about my friend. I told him how I had walked the entire way home and refused all offers of a ride. Hearing this, he embraced me. To this day, the warmth of that "Shabbat hug" remains with me.

Again and again, he asked to hear how I had walked on my own through the dark city in order to safeguard the sanctity of Shabbat. The next day, at the Shabbat meal, he called me over and related the story of my long walk the previous night in detail, in earshot of all my friends, who were very impressed.

I sensed Rabbi Rakovsky's pride in me, and I knew that he valued me tremendously. This feeling propelled me to continue to excel in my studies so as not to disappoint him.

Following Moshe's example, his siblings and parents also became observant, transforming the entire atmosphere of their home.

"I owe my entire spiritual life to Rabbi Rakovsky, who encouraged me to study Torah even after hours," says Rabbi Abutbul. "Through his devotion to the children of the orphanage, he merited to see the fulfillment of the words of the Talmud: 'Be careful with the children of the poor, for from them shall spring forth Torah.'"[41]

RABBI DAVID AZOULAY, MK, SHAS PARTY

My family made aliyah in the 1960s from Morocco. We lived in Rechasim [on the outskirts of Haifa], where I attended a mamlachti dati (government-religious) school. There I met a rabbi

who recommended that I switch to a yeshiva environment. Thus, I transferred to Zion Orphanage, the place I soon called home.

Rabbi Rakovsky attended to all our needs. He paid attention to every detail of our education, our appearance, our dorm rooms, and our emotional well-being. He would often walk among us boys and check that we had everything we needed.

Israeli Knesset Member David Azoulay, who grew up in the orphanage

Rabbi Rakovsky's calm and measured personality gave us a feeling of peace and security, but he was no pushover. We knew that when he asked for something, it had to be done. At the same time, he was supremely devoted to his charges and had a soft spot in his heart for each of us. We sensed this and didn't want to disappoint him.

I celebrated my bar mitzvah at the orphanage along with six other boys. At first, my family was disappointed that the party would not take place at home, but once they attended the beautiful orphanage celebration, the event became a cherished family memory.

---

41   *Nedarim* 81a.

When I completed eighth grade, I went on to study in yeshiva. I continued sleeping in the orphanage and served as a counselor, which gave me a steady income and a feeling of independence.

I could sense the director's love in all his deeds, in his outstretched hands, and his help in every step of my life's path. Rabbi Rakovsky's image is carved into my heart not only as a teacher but as a true father who molded my personality.

Two of the counselors at the time were Rabbi Binyamin Chen [today rabbi of the Beit HaGadi settlement in the Negev] and Rabbi Eliyahu Danino [who unfortunately passed away young]. They were our role models. At every available opportunity, they sat and studied. Rabbi Chen also led the choir, together with Rabbi Rachamim Amar. Many of the songs I learned back then have become a tradition in my own home, and to this day my grandchildren sing them at the Shabbat table.

Rabbi Rakovsky participated in my wedding and helped me with many of the expenses. Later, he attended our family bar mitzvahs and became a loving grandfather figure to my children.

SHALOM

Shalom was one of the many boys in Zion Orphanage. Like everyone else, he studied, prayed, and played. In adulthood, he experienced many difficulties and eventually abandoned Jewish tradition.

Some years later, something inside him began to call out. The memories of Rabbi Rakovsky's devotion and the familial warmth he received years earlier suddenly reawakened. He could not abandon the tradition of his youth. Shalom returned to Jewish observance, married, and built an observant home.

RABBI DANI ASSOULIN

"Rabbi Rakovsky was a real father to me. Not 'like' a father, but a *real* father!" says Rabbi Dani Assoulin of Tiberias. "He traveled all the way to Tiberias to participate in our family celebrations. I know he loved me very much."

When Rabbi Rakovsky passed away, Rabbi Assoulin tore his clothing and sat shivah like a son.

DAVID HADAD

Rabbi Rakovsky would often entrust me with money for the bank deposit. These missions gave me the feeling that he loved me and believed in me. And I never betrayed his trust. It was important to me not to diminish my standing in his eyes.

A Zion Choir performance

Rabbi Rakovsky often patted me on the shoulder and said, "David, you are a member of this house. You don't need to knock on my door. Just open it and walk in…"

On Saturday nights, he would make sure the tables were laden with delicious foods, and we sang for hours. To this day, I can conjure up the sweet memories of those times.

Many of the children received an allowance from their parents. I also received a sum, which I believed an aunt had sent for me. Years later, I discovered that Rabbi Rakovsky, who noticed that no one ever sent me money, was behind this allowance. He gave my counselor money for me from time to time, without breathing a word to me…

RABBI ILAN PERETZ

Rabbi Rakovsky was, quite simply, a great father. He showered us with unlimited warmth and love and cared for us like his sons. *If we are able to withstand the pressures of life and build beautiful families today, it is a direct result of the fatherly care we received.*

One small example of his sensitivity: Communication with parents was complicated since many homes at that time did not have telephones and the orphanage did not own a pay phone. All phone calls for the boys came in through the office during the day or through the director's house in the evenings and on Friday afternoons.

Whenever a boy's mother called, he was immediately called to the phone. Never was the mother asked to call back at a more convenient hour. Rabbi Rakovsky understood that these phone calls were like water to a thirsty traveler, and we needed to hear Mother's voice and any news from home.

Often when we played in the yard, Rabbi Rakovsky would come out and speak to us as though we were his peers. We would gather around him, expressing our opinions about different things, speaking to him about different issues of the day. These conversations imbued us with a feeling of importance and self-worth.

Sephardic boys attended the Bnei Zion school, and Ashkenazic boys attended Torat Aharon. Rabbi Rakovsky showed an interest in each child's academic progress. He encouraged and guided us constantly and would regularly remind us to behave properly on the way to and from school.

Once, I found a sum of money while walking through Geulah. Two policemen stood nearby, and in my innocence, I was sure they had placed the money in order to test my honesty. Unhesitatingly, I handed them the money, which they took without recording a thing or even asking my name.

Returning to the orphanage, I told Rabbi Rakovsky the story and saw that he was upset. The money had no identifying signs on it, and by law it belonged to me. Rabbi Rakovsky felt that the money should be returned to me, and he did not rest until the entire sum was returned.

Rabbi Rakovsky didn't forget us during vacation times. He would often come and visit us in our homes. To this day I recall the feeling of surprise when, while playing outside, I was told that a visitor was waiting for me at home. I ran there to find Rabbi Rakovsky in my parents' house in Yavneh [a city in central Israel]. For hours after he left, the neighborhood children cast admiring and envious looks my way about the special person who had honored me with a visit.

When I transferred to a yeshiva in Be'er Yaakov, my close bond with Rabbi Rakovsky remained. I felt I could ask him for anything, explain any problem, and receive a wise and immediate response.

When I was ready to get married, Rabbi Rakovsky stood by my side, guiding the process and answering all my questions. My future wife and I celebrated our engagement at the orphanage. Rabbi Rakovsky got hurt that evening and was taken to the emergency room, but he returned just in time for our engagement party. He paid no heed to his own weakness and delivered a speech in my honor.

Rabbi Eliezer Rakovsky with the children at a Hanukkah party in the orphanage during the 1970s

Rabbi Rakovsky provided me with a large sum of money to purchase an apartment, and I merited to go to my chuppah with the feeling that I had a caring father by my side.

THE LEGACY CONTINUES

Eliezer fell ill with leukemia in his mid-sixties, passing away suddenly from heart failure on May 1, 1996 (12 Iyar 5756), at the age of sixty-eight. His family and the hundreds of boys who had grown up in his home were left in a state of shock. They arrived, stunned and grieving, to accompany him on his final journey.

Three of Eliezer's daughters, Sarah (Freund), Bracha (Tauber), and Tzivia (Segal), worked in the Zion Orphanage over the years, continuing in the family tradition. With Eliezer's passing, his son Baruch became the new director, with Rivka, Eliezer's widow, assuming the role of president of the institution.

Eliezer's legacy, however, continues in another way as well: A year after his passing, Yeshivat Zichron Eliezer was established in his memory next door to the orphanage.[42]

---

42   The yeshiva, a dream of Eliezer's that did not come to fruition until after his passing, is run today by his son, Rabbi Baruch Rakovsky. It is a top-tier yeshiva high school for boys of Sephardic background.

CONCLUSION

The Orphanage Today

I n a majestic building on Yechezkel Street, a large family of children eats, sleeps, studies, and plays. Under the supervision of Mrs. Rivka Rakovsky, Avraham Yochanan's granddaughter and widow of Rabbi Eliezer Rakovsky, and her son, the current executive director, Rabbi Baruch Rakovsky, a devoted staff continues to nurture and care for 130 Zion Orphanage boys.

Each child is a world of his own, each with his own story of trials and travails that brought him here, to be accepted with open arms — and to have a new chance at childhood.

The glow in the children's eyes, the smiles on their lips, their healthy mischievousness, and the sounds of their singing — these are the sources of strength that imbue the hardworking staff with the energy to continue their unending toil. I wander through the three joint buildings, sneaking a peek into the dormitory rooms. A twelve-year-old boy is home from school this morning with a sore throat. Although there is much to keep him occupied, he is willing to give me some time to tell me about life in the orphanage — the delicious meals, the exciting holiday programs, and the wonderful extracurricular events.

With a broad smile, he describes the "store" on premises. The children earn points for good behavior, which they later trade in for a prize from the store's huge se-

lection. He proudly shows me his recent purchase, a new MP3 player.

I am amazed by how incredibly neat the rooms are. My guide explains there is an ongoing cleanliness contest, and that each room strives to win points for tidiness.

Rabbi Ovadyah Yosef visiting the orphanage. On the left is Rabbi Baruch Rakovsky, the orphanage's current executive director.

The hallways are dotted with large aquariums that create a feeling

The orphanage building today

of peace and serenity. Suddenly, I hear the sounds of sheep baaing. "That's our petting zoo," Yitzhak, another boy who is home today, informs me. "We take care of the animals ourselves. Do you want to see them?"

I think of Avraham Yochanan, who dreamed of a home for "his" children in peaceful pastoral surroundings, believing that exposure to animal life and nature was a balm to a stormy spirit. Right here in the center of Jerusalem, his great-grandson, Rabbi Baruch Rakovsky, has made this dream a reality.

The Heichal Adina Sanctuary is empty at this hour of the morning, but I can almost hear the sounds of prayer filling the air. The smell of prayer books and wooden shelves greets me as I walk through the room. I can picture Reuven's seat, with Chaim nearby. Moshe is the *gabbai* this week and Yosef is distributing prayer books…

Next, I follow the sounds of a peaceful melody to the dining room, and a nook where the children can curl up and relax. "We borrow books from the library," Yitzhak explains, leading me to the nearby room lined with bookcases.

"And here," he points to another door, "is the computer room. There's also an exercise room for anyone who needs to let off energy, and the jungle gym in the yard is a popular spot during the afternoon hours.

"We have many extracurricular classes to choose from," he continues. "We can learn English or carpentry. I study electricity and I'm in the choir. We even put out a CD," he says, chest puffing out with pride. "You can ask Rabbi Rakovsky to give you a copy."

The children's free time is filled with fun and challenging activities. During vacation, they attend an action-packed day camp run on the premises.

The family unit program (*mishpachton*) was established for children in need of a smaller and more supportive environment. A pair of adoptive parents cares for a group of eight children who belong to the "family." The family units function within their own apartments on premises. They eat their meals in a special dining room, and the parents care for each child devotedly. The program has met with tremendous success.

Shalom the cook, an alumnus of the orphanage, invests heart and soul into preparing the children's meals. His years of experience in several high-class hotels stand him in good stead. When I enter the clean and modern kitchen, he is busy stirring the soup, seasoning the vegetables to perfection, and keeping an eye on the quiche in the oven.

A large professional staff is on hand to attend to all the children's needs. A warm-hearted housemother supervises much of the running of the household. A psychologist and social workers oversee the children's emotional health. The resident doctor monitors their physical health, while the nurse bandages the inevitable cuts and bruises.

NIGHT FALLS, FOLLOWING a day packed with learning, activities, and games. The moon's glow filters through the window, lighting up the pure faces of the peacefully sleeping children.

The spirit of Avraham Yochanan Blumenthal seems to hover over the building, bringing peace and blessing to the sweet children within.

The Talmud states that if one saves a single Jewish soul, it is as though he has saved the entire world.[43] Indeed, Avraham Yochanan built thousands of worlds that continue to positively impact the world.

The seeds Rabbi Blumenthal planted over a hundred years ago have sprouted into a sturdy and life-giving tree. In his merit and in the merit of Rabbi Eliezer Rakovsky, who saved the orphanage from financial collapse and became the father to three decades of new orphans, that tree continues to bring forth new fruit. The first children of the orphanage have long moved on, the laughter of today's children now filling the house. For as long as a Jewish child needs a place to call home, he will gain a singular fresh start at the Zion Blumenthal Orphanage.

---

43   *Sanhedrin* 4:5.

Epilogue

This book is being published as we commemorate the fiftieth *yahrtzeit* of Rabbi Avraham Yochanan Blumenthal.

Rabbi Blumenthal pioneered for modern Israel the practice of providing homeless children with not just a place of refuge, but also the warmth, care, and security of a loving family — providing each child with the tools to become a self-supporting member of society.

Today, the Blumenthal legacy continues to grow and flourish. The self-contained campus, located on an acre of land in the heart of Jerusalem, is home to more than one hundred and thirty boys, ages seven to nineteen. From diverse backgrounds, these boys band together as brothers in the safe and nurturing environment of Zion Orphanage.

Following an assessment by the team of educational psychologists, the social workers and therapists develop a program to meet the emotional and physical needs of each child. The academic counselors decide on an appropriate educational framework for each child to ensure he receives a suitable academic and Jewish education — supplemented by tutoring and mentoring in order to maximize his potential.

In the morning and early afternoon, most Zion boys study at schools throughout Jerusalem; others study on the Zion campus.

The boys return in the afternoon for a hot lunch and then launch into an array of extracurricular activities and therapies. Activities include computer proficiency, photography, sports, electronics, martial arts, and acting. The music program includes lessons in guitar, keyboard, and drums, as well as a choir. Participants enjoy performing for live audiences, as well as time in a professional recording studio.

The on-campus mini-zoo and its therapists assist each boy in surfacing his inner world, as do the play and speech therapists.

Evenings at Zion Orphanage are "family time." All the younger children reside in a Family Unit (*mishpachton*). Each of these seven custom-built apartments is led by an idealistic, energetic young couple who care for up to twelve boys as their own children. Suffering from little or no knowledge of being a part of a nurturing family, the children are given the opportunity to grow up with a model of a loving family environment.

Besides sleeping and eating in the same apartment, most daily activities are done together, such as playing soccer on the rooftop Sports Center, creating arts and crafts, or spending time in the well-stocked library.

Additionally, regular visits to swimming pools, picnics in beautiful Jerusalem parks, and traveling throughout the Land of Israel are thoroughly enjoyed as the children get a healthy change of scenery. For many boys, this is their first time experiencing childhood fun.

The Zion boys participate in a variety of voluntary activities—visiting hospitals, assisting the disabled, and helping the elderly—and experience the contentment and gratification that comes from giving to others and contributing to the community.

Each devoted staff member of the eighty-eight experts in education, therapy, healthcare, and vocational training working for the orphanage pours his or her heart and soul into an individualistic approach, providing each child with the skills and resources he needs to succeed.

Secure in the knowledge that people sincerely care and are taking an active interest in their lives, the boys grow and mature.

For more information or if you would like to visit the Zion Orphanage campus in Jerusalem, please email jerusalem@zionorphanage.com or visit the Zion website at www.zionorphanage.com.

Glossary

Achashveirosh: Ahasuerus, the Persian king at the time of the Purim story

Ashkenazic: relating to Jews descended from and following the customs of the medieval Jewish communities of Germany and France

Av: the Hebrew month generally coinciding with August

bey: a Turkish officer or governor

chacham: literally, a wise person; used as a term of respect

chametz: leavened bread or grain products forbidden on Passover

chuppah: wedding canopy

Edah: the informal name given to the legal entity founded by the Old Yishuv Jews

Haganah: a paramilitary group formed to protect Jews against Arab violence in the years before the founding of the State of Israel

Havdallah: the ceremony marking the conclusion of the Sabbath

Judah HaLevi, Rabbi: a Medieval Jewish rabbi and poet

Kaddish: a prayer recited to commemorate a loved one

kippot: skullcaps

lulav: the palm branch waved on the holiday of Sukkot

matzah: unleavened bread eaten on the holiday of Passover

mikvah: a ritual bath

mitzvah: good deed or commandment

Old Yishuv: the religious Jewish community that lived primarily in Jerusalem prior to the waves of mass immigration at the end of the nineteenth and early twentieth centuries

Purim: a Jewish holiday celebrated in Adar in commemoration of the deliverance of the Jews from the massacre plotted by Haman

Rosh Hashanah: the Jewish New Year

sandak: the person honored with holding a baby during his circumcision

Sephardic: Relating to Jews descended from and following the customs of the Jewish communities of medieval Spain

Shabbat: the Sabbath

sheva berachot: a party in honor of a newly married couple, held within the seven days after the wedding

shivah: the seven day mourning period observed after the loss of an immediate relative

sukkah: a booth constructed for the seven-day holiday of Sukkot

Sukkot: the fall holiday of Tabernacles

shuk: open-air market

Tisha B'Av: the ninth of Av, the day of mourning for the loss of the Holy Temples

tzaddik: righteous person

yahrtzeit: the anniversary of a death

Yishuv: literally, a settlement; see "Old Yishuv"

Index of Names

◀ *Cantor Benzion Miller visiting the orphanage. Rabbi Baruch Rakovsky is on the right, Gershon Unger on the left*

Zion boy celebrating his birthday
▼

◀ *Zion boy creates a menorah in arts and crafts*

Zion boys play in the courtyard during the winter
▼

Zion boy wtih a coati (a member of the raccoon family) during an animal therapy session

Zion boys perform martial arts

◀ Rabbi Eli Mansour lighting the custom campus bonfire during Lag B'Omer

A Zion boy during an animal therapy ses

◀ The Zion
Orphanage
rooftop
sports center

Child playing
pickup sticks ▶

Cantor Yechezkel
Zion, who grew up
in the orphanage,
sings a duet with
celebrated singer
Yaakov Shwekey
at a Zion benefit
in New York
▼

Yaakov Shwekey performs
for the Zion boys on campus
▼

A Zion boy in the
campus courtyard

train with the letters "Chloe's Candies" for his daughter; a coal tower with "Okie's" on it, in honor of his father.

The ads on the sides of the little buildings pay tribute to some of New Haven's beloved institutions, such as Anna Liffey's bar-restaurant and Lulu's, the coffee shop in East Rock.

And because O'Connell loves jazz, he has worked in references to famed jazz musicians. "Bird lives" is inscribed on a trestle as homage to the legendary Charlie Parker.

Mixed in with all the structures are assorted tiny humans, all of them hand-painted by O'Connell. If you look closely you can see that at least one of them is holding a glass of Guinness.

O'Connell picked up a caboose. "I was fixing this today because a wheel had come off. It's an old American Flyer caboose. This is how I tinker.

"It's a fun hobby," he said. "People always ask me, 'Where do you find the time to do this?' The answer is very simple: I don't watch TV."

Now that he is retired, O'Connell and his wife also have time to ride on real trains. "I've been across the country twice on Amtrak. My wife and I go to Florida every year by train. We've also been to Nova Scotia and we've ridden trains in Italy." He figures he has surpassed 20,000 miles on the rails.

When O'Connell wrote an article in 1985 for American Flyer Features magazine, he finished by saying: "I see part of my father invested in these toys. I hope to pass on that tremendous sense of pride, awe and delight to my own daughter, for today American Flyer trains can be enjoyed by little girls too."

Now his "little girl" Chloe is all grown up, with kids of her own, who are awed and delighted by what they see in their grandfather's basement. O'Connell proudly noted: "Our grandkids love it."

69

Recalling Jack Kramer's
Steady Guiding Hands

(May 7, 2020)

THESE SAD DAYS HAVE NOW GOTTEN MUCH SADDER FOR MY COLLEAGUES at the *New Haven Register* and for this old scribe, with the news Tuesday that Jack Kramer had died.

He left us far too early, at 65, following his prolonged, brave faceoff with cancer.

Jack is the third in a distinguished trio of major players at the *Register* who were taken by cancer. Edward Petraiuolo III departed first, in 1987 at 28; Ann DeMatteo followed him in 2013 at 56.

Over the past weeks and months the coronavirus has claimed the friends and family members of many people. And so this is a time when we need friendly, upbeat folks like Jack Kramer to be around. It's not fair, not right that he is gone.

You couldn't find anybody who didn't respect and like Jack. As an example, our U.S. Representative Rosa DeLauro, D-3, reached out immediately to Jack's wife Audrey to express her condolences.

Jack and I go way back, to the 1970s, when the *Register* building was on Orange Street near downtown. Jack, a kid out of Hamden, began at the *Register* in the mid-1970s as a co-op student from the University of Bridgeport. I arrived in 1977. We were both cub reporters, not knowing we would be there for decades, forming meaningful bonds in the community.

Jack and Audrey Kramer outside Wrigley Field in Chicago. (Photo contributed by Audrey Kramer)

In those days Jack was an easygoing "jock" who loved to play baseball, golf and tennis. He joined us on Friday afternoons at Rice Field by East Rock Park for softball games that featured more beer drinking than ball playing.

Life was simple and enjoyable. Our large group of young reporters knew how to have a good time, how to party in New Haven's bars (Archie Moore's, the Jury Box, Malone's) after we had met our day's story deadlines.

This feels like it happened in another century, and indeed it was. Amid today's tense climate it's hard to imagine being that carefree. Losing Jack means we have lost another link to those fun-filled days of our youth.

After Jack proved himself as a reporter he was promoted to being bureau chief on the East Shore, then assistant suburban editor and suburban/metro editor. In 1996, he landed the executive editor's position at the *Register*. Many of us were surprised to see a former fellow reporter ascend to that job. But it never went to his head. He remained down-to-earth and approachable.

When the *Register* moved to Sargent Drive, Jack could have set himself up in one of the fancy offices on the second floor that offered a fine view of Long Island Sound. But he wanted to be down with the rest of us "in the trenches" on the first floor, turning out a newspaper every day.

The staffs of the *Register* and *Journal-Courier*, which had its last edition published in 1987, were sometimes embroiled in labor or management disputes. Jack maintained his diplomatic demeanor and unflappable nature through some bitter times. As far as I could see, he didn't make any enemies.

This was hard to pull off. When I was forced out of the *Register* in 1989 under tense circumstances with management, I figured I would never return. But I kept in touch with Jack, who had had nothing to do with my departure.

In 1997, when I decided to try to get back on board, Jack and another humane editor, Mark Brackenbury, agreed to meet with me at Brazi's Italian Restaurant, down the road from the news office. We had a warm and sentimental meal and we worked out a way for me to come back.

Yes, Jack brought me back. You wouldn't be reading this column, nor any of the columns and news stories I have written since 1997 if it weren't for Jack Kramer. I will always be grateful. I wish I had directly expressed my appreciation to him.

Jack later encountered his own problems with office politics. In July 2011, those who were in management at that time told him he was finished. We were shocked and angered but our protests could not save our old friend.

He didn't sulk. He stayed in the news business, becoming an editor at the New Britain Herald, then reporting for CTNewsJunkie.com and Patch.com. It was in his blood.

Jack and I shared a bond of being lifelong devoted fans of the New York Yankees. We never got tired of chewing over the worth of the players and the highlights of the games, the team's prospects for beating the Red Sox and other opponents.

There's a wonderfully evocative photograph of Jack and Audrey standing outside Wrigley Field in Chicago, smiling with the joy that a baseball game played in a grand old ballpark can bring.

"That was in 2012," Audrey told me Wednesday. "The Red Sox were tearing up the league at the beginning of the season and the Cubs were terrible. But the Cubs beat the Red Sox that day!"

In recent years, Jack and Audrey generously hosted annual summertime barbecues at their home in Branford. Those gatherings turned into *New Haven Register* reunions, with former and current staffers getting together again and laughing over old times. As late as last summer, when Jack was growing thinner and clearly feeling the effects of that cancer, he was still standing at the grill on his deck, cooking up dozens of burgers and hot dogs for us.

Occasionally he would take a break. Jack and I would head off to his living room and watch the Yankee game together. We were old pals, talking baseball.

When I remarked to Audrey how sad it is that Jack's old friends can't be at his funeral because of social distancing, she said: "Eventually, when things get back to normal, we will do a memorial for Jack, a celebration of life."

Remembering Our Greatest Street Thespian, Margaret Holloway

(June 5, 2020)

IN A TRAGIC ENDING TO A SOMETIMES TRAGIC BUT DRAMATIC LIFE, Margaret Holloway, long known in New Haven as "The Shakespeare Lady," has died of COVID-19.

This sad news came to me last Saturday from Joan Channick, chairwoman of the Theater Management Department at the Yale School of Drama, where Holloway received her master's of fine arts degree in 1980.

Channick befriended Holloway many years ago and stuck by her, visiting once a month in the nursing home where Holloway finally found some peace and stability for the last two years of her life.

Channick brought her toiletries, treats, notebooks, pens and a little cash. On Holloway's birthday—she turned 68 last September—Channick gave her the lipstick she so enjoyed.

"Margaret had COVID-19 and had been in a coma and on a ventilator at Yale New Haven Hospital for several weeks," Channick told me in an email. "Ultimately she died from a heart attack."

I became aware of Holloway and her street presence in the 1980s, after the effects of her mental illness had begun to set in. Anybody who spent much time in downtown New Haven knew about "The Shakespeare Lady," the nickname she acquired because of the mesmerizing sidewalk performances she did for "therapy" and spare change.

During our first interview in September 1999, she initially was wary of my intentions and how I might portray her in the *New Haven Register*. But she agreed to sit with me at a table outside Willoughby's coffee shop at the corner of Church and Grove streets, one of her favorite places to recite. Although it was a sunny afternoon, she was bundled up in a winter coat.

Holloway was always candid about what had befallen her in a life that had held so much promise. This was a creative, talented person who had earned bachelor's and master's degrees from another prestigious school, Bennington College in Vermont, before coming to Yale.

Margaret Holloway, "The Shakespeare Lady." (Photo contributed by Tom Kaszuba)

"I saw myself in a career in avant-garde theater, mostly as a director," she told me.

But she never made it to New York, where she had planned to launch herself.

"I got sick," she said. Her schizophrenia, she told me, was diagnosed as "tactile demon."

"Not only do I see and hear bad things, I also taste, feel and smell them. If I'm on the street I might feel a car has run over me. It's like the whole world has fallen in on me."

Holloway said she recited Shakespeare "more for therapy than income."

She said she became homeless in 1983, just three years after earning that Yale degree. "I've been on medication ever since, in and out of hospitals." At the time we spoke she was living in what she called "my crawl space" on Whitney Avenue for $10 a night.

When I asked her if she would please recite some Shakespeare passages for me, she walked to the corner; her eyes grew wide and intense.

She proceeded to become Hamlet on that sidewalk, then recited Middle English from Chaucer's "The Canterbury Tales" and finished with highlights of Euripides' "Medea."

I thanked her, made a donation and asked her what she wanted to do with the rest of her life. She replied, "I want to know that God isn't punishing me for something. I want that more than anything."

As we parted, she unleashed that charming smile and called out: "Thank you, Mr. Beach!"

For years afterward, no matter how many times we saw one another, she insisted on calling me "Mr. Beach." I think it was part of her proper Southern upbringing.

Often when I was rushing around by Willoughby's I would hear: "Mr. Beach! Mr. Beach!" And she would tell me of her latest run-ins with the New Haven police. She was sometimes arrested on charges of disorderly conduct, breach of peace, etc., because some shopkeepers, unlike those at Willoughby's, didn't appreciate her panhandling.

Many times she would ask me for a ride back to her rooming house on Park Street. I could never turn her down.

Holloway was also candid about her struggles with drug use. But in one of our last conversations in October 2017 she proudly said, "I've been clean for 10 years!" She added sadly, "That's why I've gained so much weight."

I was touched to hear from Channick that Holloway had told her several times: "I know if I'm ever in trouble, I can call Mr. Beach and he'll write a story about me."

Channick said the last time she was able to visit Holloway was early in March. After that, visitors were prohibited as the virus began to spread.

"She was terrified about the possibility of catching COVID-19 and being trapped in the nursing home without seeing the few friends who visited her regularly," Channick said.

Channick contacted Gregg Zuckerman, a Yale mathematics professor who also had become one of Holloway's friends through the years. Zuckerman got through to Holloway's conservator, who later called to tell him Holloway had died.

"I'm in real grief over Margaret's death," Zuckerman told me in an email. He recalled the many times they ate together at Clark's Pizza & Restaurant.

"Margaret had one of the sharpest minds of anyone I've met in the Yale community," Zuckerman said. "If she hadn't told me about her mental illness I would have believed she was an eccentric and gifted actor who was merely down on her luck."

Zuckerman added, "Margaret never lost her Southern good manners and respect for people. When she was still able to recite Shakespeare, she did so with deep reverence for 'the Bard.' She was not just performing— she was celebrating."

My final interview with Holloway was in December 2009, a week before Christmas. I wanted to give the public an update on how "The Shakespeare Lady," although rarely reciting, had gotten off drugs.

"The haunted, gaunt face and the stricken expression have been replaced by a dazzling smile, a fuller figure and a more upbeat attitude," I wrote. "There is a dancing light in her eyes."

While we sat in her pleasant but small apartment, she said sometimes she still recited Shakespeare when the police weren't nearby. "I'm real sneaky, like a fox!"

She said her friends near Clark's and Willoughby's still asked her to perform and she obliged them. "I do it because it's my passion. I'm a great thespian."

Holloway was getting by on antipsychotic medication. But she told me: "I have no peace unless I'm sleeping. It's a horrible disease."

Then, to lift her spirits and again demonstrate her passion and talent, she sang, in a sweet, emotive voice, Nat King Cole's "The Christmas Song."

Her eyes grew misty as she sang: "Chestnuts roasting on an open fire; Jack Frost nipping at your nose . . ."

This is how I will always remember Margaret Holloway.

Remembering Fred Parris*

(January 15, 2022)

AROUND MIDNIGHT, AS FRIDAY WAS SLIPPING INTO SATURDAY, I PUT ON the recording of that magic moment in New Haven history. I heard, yes, "Sha-doo, shoo-be-doo . . ."

This was the perfect way to commemorate it all, the amazing life of Fred Parris. He and the rest of the Five Satins continued to sing, with Fred in the lead: "In the still of the night, I held you, held you tight . . ."

"I remember" is a refrain of that song. And yes, I do remember the special moments I shared with Fred Parris—moments I'm recalling as I mourn his passing, announced Friday. He was 85.

Do you remember too? How many people these days know that song? I guess I have to ask because the *New Haven Register*, my alma mater, on Saturday carried the news about the death of this New Haven native, national icon and local hero, in a short article on page A11. Are you kidding me?

I remember first meeting Fred in the summer of 1980 when I was a young reporter for the *Register*. I had been assigned to write a lengthy feature story on the history of the Five Satins. Not being a native New Havener, I didn't know much about them. But I learned plenty.

My story began: "A quarter of a century ago, the Five Satins were born on the street corners of Dixwell Avenue and in the bathrooms of Hillhouse High School, where they gathered to harmonize.

---

* This column was written on my substack.com page. By then I had voluntarily left the *New Haven Register*.

"They had no thought of making musical history. Even when they recorded 'In the Still of the Night' in 1956 in the basement of St. Bernadette Church in New Haven, they couldn't imagine that that song would sell more than 10 million copies, becoming one of the most popular single records of all time."

Fred Parris. (*New Haven Register* file photo)

On a summer's day 42 years ago, eager to help me tell the Five Satins story, Fred invited me to his parents' home, an apartment in a high-rise in downtown New Haven, so he could reminisce. Although the other original members of the Five Satins had long since left the music business, he was still touring frequently with his latest band.

Fred Parris didn't merely have talent; he had ambition and drive. In 1953 and '54 he made repeated train trips to New York, seeking out record company representatives, telling them he had a band (then called the Scarlets) back in the Elm City. One of the company guys told him to cut a test record.

Fred's persistence paid off. One day a record company rep phoned the Parris home and told him to bring his group into a studio in New York. The result, "Dear One," recorded in 15 minutes, made it onto the charts across the country.

But how to follow it up? In 1955 the Scarlets became the Five Satins (Fred liked the Velvets' name and Satins was the next best thing) and they signed with a new record company.

Still unable to afford a New York recording studio for an extended session, Fred made a deal with another local kid named Vinny Mazzetta, who played jazz saxophone. Vinny knew the priest at St. Bernadette Church in the Morris Cove neighborhood of New Haven and got the priest's permission for the Satins to go into the church's basement and record a few songs. In return, the Satins let Vinny play a sax solo on one of those songs. It was "In the Still of the Night." And Vinny nailed it!

These young guys didn't know that that date—February 19, 1956—would become a big day in the history of rock music.

I asked Fred in our 1980 interview why that song had endured as one of the most requested radio station standards for decades. He laughed and said, "It beats the hell out of me! But I sure am glad."

He told me he wrote the song in 1955 in the early morning hours of guard duty for the U.S. Army, while he was stationed in Philadelphia. He said "my girl" inspired him to write that song. "I was so much in love with her." But he added: "She left me and went to California. I never saw her again."

However, Fred never got tired of singing that song, and his audiences always called on him to sing it. In October 1983, I heard him sing "In the Still of the Night" at Toad's Place in New Haven. "I was nothing but a teenager in love when I wrote this song," Fred said before singing it. "I took those words in my head and my heart and wrote them on a piece of paper."

The Toad's crowd loved it, of course.

Through the years, Fred was always willing to take my calls, answer my questions and give me all the time I needed. In 2006, he married a wonderful woman. Emma Parris is as kind as Fred, often sending gifts to my home: a Five Satins pen, a Satins cloth bag and one of the CDs Fred recorded in his later years.

Fred forever loved to perform, even when his advancing age sometimes made it difficult. In July 2013, on a sultry summer's night with temperatures in the high 90s, I watched him sing at Hamden High School. He had earlier greeted me backstage, as friendly and personable as ever. But he acknowledged the shows could be wearying. He was then in his late 70s.

That night, after several songs, Fred started to sway, and not in a good way. Stagehands rushed forward with a chair and he was carried off stage. I was relieved to see him in the lobby, sitting upright in a wheelchair. The medical crew that had responded convinced him to go with them to the hospital. He had become dehydrated.

But Fred wasn't done. He kept doing occasional shows for his fans. Then in 2020, he and Emma invited their many friends to a double birthday party for the two of them. They booked the American Legion Post 88 on Dixwell Avenue for March 21.

Then Covid hit Connecticut. Fred and Emma were heartbroken but they had to postpone their big night. (I was upset too; I had been honored to be on the list of people invited.)

In July 2020, Fred and Emma were still quite worried about contracting Covid. I spoke to them over the phone as they sat in their Hamden home. They were continuing to anticipate that double birthday celebration but knew it would have to wait until at least the following year. Acknowledging the preciousness of time, Fred told me, "I'm no kid." But Emma quickly said, "He's a young guy at heart!"

Looking back on his life, Fred told me, "It would really make a nice movie. I've had people approach me about it. I just never got around to it."

Emma interjected, "Sometimes my husband will say, 'Not now.' And I tell him, 'Fred, you've got to take advantage of it now.'"

That movie still hasn't been made—somebody should do it!—but Fred and Emma finally got to have their birthday party, last August, at a restaurant not far from St. Bernadette Church.

That was the last time I saw Fred. He had slowed down considerably since our previous in-person meeting—Emma supported him as he walked—but as ever he was smiling, polite and friendly when I greeted him. There was a long line of well-wishers behind me.

Thanks for the memories, Fred. Oh yes, I remember.

Afterword

In the years after I met and wrote about these characters I tried to keep in touch with them. Many have since died but some have persevered.

Randy Burns continues to perform wherever he can. In 2019, he revealed he has neck cancer.

"Little Richard" died on May 9, 2020 at 87 from bone cancer.

"Smoky Joe" Wood died on July 27, 1985 at 95.

Nick Apollo Forte continued to make a living as a Connecticut lounge singer after his starring role in "Broadway Danny Rose." He died on February 26, 2020 at 81 in his hometown of Waterbury.

Alan Abel, who had hoodwinked the *New York Times* into prematurely printing his obituary, "apparently actually did die," the *Times* reported, on September 14, 2018 at 94.

Steve Papa, New Haven's Santa Claus, died in May 2010 at 93.

The iconic photo-mural of Denny McGill scoring a touchdown for Yale was covered over by sheet rock after Kavanagh's changed hands. The property is now a Chi Chi's Restaurant.

Elizabeth Tashjian, "The Nut Lady," died in Old Saybrook on January 28, 2007 at 94.

Charles Webb died June 16, 2020 in England at 81. His wife "Fred" (Eve Rudd) died a year earlier. They had continued to dodge money and attention stemming from his book "The Graduate." In 2007, Webb issued a sequel, "Home School." It was not a hit.

Robert Spodick died from throat cancer on December 22, 2009 at 90. His cousin and business partner Leonard Sampson died May 18, 2004 at 85. Their Lincoln Theater had closed in September 1982 but was spared the wrecking ball when preservationists rallied to save it. The building was renovated and is now used by arts students. The York Square Cinemas closed in July 2005, one year after BowTie Criterion Cinemas opened in downtown New Haven.

George "Spanky" McFarland died on June 30, 1993 at 64 after suffering a heart attack.

Elliot Brause died on September 6, 2020 at 83.

The Yankee Doodle Coffee Shop closed in January 2008 after a run of 58 years.

Kurt Vonnegut died in New York City on April 11, 2007 at 84, several weeks after falling at his home.

Madison's Good Humor Man Joseph "Papa Joe" Barbato died on February 25, 2020 at 89.

Leo Vigue died the day after Thanksgiving in 2011. But he could give thanks for finally seeing his Red Sox win a World Series in 2004. (I celebrated with him that night at Rudy's.) He was buried wearing his Red Sox jacket, his casket draped in his Red Sox flag.

James Weil died on November 19, 2012 at 68. The Stony Creek Puppet House has been remodeled as the Legacy Theater.

The Forest Theater was demolished in 2011.

Lula White died on September 10, 2019 at 80.

"Big John" Vessichio died on November 2009. Fran Squillo Vessichio has closed the cigar store.

This is the saddest one of all: Paul Hammer did not survive his second suicide attempt. On June 27, 2021 he jumped off the Air Rights Garage in downtown New Haven. He was 64.

Vincent Scully died November 30, 2017 at his second home in Virginia. He was 97. He had taught at Yale until 2009.

Phil Linz died on December 9, 2020 at 81.

Sidney Glucksman died on November 23, 2014 at 87.

William Brinley died on September 8, 2016 at 99.

Angelo DeSorbo died on April 24, 2015. He was 106!

Ellen Ruth Hourigan died on July 14, 2017 at 74. Linda Ruth Tosetti is working on a book about her grandpa, Babe Ruth.

Rick Kaletsky's Muhammad Ali Museum is still open.

Donald "Red" Beatty retired from the U.S. Postal Service in 2011 after 44 years. He died January 12, 2016 at 74.

Hy Katz died on August 18, 2019 at 85. His family handed out joke books at his funeral.

Clark's Pizza and Restaurant, the "sister" to Clark's Dairy, closed on June 5, 2020, another victim of the Covid pandemic.

Vinny Mazzetta died on October 14, 2018. He was 83. His death notice credited him for his sax solo on "In the Still of the Night."

Cine 4 unfortunately closed in 2022.

Joe Lentine died at his home in Hamden on February 12, 2015. He was 70.

Donald Hall died at his farmhouse in Wilmot, New Hampshire on June 23, 2018. He was 89.

William Cameron died on June 3, 2016 at 85. Two months later, on August 29, 2016, his wife Joan Cameron died at 79. They are buried side by side at the Grove Street Cemetery, which they tended for four decades.

Jimmy Negretti is still selling hot dogs in all weather in front of New Haven City Hall.

Bob Barton died on January 13, 2019 at his home in Farmington. He was 83.

ACKNOWLEDGMENTS

Journalism is a team effort. My columns were supported and enhanced by dozens of editors at the *New Haven Register* stretching back to 1980. They found typos, occasionally challenged my facts or interpretations and usually wrote stellar headlines—until I finally convinced them to let me write my own.

I also owe a debt to the *New Haven Register* photographers who helped these characters come alive. One of those photographers, Pete Hvizdak, provided valuable input for this book.

New Haven Register Librarian Angel Diggs, who really is an angel, valiantly unearthed almost all of the photos that were used here. I would have been lost without her.

Mara Lavitt, another former Register photographer, went up into her attic as well as combing through her digital archive to find several photos of hers that were used in this book.

Frank Rizzo, yet another old friend from my newspaper days, came up with the organizing concept for this book: that it be about specific characters I have met and profiled.

Amy Lyons of Globe Pequot deserves credit for giving the green light to my idea of creating a book from newspaper columns.

And as always, I am grateful to my wife, Jennifer Kaylin, who provided endless advice as well as computer and photo help as I put together this book. I also thank our daughters, Natalie and Charlotte Beach, for their advice, love and support.

ABOUT THE AUTHOR

Randall Beach spent most of his working life as a columnist and reporter for the *New Haven Register*, where he got his start in 1977. He left the *Register* voluntarily in November 2020 but continues to write his "Beachcombing" column for *Connecticut* magazine. He also writes essays on substack.com. He is the co-author, with Brian Phelps of *The Legendary Toad's Place: Stories from New Haven's Famed Music Venue* (Globe Pequot). He lives in New Haven with his wife, Jennifer Kaylin.